THE €URO AND THE DOLLAR IN A GLOBALIZED ECONOMY

Papers presented at
a conference organized by
the European Union Center and
the Jean Monnet Chair of the University of Miami
with the support of the European Commission

For more information: Jean Monnet Chair/European Union Center.
101 Ferré Bldg., University of Miami, Coral Gables, Fl. 33131
Phone: 305-284-3266 / Fax: 305-284-4410:
Web: www.miami.edu/eucenter

The €uro and the Dollar in a Globalized Economy

Edited by

JOAQUÍN ROY and PEDRO GOMIS-PORQUERAS
European Union Center/Jean Monnet Chair
University of Miami, USA

ASHGATE

Published by
Ashgate Publishing Limited
Gower House
Croft Road
Aldershot
Hampshire GU11 3HR
England

Ashgate Publishing Company
Suite 420
101 Cherry Street
Burlington, VT 05401-4405
USA

Ashgate website: http://www.ashgate.com

British Library Cataloguing in Publication Data
The Euro and the dollar in a globalized economy
1. Euro 2. Euro area 3. Euro-dollar market
I. Roy, Joaquín II. Gomis-Porqueras, Pedro
332.4'94

Library of Congress Cataloging-in-Publication Data
The euro and the dollar in a globalized economy / edited by Joaquín Roy and Pedro Gomis-Porqueras.
p. cm.
Includes index.
ISBN 978-0-7546-7153-4
1. Euro. 2. Euro-dollar market. 3. Dollar, American. 4. International finance. 5. Monetary policy--European Union countries. I. Roy, Joaquín, 1943- II. Gomis-Porqueras, Pedro, 1971-

HG925.E8676 2007
332.4'94--dc22

2007002940

ISBN 978-0-7546-7153-4

Printed and bound in Great Britain by TJ International Ltd, Padstow, Cornwall.

Contents

PART IV: THE EURO AND THE EUROPEAN ECONOMIC GOVERNANCE

PART V: THE EURO IN THE GLOBAL ECONOMY

List of Figures

List of Tables

Notes on Contributors

Joaquín Almunia was born in Bilbao, Spain, on June 17, 1948. He graduated in Law and Economics from the University of Deusto (Bilbao). He did postgraduate studies at L'École Practique des Hautes Études de Paris and also completed the Senior Managers in Government program at the Kennedy School of Government, Harvard University. He was associate professor at the University of Alcalá de Henares (Madrid) on Employment and Social Security Law. From 1976 to1979 he was chief economist of the UGT, a Spanish trade union, and from 1972 to 1975, economist at the Council Bureau of the Spanish Chambers of Commerce in Brussels. From 1979 to 2004 he was a member of the Spanish Parliament. He was Minister of Public Administration and Minister of Employment and Social Security. He was Secretary General of the Spanish Socialist Party (1997–2000). From 1994–1997 he was the party's Spokesperson in Congress. In 2000 he was candidate for prime minister. He is the author of several books and numerous press columns. Since April 2004 he has been a member of the European Commission, responsible for economic and monetary affairs.

Angel Calderón-Madrid has been a senior researcher at the Center of Economics of El Colegio de México since 1989. He studied economics at ITAM, London School of Economics and Cambridge University, where he received his doctoral degree. He was invited in 2002 and 2003 by Science-Po, Paris to teach international development. He has specialized in macroeconomic policy, applied economics and evaluation of social programs. He has published the book *The Role of Private Financial Wealth in a Portfolio Model: A Study of the Effects of Fiscal Deficits on the Real Exchange Rate* edited by MacMillan Press in 1995 and papers on macroeconomic adjustments of the Mexican economy. He was awarded the 2005 "Victor Urquidi National Prize" for his paper "Assessing heterogeneity of plant responses to trade liberalization in Mexico: Productivity, Labor Reallocation and Survival of Manufacturing Plants in NAFTA". Professor Calderón-Madrid has been a consultant for the OECD, Inter American Development Bank, World Bank and Corporación Andina de Fomento.

Miriam L. Campanella (licensed in political science, University of Catania 1968; specialization in international relations and economic history, University of Turin 1969–1971) teaches a Jean Monnet permanent course on "EMU Policies and Institutions" at the faculty of political science at the University of Turin, and a course on international political economy. Since 1980, she has been a fellow at the MIT Center for International Relations, where she attended Ph.D. courses in International Political Economy. In 1997, she lectured as a Fulbright Professor at the University of Pittsburgh. In 2001, she was appointed to serve at the Ministry of Economy and Finance in Rome. She is the author of numerous publications in journals and books with a focus on EMU targeting exercise and post EMU issues (pact of stability and growth, EU budget reform, ECB monetary policy). Most recently she has co-edited, with Sylvester C.W. Eijffinger, a volume entitled *EU Economic Governance and Globalization* (Edward Elgar 2003).

Benjamin J. Cohen is Louis G. Lancaster Professor of International Political Economy at the University of California, Santa Barbara, where he has been a member of the political science department since 1991. He was educated at Columbia University, earning a Ph.D. in economics in 1963. He has worked as a research economist at the Federal Reserve Bank of New York (1962–1964) and has taught at Princeton University (1964–1971) and the Fletcher School of Law and Diplomacy, Tufts University (1971–1991). A specialist in the political economy of international money and finance, he serves on the editorial boards of several leading academic journals and is the author of ten books, including most recently *The Geography of Money* (1998), *The Future of Money* (2004) and *The Future of the Dollar* (2005). He has won numerous awards and in 2000 was named Distinguished Scholar of the Year by the International Political Economy Section of the International Studies Association.

J. Onno De Beaufort Wijnholds started his career at the Netherlands Bank in 1968 after graduating from the University of Amsterdam from which he holds a Ph.D. in economics. In the early 1970s he spent two years at the World Bank and the International Monetary Fund. He returned to Washington in the mid-1980s to serve as an alternate executive director in the IMF. Back at the Netherlands Bank he became a deputy executive director in charge of monetary policy and financial markets. He also held a part-time professorship in money and banking at the University of Groningen and was an alternate member of the Social Economic Council of the Netherlands. In 1994 he became an executive director of the IMF, representing his own country plus eleven others, mainly in the Balkans and the former Soviet Union. After leaving the IMF Board he was appointed as the permanent representative of the European Central Bank in Washington DC and the ECB's observer at the IMF. He has written extensively on international monetary and financial issues.

Pedro Gomis-Porqueras is an assistant professor of economics at the University of Miami. A graduate in economics from the University of Barcelona, he received his Ph.D. from the University of Texas at Austin. His research and teaching interests focus on the relationships between monetary policy, financial sector behavior and macroeconomic performance as well as assessing how volatility in macroeconomic aggregates affects optimal monetary policy. He has published articles in the *Journal of Economic Theory*, *Economic Theory*, *Macroeconomic Dynamics* and *Journal of Economic Dynamics and Control.*

Francesc Granell is professor of economic international organization at University of Barcelona and honoree general director of the European Commission. His academic background comprises a Ph.D. in political, economic and trade sciences from the University of Barcelona and studies in the same area at the Institute of European Studies (Geneva), the International Marketing Institute (Cambridge), and the Fletcher School of Law and Diplomacy. He has also been visiting professor at Georgetown, Bocconi, Brussels, Madrid and Praha Universities. He served with the Barcelona's Chamber of Commerce International Studies Centre, the International Trade Centre UNCTAD/GATT, the Autonomous Government of Catalonia and the European Commission. Among his professional activities in the European Commission, he was head of the Commission negotiating team for the accession of Finland as well as head of the area of relations with the Pacific, Caribbean and Indian Ocean countries and coordinator of the Third United Nations Conference on Least Developed Countries held in Brussels. He has published fifteen books and an extensive number of articles on external trade, economic international relations and European integration.

José Manuel González-Páramo was born in Madrid in 1958. He was awarded a Ph.D. in economics from the Universidad Complutense de Madrid (UCM) in 1985 and another, also in economics, from Columbia University in 1986. In 1988 he was appointed professor of economics at UCM, where he has taught courses in public finance, European economics and public management. His publications and research have focused primarily on fiscal policy, the economic effects of public spending and taxation, and the costs and benefits of disinflation. From 1985 to 1994 he was an economic advisor to and consultant for various public and private institutions, including the Spanish Ministry of Economics and Finance, the Fundación Fondo para la Investigación Económica y Social, the Banco de España, the European Commission and the World Bank. He has been involved in working groups on economic and financial matters at the Bank for International Settlements and the Organisation for Economic Co-operation and Development. He was appointed member of the Governing Council of the Banco de España in 1994 and subsequently of its Executive Board in 1998. In this capacity, he has been jointly responsible for setting the policy line on major issues encompassing monetary policy, economic analysis, preparations for Economic and Monetary Union and financial supervision and regulation. In 2004 he joined the European Central Bank as a member of the Executive Board.

David Howarth (D.Phil., M.Phil., Oxford; diplôme, ENA (Paris)) is a senior lecturer in European political economy in the department of politics at the University of Edinburgh in Scotland. His principal research interests include the political economy and politics of economic and monetary union (EMU) and specifically the role of the European Central Bank in EMU and French perspectives on economic and monetary integration. His recent publications include *The French Road to European Monetary Union* (Palgrave 2001), (with Peter Loedel) *The European Central Bank: The New European Leviathan?* (with Peter Loedel; Palgrave 2003, 2005), in addition to several academic journal articles and book chapters on these subjects. He also edited *EU Economic Government: Revising the Rules?*, for the Journal of European Public Policy (2004). David Howarth maintains a parallel interest in French political economy (notably the role of the French state in the economy) and is currently preparing the monograph *Managing the French Economy* (Palgrave forthcoming).

Kurt Hübner is a trained macroeconomist who holds a full professorship in the political science department of York University, Ontario. He completed his Ph.D. at the Free University of Berlin where he taught and researched for eleven years before he moved to the Berlin School of Economics. Hübner is a member of the Canadian Centre for German and European Studies. His current research focuses on currency regimes, innovation theories and policies, globalization and European modes of regulation. He recently edited *New Economy in a Transatlantic Perspective. Spaces of Innovation* (Routledge 2005). Together with Hansjoerg Herr, he coauthored in 2005 *Currency and Uncertainty in the Global Economy* (only in German).

Hans Martens is chief executive of the European Policy Centre, a leading Brussels-based think tank set up to promote European integration. Born in Denmark, Hans Martens studied political science at Aarhus University and went on to become associate professor in international political and economic relations. In 1979 he joined the Danish Savings Bank Association as editor-in-chief and head of information. From 1982–1985 he was head of the international department of a Danish trade union, the Salaried Employees Federation, where he took charge of the organization's international relations, including with the OECD and the ILO. In 1985 Hans Martens joined the Copenhagen Handelsbank initially in charge of the economic department and later as head of the International Private Banking Department. There he was responsible for economic analysis and forecasting and for developing the bank's investment and capital market products. In 1989 he set up Martens International Consulting, specializing in international consultancy and customized training (including in EU affairs) for a number of major companies. He joined the European Policy Centre as chief executive in 2002. He has been visiting professor at the Universities of Aarhus and Copenhagen and he is a regular lecturer at the Executive MBA Programme at Virginia Commonwealth University. He is an expert on the new economy, European competitiveness issues and on eBusiness and eGovernment.

Julie McKay is currently the senior advisor to the European Central Bank Permanent Representative at the IMF in Washington DC. Her work focuses mainly on Eurosystem-relevant policy topics as well as issues pertaining largely to the global economy and EU and euro area countries. Prior to this, she was Senior Economist in the International Policy Analysis Division of the ECB's Directorate General International and European Relations in Frankfurt for five years to 2005, where she specialized in regional and exchange rate issues related to emerging markets in Asia and Latin America. She worked for the Reserve Bank of Australia in Sydney for three years in the early 1990s as Senior Analyst on financial systems and supervision. As committed to teaching as she is to policy, she has lectured at the University of Cambridge, UK, held visiting professorships for the EERC Master's Program in Economics at the Kyiv-Mohyla Academy,

National University Ukraine, and was Dolph Zink Teaching Fellow at Curtin University in Perth, Australia. Her areas of specialization, in which she both teaches and publishes, include international finance, regional trade, and European economic integration. She holds a Ph.D. and M.Phil. in Economics from the University of Cambridge.

Joaquín Roy (Lic. Law, University of Barcelona, 1966; Ph.D., Georgetown University, 1973), is Jean Monnet Professor of European Integration, director of University of Miami European Union Center and co-director of the Miami-Florida European Union Center of Excellence. He has published over 200 academic articles and reviews, and he is the author, editor, or co-editor of twenty-five books, among them *The Reconstruction of Central America: The Role of the European Community* (North-South Center, 1991), *The Ibero-American Space/El Espacio Iberoamericano* (University of Miami/University of Barcelona, 1996), *Cuba, the US and the Helms-Burton Doctrine: International Reactions* (University of Florida Press, 2000), *Las relaciones exteriores de la Unión Europea* (México: UNAM, 2001), *Retos de la integración regional: Europa y América* (México: UNAM, 2003), *La Unión Europea y el TLCAN* (México: UNAM, 2004), *The European Union and Regional Integration* (Miami: EU Center, 2005), *La Unión Europea y la integración regional* (Buenos Aires: CARI/ U. Tres de Febrero, 2005), *Towards the Completion of Europe* (Miami: EU Center, 2006) and *A Historical Dictionary of the European Union* (Scarecrow Press/ Rowman and Littlefield, 2006). He has also published over 1300 columns and essays in newspapers and magazines. Among his awards is the Encomienda of the Order of Merit bestowed by King Juan Carlos of Spain.

Sebastián Royo is the director of the Suffolk University Madrid Campus. He is an associate professor in the government department at Suffolk University in Boston and affiliate and co-chair of the Iberian Study Group at the Minda de Gunzburg Center for European Studies at Harvard University. He received a five-year law degree from the University of Madrid, and a Masters in Business Administration, a Masters in International Relations and a Ph.D. from Boston University. Royo's articles and reviews on Southern European and Latin American politics have appeared in *South European Society and Politics*, *West European Politics*, *SELA*, *Democratization*, *Perspectives in Politics*, *Mediterranean Quarterly* and other publications. Publications include: *From Social Democracy to Neoliberalism: The Consequences of Party Hegemony in Spain, 1982–1999* (St. Martin's Press 2000); *A New Century of Corporatism? Corporatism in Southern Europe* (Praeger 2003); *Spain and Portugal in the European Union: The First Fifteen Years* (co-edited with Paul. C. Manuel, Frank Cass 2003).

Ramunas Vilpisauskas is an associate professor at the Institute of the International Relations and Political Science, Vilnius University. The main areas of his scholarly interest include European integration, international political economy and policy analysis. He studied and did research in a number of scholarly institutions including Oslo University, Lancaster University in Britain, European University Institute in Florence and Columbia University, where he stayed as a Fulbright

Scholar. In 2002–2003 he was a visiting fellow at the EU Center, GAI, Syracuse University where he taught a course on EU enlargement. In September, 2004, he gave lectures on European integration as a visiting fellow at Carleton University. During the EU accession negotiations, he has been a consultant to the Lithuanian government. Since 2003, he has been a president of the Lithuanian Political Science Association and a member of the board of the Open Society Foundation. Since November 2004, he has been a chief economic advisor to the president of the Republic of Lithuania. He has an extensive list of publications on EU enlargement, transition reforms, political economy of European integration and regionalism.

Preface

This volume, the result of an elaborate research project, was developed in a historical and current background setting composed of a certain consensus and a general understanding regarding monetary issues in Europe and the world. However, the new circumstances posed by the appearance of the European common currency presented some additional challenges.

On the one hand, it is a widely accepted fact that the US dollar has been the dominant currency of the world economy for almost a century for a single overwhelming reason: it has had no competition. No other economy has come close to the size of that of the United States. The dollar had been the *de facto* world reserve currency: the US currency accounted for approximately two-thirds of all official exchange reserves. More than four-fifths of all foreign exchange transactions and half of all world exports are denominated in dollars. In addition, all IMF loans are denominated in dollars.

However, on the other hand, the introduction of the euro created a motive for diversification into dollars for those investors who had previously obtained some portfolio balance by holding several European currencies. To the extent that the capital flows from Europe to the United States are critical, the future will be determined, at least in part, by the success in Europe of matching the expected rates of return on US assets. But market pressures toward portfolio diversification are clearly also going to play a major role in the future relative positions of the dollar and the euro. The world can only benefit from the competition.

In 1999, twelve European Union countries adopted the euro as their common currency directly competing with the dollar. Since 2002 the euro has gained widespread international acceptance resulting in important institutional, economic and financial changes for the eurozone, the United States and the world's economies, affecting foreign exchange and financial markets as well as economic activities around the world.

A clear example of the euro's impact in the world economy is the fact that Russian banks have been significantly increasing their euro-denominated debt. Deposits outside Russia have been on an upward trend since the end of 1998 and have continued to migrate from banks in the United States to banks resident in Europe. Moreover, President Hugo Chávez of Venezuela has diversified a large amount of assets from dollars to euros. Similarly, Asian central banks have been holding more euros, with the Japanese proving to be the most enthusiastic about the new single European currency. Japan's major corporations have also initiated their own shift to the euro.

The effect of the euro has been far reaching in Latin America. Comparatively, this region is not noted for its strong trade links with the eurozone. Latin America's indisputable reference currency is the US dollar. Nonetheless, the recent considerable increase in economic ties between many of the countries of

Latin America and Europe due to a spectacular European investment trend has a direct impact of the euro and the performance of the economies in the region. In particular, as trade between Europe and Latin America and the Caribbean grows, euro-denominated debt may well account for a larger share of the latter's total foreign debt. Hence, countries in the region need to reassess their hedging strategies. As a result, the euro may benefit from enhanced investment inflows from Europe to Latin America. Moreover, during the last decade the flows of direct European investment toward Latin America reached levels comparable to those from the United States, and the commitment of European banks in the region increased considerably. Probably the biggest driver into the Latin American banking system has been from Spanish and Portuguese banks, increasing the importance of the euro in the region.

In the future, the international role of the euro will eventually hinge on the validity of the fundamental idea underlying its creation, namely that important components of sovereignty can be pooled and shared among nations in the pursuit of common economic and political objectives. There are several issues that are going to be crucial for the presence of the euro in the world economy in the years to come. For example, what are going to be the implications of the failure to ratify the constitution on the euro? How is breaking the barriers for cross-border banking in Europe going to affect the value of the euro and spur growth? How are competitive policies and protectionism going to affect the valuation of the euro?

In consequence, the central mission of "The Euro and the Dollar in a Globalized Economy" project was to involve various disciplines (economics, business, and political science) in order to foment sharing of thoughts intended to facilitate an exchange of ideas among academics, practitioners and the business community.

Participants consulted with a prestigious and select group of economists, political scientists, business leaders and central bankers, assessing the international role of the euro to evaluate its impact on global financial markets, shifting global exchange rate relationships and their implications, and to recount lessons learned and identify future challenges.

In sum, the project adopted the task of covering the following general themes: the dollar and the euro as competing currencies in a globalized economy; EU enlargement and its effects; the euro and the dollar monetary policies; and risks and opportunities in Latin America and the Caribbean.

The Euro and the Dollar in a Globalized Economy is the final result of the discussion and subsequent editing of individual contributions that were finally collectively exposed and commented on at a symposium organized by the European Union Center and the Jean Monnet Chair of the University of Miami, with the support of the European Commission, held at the Biltmore Hotel, Coral Gables, on Tuesday, April 25, 2006. The whole project was made possible by the agreement between the Delegation of the European Commission in Washington DC and the University of Miami. This honor for the academic institution was awarded through a competitive selection among other universities in the United States. The University of Miami had as part of its credentials the record of being the first higher education entity in the United States to organize a pioneer briefing seminar introducing the euro, just after it became an official currency for twelve countries in January of 2002.

The understanding of this mutually beneficial endeavor was signed by Dr. Tomas Leblanc, Provost of the University of Miami, and Ambassador John Brutton, head of the EU Delegation. Research and publication details were developed by Dr. Joaquín Roy, Jean Monnet Professor and Director of the University of Miami EU Center, and Mr. Moreno Bertoldi, head of the outreach programs on the euro at the EU Delegation.

The final event was opened by a brief ceremony co-presided by Ambassador Santiago Cabanas (Consul General of Spain in Miami) and the Honorable Philippe Vinogradoff (Consul General of France). Provost Leblanc introduced Mr. Joaquín Almunia, EU Commissioner of Economic and Monetary Affairs, who in turn offered the opening address, available now as the introductory chapter for this volume. The evening before, Commissioner Almunia was the guest of honor at a reception and dinner presided by the Mayor of Coral Gables, the Honorable Don Slesnick, who presented Almunia with the key to the city.

Sessions of the discussion symposium were chaired by Dr. Claustre Bajona-Xandri (professor of Economics at the University of Miami), Ambassador Ambler H. Moss, Jr. (professor of International Studies at the University of Miami) and Dr. Nicol Rae (professor of Political Science and co-director of the Miami-Florida European Union Center at Florida International University). Comments were made by Dr. Pedro Gomis-Porqueras (professor of Economics at the University of Miami), Dr. Robert A. Einsenbeis (Vice President of Research at the Federal Reserve Bank of Atlanta) and Dr. Roger Kanet (professor of International Studies at the University of Miami). Dr. Michael Halleran (Dean of the College of Arts and Sciences at the University of Miami) introduced Dr. José Manuel González-Páramo (Member of the Executive Board, European Central Bank), who offered a keynote speech, included in this volume.

The symposium proceedings were attended by 149 participants from the faculty and students of local universities, the local business community, government and media. Editing and organizational tasks were carried out by a team of tireless staff members of the EU Center and Jean Monnet Chair, composed of Wendy Grenade (Associate Director of the EU Center), Markus Thiel (Research Associate), María Lorca (Research Assistant), Eloisa Vladescu (Research Assistant), Catherine Cottrell (Editorial Assistant) and Abhay Sudhindra (Research Assistant).

Co-sponsoring institutions and organizations have been the Federal Reserve Bank of Atlanta, the Miami-Florida European Union Center of Excellence (a partnership of the University of Miami and Florida International University), the College of Arts and Sciences and the School of Business Administration of the University of Miami, the Florida International Bankers Association (FIBA), the German American Business Chamber, the Greater Miami Chamber of Commerce, SAF-T-PAY, Greenberg Traurig, the City of Coral Gables, and Diario las Américas. Special gratitude is due to Rosa Sugrañes (Iberia Tiles), Amy Medearis (European Commission), Juan del Busto (Federal Reserve Bank, Miami), Peter Bekx (EU

Commission), Julie McKay (European Central Bank, Washington), Walter Loy (German Chamber of Commerce), Horacio and Helen Aguirre (*Diario las Américas*) and Humberto Castelló (*El Nuevo Herald*).

PART I
The Euro, This Unknown!

Chapter 1

Introduction to the Dollar and the Euro

Pedro Gomis-Porqueras

Introduction

The first seeds of the euro can be traced back to the Treaty of Rome in 1958, establishing the European Economic Community. At this time, the monetary exchange rate between countries was controlled by the Bretton Woods system, which connected all currencies to the US dollar, allowing for only a one point fluctuation around previously designated values. This system worked well for twenty years, helping to stabilize exchange rates and restore economic growth in the postwar period. By 1960, however, the system began to fail, and exchange-rate agreements became the prevalent topic among European political and economic leaders.

By December 1969, Luxembourg's Prime Minister, Pierre Werner, was asked to write a European Community report covering the need for a complete monetary union among the European economies. The 1970 Werner Report brought the idea of a single European currency as part of a cooperative monetary effort. The report was the first to use the term "Economic and Monctary Union".

It was not until 1979 that the European Monetary System was developed, which locked exchange rates among the participating countries into predefined trading zones. This arrangement, in itself, stabilized the economy by creating predictable trading zones (Dyson 1994).The process of creating the euro got its real start a decade later in 1989, when the Delors Report was published. This important report outlined a three-stage transition plan that would create a single European currency. The Delors Report established the transition to a single European currency following a three-stage plan: (1) Stage one began on July 1, 1990, and immediately abolished (at least in principle) all restrictions on the movement of capital between the member states. It also began to identify issues that needed to be dealt with and to develop a working program to implement the upcoming changes. (2) Stage two began on January 1, 1994, and marked the establishment of the European Monetary Institute. This Institute was responsible for coordinating the monetary policy and strengthening the cooperation of the central banks, as well as making preparations for the establishment of the European System of Central Banks, which included the single monetary policy and single currency. (3) Stage three began on January 1, 1999, with the establishment of "irrevocably fixed exchange rates" of the currencies of the current eleven member states (Delors 1989). At this point, the euro was the official currency of those countries, but could only be used in non-cash transactions such as electronic transfers and credit. Greece joined the European Monetary Union in January 2001.

Given the long process required to create the euro it is not too surprising that the dollar has been the dominant currency of the world economy for almost a century. The dollar had no competition for a long time since no other economic block came close to the size or importance of the United States. As a result, the dollar had been the *de facto* world reserve currency. In the past, the US currency accounted for approximately two-thirds of all official exchange reserves. More than four-fifths of all foreign exchange transactions and half of all world exports are denominated in dollars.

There are several benefits to being a reserve currency. If the euro were to become one it would benefit member countries by lowering the service charges on their debts. Since the currency would be so broadly acceptable it would make the premiums paid to debt holders lower, since the risk to the borrower would be lower. The issuer of the reserve currency is freer to pursue macroeconomic policy adjustments to suit its own needs in terms of financing its debt, or influencing other countries. Reserve status would also lower the cost of many commodities for Europeans. Thus a currency gaining reserve status is not just a sign of power but also has important economic benefits.

Since 2002 the euro has gained widespread international acceptance resulting in important institutional, economic and financial changes both for the euro zone, the United States and the world economies, affecting foreign exchange and financial markets as well as economic activities around the world.

A clear example of the euro's impact in the world economy is the fact that, according to the Bank for International Settlements, Russian banks have been significantly increasing their euro-denominated debt. Deposits outside Russia have been on an upward trend since the end of 1998 and have continued to migrate from banks in the United States to banks resident in Europe. Moreover, President Chávez of Venezuela has said that he will diversify a large amount of assets from dollars to euros, obviously a politically motivated measure. Similarly, Asian central banks are holding more euros. Of the Asian nations, it is the Japanese who are the most enthusiastic about the new single European currency.

To the extent that the capital flows from Europe to the United States are critical, the future will be determined, at least in part, by the success in Europe of matching the expected rates of return on US assets. But market pressures toward portfolio diversification are clearly also going to play a major role in the future relative positions of the dollar and the euro. The world can only benefit from the competition.

In order to understand these recent and future trends it is important to analyze the history and characteristics of the underlying institutions that control the two major currencies in the world: the Eurosystem and the Federal Reserve System. The Federal Reserve System was created in 1913 and it is comprised of the Board of Governors and the twelve regional Federal Reserve Banks (FRBs). The location assignment of the FRBs in the individual districts was decided according to the political and economic importance of the individual cities. However, the individual districts have developed differently since the foundation of the Fed. Until 1935 the decisive role was played by the FRBs. The Federal Open Market Committee (FOMC) was founded in 1933 and, at that time, it could only give recommendations whereas the individual FRBs had the right to decide. In order to have a common monetary policy directed to the whole economy in the United States, a basic reform of the Fed occurred in 1935. Open market policy was now placed into the responsibility of the FOMC and the influence of the FRBs in the FOMC was reduced.

On the other hand, the European System of Central Banks comprises the legally independent national European Union central banks (NCBs) (currently fifteen) and the legally independent European Central Bank (ECB). The ECB was established on June 1, 1998, as a common subsidiary of the national central banks located in Frankfurt. In addition to the ECB, the Eurosystem only comprises the national central banks of the countries participating in the monetary union. The Eurosystem bears the exclusive responsibility for monetary policy in the European Monetary Union. The ECB is the "heart" of the Eurosystem. It is responsible for carrying out all tasks of the Eurosystem either through its own activity or through the national central banks. This means that the national central banks are, by function, subordinated to the ECB to allow the Eurosystem to operate efficiently as a single entity with a view to achieving the objectives of the Treaty of Maastricht.

Since both systems were created for different purposes and face different institutional structures, it is not surprising that both systems have some important differences. In particular, the Eurosystem and the Fed have different jurisdictions and laws; they also have different targets in their monetary policies, and they have different fiscal policies. In particular, the Economic and Monetary Union in the EU lacks the equivalent of a national government responsible for monitoring and overseeing the operation of the Central Bank and controlling fiscal policy. This lack of oversight means that the coordination of the two major instruments of macroeconomic policy is difficult, potentially weakening the credibility of the European Central Bank to deliver price stability. Thus, legal requirements are used to influence the behavior of the active participants in the euro, for example, the convergence criteria for Economic and Monetary Union membership. Moreover, an attempt is made to shape a value system by striving to achieve a consensus on what is required in economic policy through various European Council initiatives. These two approaches are apparent in fiscal policy: the control of the balance between the overall level of public expenditure and taxation (Obstfeld and Peri 1998). The fiscal decision remains a national government responsibility, subject to the restrictions of the Stability and Growth Pact and attempts at broad economic policy coordination. The Stability and Growth Pact contains the excessive deficit procedure which is clearly rules-based, while multilateral surveillance attempts to mold the behavior of national governments through consensus and cooperation.

Because the eurozone has a single monetary policy, and so a single interest rate, set by the European Central Bank, it cannot be fine-tuned for the economic situation in each individual country. Public investment and fiscal policy in each country is thus the only way in which government-led economic stimulus can be introduced specific to each member state. This inflexible interest rate might stifle growth in some areas, while over-promoting it in others. These considerations are irrelevant when examining the dollar. As a result, the United States has more flexibility, in other words it has the potential to use fiscal policies to stimulate the economy. Thus, these structural differences between systems are going to have vastly different consequences for the type of policies that both members of the eurozone and the United States can implement, having then real effects on the value of their respective currencies, the euro and dollar.

In terms of monetary policy, both central banks were created for different purposes and face different institutional structures; thus both systems have some important differences directly affecting the underlying value of the euro and the dollar. In particular, the European System of Central Banks and the Federal Reserve System have different jurisdictions and laws; they also have different targets in their monetary policies (Wynne 1999).

The primary objective of the European System of Central Banks is to maintain price stability. The European Union Treaty does not specify a precise timeframe within which this objective should be attained. Without prejudice to the primary goal of price stability, the European System of Central Banks should support the general economic policy in the EU. The monetary policy strategy of the European System of Central Banks was announced at the meetings of the ECB Governing Council in October and December 1998. It is comprised of three main elements: a quantitative definition of price stability, reference value for M3 and a broadly based assessment of price developments. On the other hand, The Federal Reserve Act states the following: "The Board of Governors of the Federal Reserve System and the Federal Open Market Committee shall maintain long run growth of the monetary and credit aggregates commensurate with the country's long run potential to increase production, so as to promote effectively the goals of maximum employment, stable prices and moderate long-term interest rates."

Since its inception then the policy of the Fed may be characterized as a multi-indicator approach without an explicit intermediate target. Within this approach real variables play a decisive role. Major attention is paid to real interest rates and to the (real) term structure. However, before now no variable has become an official intermediate target. These two variables are incorporated into a multi-indicator system for forecasting price developments and the business cycle. The Fed predicts inflationary pressures mainly in the case of rising GDP growth, which manifests itself in increasing capacity utilization (Ruckriegel and Seitz 2002).

These different operating procedures for monetary policy between the eurozone and the United States have vastly different consequences for the corresponding exchange rate policies as well as the potential fiscal policies consistent with the monetary policies followed by the central banks. Given the different structure and nature of the institutions that conduct monetary policy for the euro and the dollar, one can not really ignore these structural differences when predicting the future role of the euro and the dollar.

In the future, the international role of the euro will eventually hinge on the validity of the fundamental idea underlying its creation, namely the idea that important components of sovereignty can be pooled and shared among nations in the pursuit of common economic and political objectives. There are several issues that are going to be crucial for determining the future presence and importance of the euro in the world economy in the years to come. For example, are the euro and the dollar really competing currencies? How has the presence of the euro and the dollar affected the global economy? How is European enlargement going to affect the euro and the dollar? And what risks and opportunities does the euro represent for Latin America and the Caribbean?

The sections in this book try to answer some of these important questions as well as assess the international role of the euro, discuss its impact on global financial markets, shifting global exchange rate relationships and their implications. In Part I, Gomis-Porqueras gives an historical perspective of the euro and the dollar. Almunia then summarizes the accomplishments of the euro over the past few years. Finally, Roy recognizes the non-economic dimension of the euro, emphasizing its symbolism. In Part II, Hübner and Martens analyze the euro and the dollar in the global market. Hübner argues that the appreciation of the euro against the US dollar since 2002 is not a sign of relative economic strength on the side of the economies of the eurozone but, on the contrary, reflects the combination of political and economic weaknesses. This stems from the political and institutional flaws of the euro project. In particular, Hübner suggests that the appreciation of the euro reflects the successful efforts of the US government to talk the dollar down in order to improve its external position. As he points out, the rise of the euro towards the US dollar is the outcome of a deliberate strategy by the United States to deal with its rising trade balance deficit and the explosion in the deficit of its current account. This strategy could work only, however, due to the neutral policy stance of the European Central Bank.

Finally, Martens suggests that analyzing the real and fiscal economies at the same time provides a better understanding of how economies perform. If we analyze the development within the framework that Martens proposes, the recent exchange rate movements of the euro relative to the US dollar may not be too surprising even though the US's macroeconomic performance has been better than Europe's. It is the difference in deficits that help explain the observed trends. The author points out that Greenspan issued a serious warning about the current account deficit and its important implications for the US economy – not only in relation to financing the deficit, but also the question of American dependence on foreign investors, as an increasing proportion of the future wealth created in the United States would have to be paid to investors who had helped finance the deficit. Thus distinguishing between the economic growth and employment and the current account and government budgets are important in determining the future role of the euro and the dollar. The second aspect he considers is the size of the underlying economy since it reduces the sensitivity to external shocks as well as the larger absolute flows of private investment, government debt issuance and gross trade. These higher volumes allow economies of scale and scope in transactions in the domestic currency and exert an implicit pressure for international transactions to be denominated in the domestic currency.

In Part III, with a different perspective, Wijnholds and McKay argue that, based on currency stability and relative economic performance, the euro has been well received internationally but it is not a rival to the US dollar. Their chapter examines what impact the euro has had so far in the international arena using three important criteria. They point out that first aspects to be analyzed are the strength of the underlying economy and the stability of the currency. Internal stability of the currency through low and stable inflation rates as well as external stability through a reliable rate of exchange is crucial. The soundness and credibility of economic policies are key determinants in the emergence of an international currency. Campanella, on the other hand, argues that the current strength of the euro is not necessarily by choice but by coincidence. In particular, the author points out that the current value of the euro is because the United States has the highest external deficit in history, thus reducing the value of the dollar relative to the euro. Asian countries hold large US dollar assets as a guarantee against exchange rate upswings, and Japanese and European exports of goods and capital surplus hedge against weak internal demand and weak potential and actual growth rates. Campanella suggests that this appreciation of the European currency might have mixed blessings since the eurozone economy is more open than larger economies. Therefore, eurozone economies will tend to respond much more to exchange rate movements. Moreover, the euro's appreciation is regarded as a deteriorating factor in the area's competitiveness as structural reforms have not been taken place in Europe.

Finally, Cohen argues that the Eurosystem so far has not been clear regarding the delegation of monetary authority among governments and European Union institutions. Thus the addition of a diverse collection of new members with the recent enlargement can only make the challenge of governance worse. As a result, Cohen argues that these new member countries will intensify the ambiguity at the expense of transparency and accountability. Moreover, the author points out that enlargement will increase the segmentation of Europe's financial markets, increasing the cost of doing business in euros. Cohen argues that with the addition of these new members there is going to be increased complications on an already complex governance structure; the new entrants will cloud even more the fundamental question of who is in charge. As a result, enlargement will diminish the global attractiveness of the euro.

In Part IV Howarth and Royo analyze the governing of the euro and its potential effects on the economy. Howarth analyzes the reform of decision making in the European Central Bank's Governing Council. The author points out that the impact of eurozone enlargement looms large for the European Central Bank, principally because it highlights existing problems with the operation of the Governing Council – problems that reflect the uneasy balance between equality, representativeness and decision-making efficiency. Howarth argues that, given the lack of transparency surrounding the intra-ECB discussions and negotiations on Governing Council reform, the precise policy positions of the different member states and the precise nature of internal debates is impossible to determine for the time being. The impact of these reforms on the economy will be seen in the future and will have a direct impact on the underlying value of the euro. The chapter by Royo examines the impact of EMU integration in Spain. Contrary to expectations it has not led to a process of deep economic structural reforms that would have fostered the development of an economic growth model based on value added and productivity. The examination of the Spanish case will show that the process of economic reforms has to be a domestic process led by domestic actors willing to carry them out.

Vilpsiauskas has a more optimistic view regarding the effects of the new member countries on the euro. This author argues that the first round of new member's accession into the eurozone could have important implications for the discourse about the monetary policy in the European Union, its relationship to domestic structural reforms and the new projects of further integration. In particular, Vilpsiauskas stresses the importance of the political effect of enlarging the monetary union to the domestic discourses about structural reforms in the founders of the EU and the eurozone linked to the broader debates about competitiveness; especially in the labor arena. According to Vilpsiauskas this increased competitiveness in the labor and financial markets have the potential to strengthen rather than weaken the value of the euro.

In Part V, Calderón-Madrid and Granell discuss the role of the euro in developing countries, giving special emphasis to Latin America and the Caribbean countries. Calderón-Madrid examines currency crises in Mexico. The author suggests that crisis might be a powerful instigator of reforms. In the case of Mexico, after the 1985 exchange rate crisis, the economic administration embarked on far-reaching fiscal reform, significantly reduced government subsidies, privatized the majority of state owned enterprise and successfully renegotiated its foreign debt. The 1994–1995 crisis, on the other hand, made evident the need to have more efficient bank regulation, prompting new deposit insurance mechanisms. Finally, in signing the 1993 Free Trade Agreement with the United States and Canada (NAFTA), the authorities took a final – and major – step to ensure a credible and predictable rule-bound behavior to minimize the economic costs of experiencing financial crises. Mexico's experiences with different financial crises and its link to the dollar can serve as useful guides for the new member countries in Europe. Having structural and transparent reforms in the financial system is going to be a crucial element for the new members of the European Union.

On the other hand, Granell studies how the internationalization of the euro is affected by developing countries through bilateral and multilateral transactions with European countries, and the role played by the European countries in the governance and action of the international institutions in these developing countries. The author argues that the expansion of the euro among developing countries is not supported by the attractiveness of high European interest rates, but by a progressive engagement of the European countries with developing nations through trade, investment, aid and other economic relations. Granell argues that the political dimension of the European Union is crucial to understand the future role of the euro in developing countries. Moreover, he points out that, in any case, additional internationalization of the euro would never be dramatic enough to change monetary traditions and inertia would continue to play in favor of the US dollar.

Finally, González-Páramo contemplates different scenarios in the world economic arena and their effects on the euro. In particular, the author discusses the role of the growth of the Chinese economy as well as the importance of the new acquired wealth by oil producing countries in determining the future of the euro.

The contributors of this book try to understand the two major economic blocks and monetary systems in the world and their effects on the evolution of financial markets in this new environment and in determining the world's reserve currency. The different operating procedures for monetary policy in the eurozone and in the United States have vastly different consequences for the corresponding exchange rate policies as well as the potential fiscal policies consistent with the monetary policies followed by the central banks. Given the different structure and nature of the institutions that conduct monetary policy for the euro and the dollar, one cannot really ignore these structural differences when predicting the future role of the euro and the dollar, and this book tries to shed some light on these complicated issues.

References

Delors, J. (1989), "Report on Economic and Monetary Union in the European Community", a report to the European Council by a Committee chaired by J. Delors, Brussels Commission of the European Community.

Dyson, K. (1994), *Elusive Union: The Process of Economic and Monetary Union in Europe* (London: Longman).

Obstfeld, M. and Peri, G. (1998), "Regional Non-Adjustment and Fiscal Policy", Economic Policy 26, 207–47.

Ruckriegel, K. and Seitz, F. (2002), "The Euro System and the Federal Reserve System Compared: Facts and Challenges", Working Paper Center for European Integration Studies.

Wynne, M. (1999), "The European System of Central Banks", *Economic Review*, First Quarter.

Chapter 2

Seven Years with the Euro

Joaquín Almunia

In the eight years since the creation of the Monetary Union, the euro has emerged as a strong and stable currency. The aim of this chapter is to discuss the main achievements of these first eight years with the euro in terms of macroeconomic stability, reduced transaction costs, greater competition and financial stability. The chapter will also assess the euro's progress in establishing itself as an international currency and consider the prospects for further strengthening the euro's global role. Before developing these themes, however, the chapter first examines the evolution of the euro–dollar exchange rate since the introduction of the euro.

Since the birth of the euro in January 1999, the euro–dollar exchange rate has seen some marked gyrations. The first three years of the single currency were characterized by euro depreciation, with the value of the euro falling from about US$1.17 to below 83 cents at its lowest point in October 2000. Starting in early 2002, the euro then recovered and peaked at slightly above US$1.36 in late 2004, before falling back somewhat during 2005. Since early 2006, the euro has started strengthening again, to historical heights – over US$1.36.

In real effective terms, and taking a slightly longer perspective, the euro – or its legacy currencies before 1999 – is now close to its historical average for the last twenty-five years. This reflects the confidence that market participants are investing in the euro, a confidence which partly explains why, relatively soon after its introduction, the euro has succeeded in establishing itself as a major international currency.

The introduction of the euro in 1999 was a logical step in the process of European economic integration, a process which extends as far back as the 1950s. Initially, the main priority of Europe's integration was to foster trade between the European Union (EU) member states by making their economies more interdependent.

Of course, the liberalization of trade is a centuries-old historical phenomenon, and is not confined to Europe. But never before has any regional grouping of countries succeeded in pursuing economic integration to the extent that Europe has done. Customs duties between European countries came down steadily in the 1950s and disappeared entirely in 1968 with the completion of the customs union. Subsequently, Europe was to see the harmonization of standards and the gradual dismantling of non-tariff barriers, finally resulting in their abolition following the completion of the single market in 1993.

However, by strengthening economic interdependence between member countries, the single market had reduced the room for independent policy maneuvers and amplified the cross-border effects of developments originating in each member country. With full freedom of capital movements and fully integrated financial markets, incompatible national economic policies would quickly give rise to exchange rate tensions and put an increasing and undue burden on monetary policy. The single market therefore made a more intense and more effective co-ordination of economic policies indispensable.

It is no coincidence that, historically, a single market and a single currency develop alongside one another. The efficiency gains brought about by market integration are amplified by monetary integration. It is therefore hardly surprising that against a background of progressive trade integration, exchange-rate arrangements have become a major concern for EU policy makers. The concept behind this is both very strong and quite simple: one market, one money. Research has shown that the full benefits of the internal market can only be reaped with a high degree of exchange-rate stability.

The euro is now the single currency of the thirteen member states that have fulfilled the conditions for its adoption. It delivers economic and financial benefits primarily through the four following channels.

First, the single currency establishes a culture of macroeconomic stability across the euro area. The economic policy framework that underpins the euro is strongly oriented towards stability. Notably, the independent European Central Bank has a clear mandate to maintain price stability, defined as an inflation rate below, but close to, 2 per cent, while the fiscal rules – as defined in the reformed Stability and Growth Pact (SGP) – are designed to guard against excessive deficits and the unsustainable accumulation of debt. The reformed SGP maintains the overall focus on fiscal stability, while addressing a number of problems that were identified over the first five years of its existence. In particular, the new pact puts increased focus on debt sustainability and the need to make greater adjustment efforts in economic good times.

This framework has already delivered low inflation and historically low interest rates throughout the euro area. Such progress is particularly noteworthy in those countries with a previous history of high inflation, such as Greece, Italy, Portugal and Spain. In these countries, the annual inflation rate has decreased from an average of approximately 7.5 per cent in the first half of the 1990s to an average of around 3 per cent since the introduction of the euro in 1999.

The reduction in inflation has allowed average long-term interest rates in the euro area countries to fall by almost two-thirds from above 9 per cent in the mid-1990s to the current level of approximately 4 per cent. Needless to say, the stable macroeconomic framework brought about by the introduction of the euro is also conducive to higher sustainable growth and employment.

The second channel through which the euro delivers economic benefits to its members is by lowering transaction costs. Preceding the introduction of the euro, such transaction costs amounted to 0.5 per cent of gross domestic product (GDP) in the European Union. Costs associated with foreign exchange management and cross-border transfers by companies have also been removed. The lowering of transaction costs has allowed for a more efficient allocation of resources, and has led to increased trade in goods and services. Consequently, exports and imports of goods within the euro area have increased from approximately 26.5 per cent of GDP in 1998 to around 31 per cent of GDP in 2005, whereas intra-euro area trade in services increased from 6 per cent of GDP to 7.5 per cent of GDP over the same period. Euro area trade in services with countries outside the euro area has also increased, but not at the same pace, suggesting that the introduction of the euro has accelerated trade integration among its members.

The euro has also acted as a catalyst for integration in the field of foreign direct investment (FDI). During the decade leading to 2005 , the stock of intra-euro area FDI grew from less than 14 per cent of euro area GDP to around 26 per cent. This considerable increase represents an important process of catching-up with extra-euro area FDIs, which however still amount to 34 per cent of euro area GDP.

The third means by which the euro supports European economies is by making markets more transparent. The introduction of the euro has increased price transparency, allowing consumers to compare prices more directly, and firms to compare costs more easily. This has helped to boost price competition and has improved the efficiency of markets.

Operating via these channels, the euro creates the conditions for greater prosperity in Europe. Moreover, there is a fourth key benefit brought about by the introduction of the single currency: financial stability, both within the euro area and globally. Undoubtedly, the euro has added to financial stability within the euro area by eliminating the risk of exchange rate tensions among the member states. By creating deeper, more liquid and diversified pan-European financial markets, the euro has also enhanced the resilience of the EU to external financial shocks. Nevertheless, it is true that the increasing cross-border financial linkages within the EU heighten the risk of contagion from one member state to another.

Appropriate procedures and institutional arrangements for prudential supervision are therefore required. These include comprehensive cooperation and exchange of information between all relevant authorities in addition to improved arrangements for cross-border supervision. This commitment to enhanced supervisory co-operation applies not only to relations within the EU, but also to relations between the EU and its partners in multilateral or bilateral fora. As the international role of the euro has expanded, its importance for global financial stability has also increased.

Examining the global role of the euro in more detail it is clear that, since its creation, the euro has increased its weight in some areas, such as cross-border bond issuance and trade, but shows less progress in others, such as official foreign exchange reserves. For example, in September 2006 the euro accounted for 30 per cent of the sum of outstanding international debt securities. This compares to little over a fifth in 1999. Over the same period, the share of the US dollar declined moderately from almost half to approximately 46 per cent. The euro's share as an invoicing and settlement currency has been on a clear upward trend, exceeding 50 per cent for both imports and exports in many euro area countries in 2004. Conversely, in the foreign exchange markets, the euro's share has remained fairly stable at less than a fifth of all transactions. This is still far behind the US dollar, which accounts for 44 per cent of all transactions.

Meanwhile the euro's share in international reserves has, in recent years, stabilized at around 25 per cent following a rapid increase in the first few years of the currency's introduction. However, it is necessary to interpret these numbers with some caution, as they do not include data for some of the biggest reserve accumulators in recent years – notably in Asia – which do not report the currency composition of their reserves.

The use of the euro is particularly high in the new member states and in the immediate neighborhood of the EU, such as Eastern Europe, the Western Balkans and North Africa. Many of the countries in these regions have exchange rate regimes linked to the euro, which has helped stabilize their exchange rates. In this way, the stability-oriented economic framework underlying the euro provides an anchor for countries seeking to import economic stability.

A look at the key economic criteria found in the literature on international currencies – such as the size of GDP and trade flows, the size and efficiency of the domestic financial system and the existence of a stable macroeconomic framework – suggests that the euro could eventually play an international role to rival the importance of the dollar. This would continue a trend observed since the early 1970s pointing towards a decline in the international role of the dollar and the emergence of a 'bipolar' or 'tripolar' currency system.

This issue gains particular relevance in the current context of large global imbalances. Over the last decade, the US current account deficit has gradually increased, reaching 6.5 per cent of GDP in 2006. The counterpart to this deficit is the development of large surpluses in Asia and the oil-exporting countries. Such imbalances are due to unsustainable trends in the international distribution of savings and investment, with the United States saving too little and the rest of the world, particularly Asia, either investing too little or, in the case of China, saving too much.

The manner in which these imbalances unwind is not only crucial for the outlook of the global economy, but could also have implications for the role of the US dollar as the world's preferred reserve currency. Should the rest of the world become less willing to finance the US deficit by continuing to accumulate US dollar assets, it could result in higher interest rates and a sharp depreciation of the US dollar. With the introduction of the euro and its stability-oriented institutional framework, there is now an attractive alternative to the US dollar. This should function as a stabilizing factor should the international economic environment turn more volatile.

The above assessment of the euro and the evidence provided in this paper clearly prove that, by contributing to macroeconomic stability and economic integration, the euro has been supportive of growth. However, in order for the euro area economy to reach its full potential it is necessary to step up progress on structural reforms. Therefore the re-launching of the Lisbon Strategy for Jobs and Growth, comprising a comprehensive agenda of structural reforms, is a particularly welcome step forward.

In conclusion, one can justifiably state that the euro, despite its short existence, has already proven its worth. The single currency represents a milestone in Europe's quest for deeper EU integration. By inspiring confidence among consumers, producers and investors both within the euro area itself and well beyond its borders, the euro has strengthened macroeconomic stability and firmly established itself as the second most important international currency.

Chapter 3

A Financial and Politically Symbolic Tool*

Joaquín Roy

Introduction

When an officer of the European Commission was once asked what he did for a living, he answered: "I work for the European Union". "Oh, I did not know that you were in insurance" – responded the apparently surprised US businessman. "I am" – the witty officer cleverly retaliated. We are all in fact involved in the business of insuring the European future. The euro, the new currency, can be considered as the new Portuguese *escudo* (shield).

A New Bold Action

Since Robert Schuman, French Minister of Foreign Affairs, issued his famous "Declaration of Inter-Dependency" (as some innovative commentators like to call it) on May 9, 1950, announcing the establishment of the European Community of Coal and Steel (an original idea of his advisor Jean Monnet), no other European Union (EU) move has been as dramatically symbolic as the adoption of the euro. The name of the new currency came after much debate. According to insiders, no one really liked the name too much, and that is what convinced all sides. The EU has been built largely by consensus and avoidance of confrontation. The naming of the currency was executed the same way. France apparently was the only country persisting in keeping the ECU, an abbreviation of European Currency Unit, the accounting measure used for a decade, actually the name of an old French coin used in the eighteenth century. Diverse names as euromark, caesar (a Spanish suggestion, honoring the first recognized European citizen), and franken, were considered, but finally euro prevailed. French President Chirac proposed delaying the decision until 2002, after a popular survey, an idea that

---

* This chapter reflects an expansion and update of an essay presented at the introductory conference on the euro held on January 2002, as part of the activities of the Miami European Union Center. The author would like to express gratitude for the editing efforts provided by Aimee Kanner, Wendy Grenade, Eloisa Vladescu, Catherine Cottrell, and the suggestions made by Tomas Gronberg.

was rejected by his colleagues led by Germany's Helmut Kohl. Greece did not succeed either in stopping the endorsement of the euro, claiming difference in its alphabet. Finally, pressure came from other leaders (among them Spain's Felipe González) advocating the symbolism of Europe. The consensus then was that it was not very original, but its lack of any source for friction made it acceptable to all. For the adoption of a logo, the European Commission asked for no fewer than thirty sketches from a team of skilful designers. Ten were chosen and submitted for public scrutiny. Two of these were selected, and the final choice was made by EU Commission President Jacques Santer and Finance Commissioner Yves-Thibault de Silguy. It was a winner: inspired by the Greek letter epsilon (born in the cradle of Europe) and two parallel lines symbolizing stability, a thought tenaciously sought by the EU leadership. The final decision was made at the Madrid European Council of December 1995.

On January 1, 2002, twelve European countries began to use a common currency.[1] The culmination of a long series of efforts to respond to the formidable challenges in this new and crucial stage in the history of the EU was more political than financial. The technical and financial doubts raised in Europe about the efficacy and the benefits of adopting a common currency were muted by the political will to proceed. To rephrase the comment made during the 1992 US presidential campaign that propelled Governor Bill Clinton to defeat the incumbent President George H. Bush, it could be said that the reason for adopting the euro "was politics, stupid" – not economics. The move marked the end of a cycle that had begun in the mid-1980s (during the uncertainty of the political changes to come with the end of the Cold War) when what was then the European Community (EC) decided to take the road that led to the Single European Act of 1986, which completed the Common Market, and the Maastricht Treaty of 1992, which transformed the EC into the more ambitious European Union. The euro was a new "bold act", as was Schuman's declaration.

In the closing act of the Belgian presidency at the Laeken European Council held on December 14–15, 2001, and as a prelude to the Spanish presidency, the EU opted to call for a Convention presided over by the former president of France, Valèry Giscard D'Estaing (Ludlow, 2002). This extraordinary gathering was given the high mission of drafting what was grandly branded as a Constitution, although it was in fact an elaborate EU treaty with the task of collectively codifying and superseding the series of treaties that have held together the European project for more than half a century (Borrell, Carnero and López, 2003; Norman, 2003; Lamassoure, 2004; de Poncins, 2003). Mistakenly modeled by some observers and protagonists after the US Constitutional Convention held in Philadelphia, this unprecedented meeting of European notables delivered a thick, convoluted and complicated document to the customary intergovernmental conference to decide the future structures of European integration.

Unfortunately, after a series of give-and-take actions among governments over details of the qualified voting system, the national voters of France and the

1 Two other EU member states have a formal opt-out clause (the United Kingdom and Denmark) and one rejected the adoption of the euro in a referendum (Sweden).

Netherlands derailed the ratification process (a must, according to the regulations). The European Council then placed *since die* the whole project in mothballs, giving the EU time to decide on a future coursebecause, in order for the Constitutional text to be approved, it has to be ratified by either parliamentary vote or national referendum in each and all of the 25 member states.[2] With two negative votes, the Council interpreted that the project was dead, in fact violating the explicit mandate to hold ratification processes in all the countries and denying the right of citizens and its representatives in the countries still pending the referendum or parliamentary motion to enjoy what their counterparts in other states experienced. The balance is that a majority of fourteen states and a substantial majority of citizens have indeed approved the Constitution.

In any event all this extraordinary activity around the adoption of the euro commenced while the EU was facing the consequences of the decision taken during the French presidency at the Nice European Council in December 2000 (Bond and Feus, 2001; Fukuda and Akiba, 2003; Galloway, 2001; Stubb, 2002; Vilà Costa, 2001; Martínez Cuadrado, 2001). A green light was given for the most spectacular enlargement operation of the EU's history. In fact, this enlargement was considered to be the main reason for the EU to adopt a new Constitutional Treaty: to reformat and rationalize an institutional structure meant for only six original members. The existing fifteen members of the EU in 2001 may reach a total of almost thirty by the end of the decade – definitely including Bulgaria and Romania in 2007, leaving out of Europe (temporarily, according to certain experts) only Russia, certain of its former satellites in its vicinity and in the Balkans, and possibly the perennial candidate, Turkey.

Of all of the previous developments in EU history, none carries greater symbolic weight than the adoption of the euro, which is the logical consequence of a decision taken in the mid-1980s to complete the common market, the subject of the 1957 Treaty of Rome. Since then, the vague direction in which the EU was headed has evolved into a definitive course. The goal was always to create a novel form of cooperation between states that was different from the traditional structures of federations, confederations, nation-states (in the traditional sense) and international organizations built around an intra-governmental logic (like the United Nations).

In the humorous definition of Jacques Delors, the former president of the European Commission and engine behind the drive towards Maastricht and the euro, the EU is a UPO – an "unidentified political object" (Roy, 2004). The rest of the world will have to get used to the fact that the EU is different, although

---

2 For a evaluation on this failure, see my commentary: "After the French and Dutch Rejection of the EU Constitution", European Union Center/Jean Monnet Chair, May 2005 http://www.miami.edu/eucenter/eu-france-2000final.pdf and my column: "Después del 'non' francés", *El Nuevo Herald*, 30 mayo 2005 http://www.miami.com/mld/elnuevo/news/opinion/11771118.htm; *La Opinión de los Angeles* http://www.laopinion.com/print.html?rkey=00050530134203383325; Inter Press Service (IPS); *Diario Correo* (Bilbao) 31 mayo 2005; Nueva Mayoría http://www.nuevamayoria.com/ES/ANALISIS/?id=roy&file=050531.html.

it is rather convoluted and confusing to foreign observers in its institutional and negotiating dimensions. US Secretary of State Madeleine Albright, frustrated and fascinated by dealing with Brussels, once said that in order to understand the European Union you must be French or very intelligent – or both (Roy, 2003). The same logic for not understanding the aim and purposes of the euro apparently dominates the views of extremist US observers who, for example, early predicted that the new currency would cause wars among Europeans besides posing a threat to the United States (Feldstein, 1997). No wonder the presentation of the euro on Wall Street by none other than EU's Commission President Romano Prodi turned to be an attendance disaster.[3] Although the reasons are complex and combined, the initial fall in the value of the euro in its exchange with the dollar has been balanced by its steady and spectacular rise in 2006 and 2007, reaching a rate of 1.36, leveling off at a rate of 1.20.

In any event, the EU may be still unknown or opaque, but it has followed a steady path of European integration. Although European citizens still are inclined to value high-value assets (such as automobiles and housing) in the former currencies, daily life purchases are routinely understood in euros. The adoption of the euro has certainly helped to consolidate the message of unity, though not as the sublimation of what Winston Churchill called the "United States of Europe" in Zurich in 1946. Well before that, a group of European leaders and commentators, mostly French, had alluded directly to the same project. From Victor Hugo in the mid-nineteenth century to the German socialists in the early 1900s, from the visionary Hungarian count Coudenhove-Kalergi in the 1920s to Ortega y Gasset in the context of his classic essay *The Rebellion of the Masses* in 1930, all shared the obsession of the French Minister of Foreign Affairs Aristide Briand with forging a solid federation, later buried beneath the ashes of the Second World War.

From the evolution of experiments in integration, two models have emerged. One involves the tenacious integration of all sectors of the economy to inexorably include politics as well; the other consists simply in the elimination of tariffs and the advancement of free trade (Roy, 2005). In essence, this dichotomy has surfaced during the referendum processes in France and the Netherlands that froze the ratification move. One faction of voters thought that the Constitution offered too little progress in further integration and social protection, and the other judged that it went too far and it was not pro-business and pro-national enough, that it was too liberal. The essential difference in the EU project is that each advance in the process of integration is another step towards the apparently impossible goal of maintaining the nation-state while simultaneously constructing another entity to administer a shared sovereignty. This common basket (the first pillar, in euro-speak) has been growing tenaciously since 1950, to the point that only a few detectable dimensions of national sovereignty seem to remain today – defense/foreign affairs and justice, the second and third pillars, respectively.

3 Isabel Piquer, "Nueva York desprecia al euro en una visita de Romano Prodi a Wall Street", *El País*, 13 enero 2002.

Nostalgia for National Sovereignty

However, the fever for integration and the commitment for inter-state cooperation still co-exist with a healthy resistance to a potential loss of national identity. A cursory analysis of the bank notes and coins of the euro reveal a fascinating picture worth exploring.

Owls, swans, lions and eagles; doors, bridges, windows; Zeus and Venus; Marianne and Brandenburg; Beatrice of Holland, Albert of Belgium and Juan Carlos of Spain; Mozart and Celtic harps; Dante and Cervantes. It seems that anything goes in symbolizing Europe and its nationalities. On what grounds George Wills,[4] among other US columnists, could say that the new European money is "bland" and "not pretty"?

The bank notes, elegant and sober, have been unfairly criticized for their apparent neutrality and alleged lack of identification. On the contrary, there is nothing more explicit of European self-identity than the historical and cultural stages depicted as illustrations for the €5, 10, 20, 50, 100, 200 and 500 bills. With the virtual drawings made by Robert Kalina, an Austrian artist (also selected on the basis of an open competition), different variances of windows, doors, arches and bridges (intended to express communication and integration) are used to graphically showcase the fundamental periods of European civilization and architecture: Classic Greco-Roman (€5), Romanesque (€10), Gothic (€20), Renaissance (€50), Baroque and Rococo (€100), Iron and Glass (€200), and modern of the twentieth century (€500). What unites (or should unite) the Europeans is a point of reference (to themselves) in each of these eras and is worthy of a long meditation; not only the response of an occasional op-ed piece, but also whole books.[5] Euroeskeptics could not resist commenting that the bills depicted fictional, but not real, bridges, as reflection of a negative view of the EU project. The fact is that the symbolic pictures were chosen so not to prime "tourist" sites and at the same time alluding to all samples of artistic periods.

A different, but just as complex, terrain for research is present in the inspection, not of the constructivist and shared identity reflected in the bills, but of the election of the national symbols and images used for the €1 and €2 coins, and in the smaller pieces of 1, 2, 5, 10, 20, and 50 cents.[6] While the bank notes are the prerogative of the European Central Bank, the national mints control the production of the coins.[7] The number of coins decided was based on the fact

4 "In Europe, It's a Bland New Day", *The Times-Picayune*, December 30, 2001, p. B7; Tom Zeller, "The Color of Consensus", *The New York Times*, January 6, 2002.

5 For a complete analysis of the development of the bank notes and its significance, see Jacques E.C. Hymans, "Money for Mars?: The Euro Banknotes for European Identity", included in the comprehensive volume edited with the papers presented at a conference held in 2002, edited by Robert M. Fishman and Anthony M. Messina, 2006.

6 Alicia P. Barker-Aguilar, "Iconography and Identity: Constructing the Political Symbolism of the Euro", unpublished undergraduate thesis, Princeton University, 2003.

7 Article 106 (ex 105a) of the Treaty regulates the control of the euro. Council Regulation No. 974/98 and Council Regulation 975/98 specify the conditions of the euro

that the average of national coins was 7.17. The weight and material used are the result of an elaborate process of consultation with many sectors of European society, among them the European Vending Association, and taking into account the needs of the blind. After a complete study, nickel was accepted to be used in combinations for the €1 and €2 coins (while yellow in external color). Nordic gold is used in 50, 20 and 10 cent coins (yellow in appearance), while copper-covered steel is the material of the 5, 2 and 1 cent coins (red in color).

The Ecofin council of the Spring 1996 meeting in the Italian city of Verona gave the final directive for the euro coins to have one side common and another national. A call was then made for proposing the European side. After panel evaluation and public polls came to the selection of a design made by Belgian Royal Mint designer Luc Luycx: 1, 2 and 5 cent coins would have a map of Europe in the world; 10, 20 and 50 cent coins would show a group of nations and the €1 and €2 coins would illustrate Europe as a whole. The national side was then left to the wishes of the each of the countries.[8]

By just concentrating on the €1 and 1 cent coins, there is ample field for speculation. Germany, Spain and France do not surprise with their traditionalism (the Brandenburg gate, Cervantes and republican symbols), while Greece and Portugal demonstrate their geniality and tenacity. A closer examination offers plenty of objects of study of national identity, self-restraint, a certain degree of show-off and prudence, if not lack of originality.

In general, in the coins of lesser value, France seems to try to make a solid statement with the inclusion of classic Marianne – young, feminine and republican – which represents, according to official statements, a "solid and solidarian Europe". Only two other French designs appear on the nine coins. One is a tree contained in a hexagon, symbolizing "life, continuity and growth", surrounded by the Republican motto of "liberté, égalité, fraternité". The second is a sower, which is a constant in French monetary history, illustrating France integrating into Europe. While parliamentary monarchies in the Netherlands, Luxembourg and Belgium insist on using the images of current royals (the Nordic states of Sweden and Denmark are absent from the euro family), Spain has decided to trace back its roots of national identity to the basilica of Santiago de Compostela, including the more traditional option of the portrait of Cervantes, all reinforced by King Juan Carlos I on the €1 and €2 coins. Austria has preferred to self-illustrate in a musical and ecological fashion Mozart and diverse flowers, among them the mythical edelweiss. Ireland endorses this musical resonance with a Celtic harp, and the name of the country, Eire, in Gaelic. This is a linguistic point that is replicated by Luxembourg. Republican Finland elected to be represented by blackberry flowers, two swans flying over a lake, and the heraldic lion. Animal symbols are also present in other national sides of the coins. Germany responds with the

---

coins. On October 1996, the Finance Ministers decided the subdivision of the euro into 100 cents.

8 European Commission, Directorate General for Economic and Financial Affairs, 2000, "Euro Coins: From Design to Circulation: Euro Papers 37" http://europa.eu.int/comm/economy_finance/publications/euro_papers/europapers37_en.htm.

predictable eagle, combining with the architectural emblem of the Brandenburg gate and oak twigs.

Without match, Italy outpaces all with exuberance: Roman emperors (Marcus Aurelius on horseback on the 50 cent coin), the Coliseum (5 cents), palazzos (Molle Antonelliana, 2 cents) and fortresses (Castel de Monte, 1 cent) accompany Boticelli's Venus (10 cents), works by Raphael (Dante's portrait, €2) and da Vinci's human body drawing (€1), a copy of which the United States took to the moon. It seems as if the Italian designers wanted to remind the rest of the continent that, without the richness of Italian art, Europe would not be the same. This message served to counterbalance the perception that the Italian government holding office at the time was ambivalent to the deepening process of European integration. Upon the introduction of the euro, Italy's Minister of Foreign Affairs, Renato Ruggiero, resigned over a polemic involving the Prime Minister Silvio Berlusconi and other members of the cabinet, who questioned the efficacy of the new currency.[9] Coincidentally, the present volume is the consequence of a conference held at the outcome of the April 2006 Italian elections that produced the defeat of Berlusconi by former European Commission president Romano Prodi. It came after a rocky relationship between the Italian premier and the Brussels institutions that expressed relief after his loss. Nonetheless, historians know very well that while the foundation of the EU is credited to the Franco-German alliance, an EU without Italy would be inconceivable, no matter who is in power.

Only Austria appears to challenge Italy's artistic leadership. A classic building in Vienna (50 cents), the Belvedere palace (20 cents) and St. Stephen's Cathedral (10 cents) are in the company of portraits of the 1905 Nobel Peace Price laureate Bertha von Suttner (€2) and Mozart (€1), complemented by nature's symbolism of Alpine roses (5 cents), edelweiss (2 cents) and a gentian flower (1 cent). It should be noted that, besides symbolic French Marianne, von Suttner (on her own intellectual merits) and Queen Beatrix (by virtue of lineage) are the only women honored in the twelve countries' coins, which has been blamed by European observers as sexist.[10]

A message of sobriety and tenacity is present in the coins produced by Portugal. Feeling the loss of references to Henry the Navigator, Pedro Alvares Cabral and Vasco da Gama, the Portuguese wanted to get the record straight.[11] Their early royal seals of the 1100s (precisely 1144, 1142 and 1134) reinforce Portugal's deanship as the oldest European well-defined nation-state (territory, people, language, unified state), interlacing castles and shields with the current European symbolism.

---

9 Reuters, "Berlusconi Under Attack and Foreign Minister Quits", *The New York Times*, January 6, 2002; David Williams, "Italy's Foreign Minister Resigns", *The Washington Post*, January 6, 2002, p. A18.

10 Joost Klarenbeek, "Female Heads Fail to Make Impression", Letter to *Financial Times*, April 19, 2006, in response to *FT Observer*'s note "No Harm Mint", April 11, 2006.

11 Alan Cowell, "Portugal is Losing a History Told in Bank Notes", *The New York Times*, December 30, 2001.

In addition to the fact the euro sign (€) is an adaptation of the Greek letter epsilon, Greece captured a special top prize for originality with an enigmatic owl, which originated in the now-defunct drachma coin, the oldest currency of Europe until its demise. Moreover, perhaps to remind the rest of Europe that Greece was at one point in danger of remaining out of the eurozone for lacking certain economic indicators, the rape of Europa by Zeus, transfigured as a classic bull, is illustrated on the €2 coins. Just in case, other euro coins minted in Greece add portraits of thinkers and political leaders who contributed to forge Greek nationalism and a Balkan confederacy free from Turkish domination. History is also completed by illustrations of ships placed on the lesser denomination coins.

Finally, one must note that some non-EU microstates actually issue euro coins (but not banknotes): Monaco (that ceased to use the defunct French franc), and San Marino and the Vatican (using until then the Italian lira). The Vatican State has issued three different series illustrating the changes at the head. Following the change in Spring 2005, there are already two series of Vatican circulation coins. The first series, bearing the effigy of the former Pope John Paul II, was issued between 2002 and 2005. Then, a limited special "sede vacante" issuance bearing the coat of arms of the Cardinal Chamberlain was circulated. Finally, a third series with the effigy of His Holiness Benedict XVI was issued.[12] Commemorative coins have been also issued by different states.[13]

The Next Step

Political theory and logic teaches that national sovereignty is defended through the control of territory (with its economy regulated by transactions in a given currency) and the monopoly of force (exercised by the police and the armed forces). With the national currencies no more (at least in the twelve-member eurozone), what remains is maintaining domestic order and an army as the remnants of traditional state sovereignty. There are signs that these two elements are in the process of being eroded and pooled. Since September 11, 2001, there has been spectacular progress in the adoption of a common judicial space, at least in reaching a continental definition of what constitutes a terrorist threat.

With the euro in circulation, all that remains is the integration of the national armies. Though the road is still too long, about 100 military officials from the fifteen EU member countries began to meet in Brussels to work out the logistics for the deployment of 60,000 soldiers to conflict zones as part of the Rapid Reaction Force, the nucleus of the future European army. Joint EU forces have seen action in Africa and took over the security in Kosovo from NATO control. Still, what defines the EU apart from other international alliances, especially

12 See European Commission website: http://europa.eu.int/comm/economy_finance/euro/notes_and_coins/coins_images_vat_2002_en.htm.

13 For details, see "The Euro: Our Currency" section of the EU Commission website: http://europa.eu.int/comm/economy_finance/euro/notes_and_coins/commemorative_coins_en.htm.

the ones that base their influence on the use (real or potential) of force is what has been termed as "soft power". Along the inspiration that EU integration has dispersed through different regions of the world (especially in Latin America), the integrating engine that the euro represents is a unique expression of this soft power. And it is a mechanism for protection. The Portuguese may then claim that the *escudo* has a new shape: it is a European insurance policy.

References

Bond, M. and Feus, K. (eds) (2001), *The Treaty of Nice Explained* (London: Federal Trust).

Borrell, J., Carnero, C. and López Garrido, D. (2003), *Construyendo la Constitución Europea* (Madrid: Real Instituto Elcano).

Feldstein, M. (1997), "EMU and International Conflict", *Foreign Affairs*, November/ December, 60–73.

Fishman, R. and Messina, A. (eds) (2006), *The Year of the Euro: The Cultural, Social, and Political Import of Europe's Common Currency* (Notre Dame, IN: University of Notre Dame Press).

Fukuda, K. and Akiba, H. (eds) (2003), *European Governance After Nice* (New York: Routledge).

Galloway, D. (2001), *The Treaty of Nice and Beyond: Realities and Illusions of Power in the EU* (Sheffield, UK: Sheffield Academic Press).

Lamassoure, A. (2004), *Histoire secrete de la Convention Européenne* (Paris: Fondation Shuman).

Ludlow, P. (2002), *The Laeken Council* (Brussels: Eurocomment).

Martínez Cuadrado, M. (2001), *Estructura política de la Unión Europea: El Tratado de Niza y sus efectos en los fundamentos constitucionales de la Unión* (Madrid: Universidad Complutense).

Norman, P. (2003), *The Accidental Constitution* (Brussels: Eurocomment).

Roy, J. (2003), "La Unión Europea: de la arquitectura a la alquimia", in Roy, J., Domínguez, R. and Velázquez, R. (eds), *Retos e interrelaciones de la integración regional: Europa y América* (México: Universidad Nacional de Quintana Roo/Plaza y Valdés), 53–77.

Roy, J. (2004), "La naturaleza de la Unión Europea", in *La Unión Europea y el TLCAN: Integración regional comparada y relaciones mútuas* (México: UNAM. Joaquín Roy, R., Chanona, A. y Domínguez, R. (compiladores)), 183–202.

Roy, J. (2005), "The Nature of the European Union", in Van Der Hoek, P. (ed.), *Public Administration and Public Policy in the European Union* (New York: Taylor and Francis), 77–111.

Roy, J. and Domínguez, R. (2005), *La Unión Europea y la Integración Regional: Perspectivas comparadas y lecciones para las Américas*, Roy, J., Peña, F. y Lladós, J.M. (eds) (Buenos Aires: Universidad Nacional de Tres de Febrero/ Consejo Argentino de Relaciones Internacionales), 7–19.

Stubb, A. (2002), *Negotiating Flexibility in the European Union* (Basingstoke, UK: Palgrave).

Vilà Costa, B. (2001), *El horizonte institucional de la UE tras la conferencia intergubernamental (de Biarritz a Niza)* (Barcelona: Universitat Autònoma de Barcelona/Institut Universitari d'Estudis Europeus).

PART II
The Euro–Dollar Exchange Rate: A Puzzling Relationship

Chapter 4

Euro–Dollar Puzzles

Kurt Hübner

Puzzles

The euro came with a heavy load. One of the many "bags" was filled with the expectation that the euro would foster or even create the missing European identity that is seen as essential for the further development of the European project (Hübner 2005). A next bag was filled with the hope that the new currency could become a competitor to the US dollar and fulfill the whole range of the functions of money on a global scale (Campanella 2006; Hau, Killeen and Moore 2002). A further bag was filled with skepticism about the sustainability of the new money fuelled by the fact that the eurozone was not even close of fulfilling the criteria of an optimum currency area (Feldstein 2000). A majority of university-based German economists, for example, were arguing that the euro would undermine the "inflation-fighting culture" established by the German central bank and being Europeanized via the mechanisms of the European Monetary System (EMS), (see Schroeder 2003). And then was the argument that the transfer of monetary policy to a single European Central Bank in combination with the ceiling of fiscal policy due to the regulations of the Stability and Growth Pact would destroy any chance for an optimal policy mix (Arestis *et al.* 2002).

This chapter will look into another "bag" by discussing the strong appreciation of the euro against the US dollar since 2002. I will argue that the appreciation of the euro is not a sign of relative economic strength on the side of the economies of the eurozone but on the contrary reflects the combination of political and economic weaknesses, which has its main reasons in political and institutional flaws of the euro project. This argument differs from the traditional mirror argument that reclaims the appreciation of the euro being a mere reflection of the depreciation of the US dollar.

Since the launch of the euro, its exchange rate versus the US dollar (see Figure 4.1) has undergone three distinct phases. The first phase can be described as a very brief "honeymoon" period where the euro could keep its relatively high exchange rate against the US dollar. The unexpectedly smooth substitution of national monies with the new currency was appreciated by the financial markets, which were willing to give some credit to the new currency. This period was soon followed by a strong and steady depreciation of the euro. This decline started an intense debate between economists about its reasons. Besides the usual suspects like Eurosclerosis, insufficient relative growth dynamics, interest rate differentials and the like, the debate also brought some new arguments that indicated that the depreciation is caused by extraordinary and unique reasons like the one-time need to whitewash former illegal deutschmark deposits into legal euro deposits (Sinn and Westermann 2001). Later arguments explained the weakness of the euro as a temporary phenomenon that would soon disappear. In terms of price competitiveness the depreciation came definitely at the right time, as the eurozone economies urgently needed additional stimuli for their growth-retarded economies. The depreciating euro, as the data in Table 4.1 indicate, made a positive contribution to the growth rate of real gross domestic product (GDP).

Figure 4.1 US–Euro Foreign Exchange Rate

Source: US Bureau of Economic Analysis.

In terms of creating a strong reputation for the euro, the depreciation was seen as a catastrophe by the governments as well as the European Central Bank (ECB). Fearing a free fall of the exchange rate with the consequence of depreciation–inflation spiral, the ECB decided to intervene into the global foreign exchange markets. On September 22, 2000, a coordinated intervention by the ECB, Federal Reserve, Bank of Japan and Bank of England was undertaken. November 3 and 9 of the same year saw one-sided interventions by the ECB. The official reserves held by the European System of Central Banks were not seen as large enough to impress the foreign exchange markets nor was it helpful that the coordinated interventions were a kind of one-time event and the fight against the depreciation of the euro was left to the ECB alone. The few and half-hearted efforts to talk up the euro against the US dollar did not show positive results. The findings of Jansen and de Haan (2005) show that the verbal intervention efforts

Table 4.1 Macroeconomic Indicators

	Euro Area		United States	
	1992–2001	**2002–2005**	**1992–2001**	**2002–2005**
Real GDP (percentage change from previous year)	2.10	1.25	3.38	3.025
Foreign balance contributions to changes in real GDP	0.23	–0.075	–0.46	–0.525
Labour productivity in the business sector	1.47	0.575	1.89	2.925
Standardized unemployment rates *up to 2004	9.66	8.633	5.38	5.766
Consumer price indexes	2.62	2.175	5.71	2.50
General government financial balances	–3.29	–2.775	–1.79	–4.30
Short-term interest rate	5.71	2.475	4.99	2.025
Effective exchange rates *2005 assumption	103.92	117.875	86.90	98.35
Trade balances for goods and services	95.42	176.025	–164.82	–564.825
Current account balances, bn $	21.58	20.025	–195.57	–617.175
Current account balances, as a percentage of GDP	0.32	0.325	–2.22	–5.35

Source: OECD Economic Outlook, Vol. 2005/2, No. 78, December.

did result in an increase in exchange rate volatility, but not in improvements of the euro rate.

Starting in the last quarter of 2001 and the taking speed early in 2002 the euro rushed into a rally that lifted the exchange rate with the US dollar until the end of 2005 above its launch value. Since then we have seen a brief correction in favor of the US dollar that seems to have come to an end in February of 2006. Unlike in the case of the depreciating euro, the ECB was so far neither willing to intervene on the markets to bring the euro back to a more adequate level nor did it try to down talk the euro. On the contrary, it seems that the ECB would enjoy the rise of the euro, interpreting it as an indication for the gain in reputation in the global markets.

Two questions emerge. First, how can the strong appreciation be explained given the fact, as will be argued below, that the relative fundamentals of the eurozone have not changed to the better since late 2001. Second, why did the ECB intervene in the case of a depreciating euro and not in the case of an appreciating euro if the economic costs in the latter are pretty high?

The Appreciation Puzzle

The appreciation of the euro since late 2001 is not covered by economic fundamentals. In terms of growth rates of real GDP the United States is doing much better than the economies of the eurozone as an aggregate since 2002. The same holds for the increase in the number of employed workers. The real short-term interest rate of the eurozone has been higher as in the United States but the depreciation effect of the US dollar did more than compensate any interest rate differential. Furthermore, the inflation rate has been slightly higher in the United States, contributing to a reduction of the positive difference of the short-term interest rate in favor of the eurozone. In brief, according to textbook economics there is no good reason for the euro to appreciate so strongly. The appreciation episode of 2002–2005 seems to verify the general exchange rate puzzle the recent literature agrees upon: Whatever sophisticated methods one uses, movements of exchange rates are not driven by economic fundamentals (see De Grauwe and Grimaldi 2004; see also Table 4.1). Sluggish growth dynamics in the period 1999 to 2001 was made responsible for the depreciation of the euro; an even more pronounced relative growth weakness in the period 2001–2005 went hand-in-hand with a strongly appreciating euro.

Table 4.1 gives some detailed empirical information for the periods 1992–2001 and 2002–2005 for both the economies of the United States and of the eurozone. In terms of growth rates of real GDP and of labor productivity the United States was superior to the eurozone in both periods. Short-term real interest rates were in both periods higher in the eurozone than in the United States and should have attracted short-term capital inflows in both periods. The unemployment rate was in both periods much lower in the United States than in the eurozone. Finally, in both periods the eurozone has achieved a surplus in its external accounts whereas the United States experienced huge deficits. From a theoretical point of view, it is not very convincing to hold the same variable responsible for movements of the exchange rate in opposite directions. Obvious contradictions like this turned scholarly attention towards the argument that the euro is not changing directions due to internal changes in the economic fundamentals of the eurozone but is mirroring the US dollar, in that the euro–dollar exchange rates solely reflect changes in the US political economy.

Instead of searching for more promising fundamentals or following the simple mirror argument I will argue that the appreciation of the euro reflects the successful efforts of the US government to talk the dollar down in order to get its external position right. In other words, the rise of the euro towards the US dollar is the outcome of a deliberate strategy by the United States to deal with its rising trade balance deficit and the explosion in the deficit of its current account. This strategy could work only, however, because of a specific policy stance of the ECB that reflects flaws in the set up of the architecture of the common currency.

The mirror approach usually refers to the trade balance and the current account. As widely known, both deficits are huge and dynamic in their character in case of the US. As Figures 4.2 and 4.3 show, the deficits have been pushed further since 2002. In 2004 the current account deficit showed an amount of

$668.1 billion, a share of 5.7 per cent of GDP. In 2005 the deficit rose to $804.9 billion, a share of 6.4 per cent of GDP. Given those figures, one could argue that the US dollar should have depreciated even more. Several studies indeed suggest that a further depreciation of about 20 per cent is on its way should the United States be seriously interested starting to clean up its external deficits.

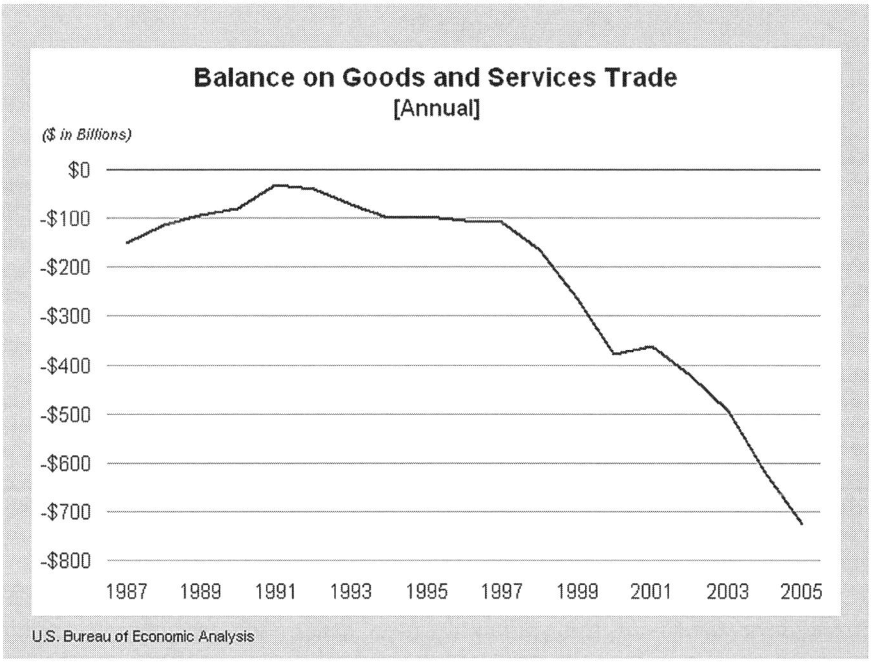

Figure 4.2 Balance on Goods and Services Trade

Source: US Bureau of Economic Analysis.

Referring to the external deficits of the United States is a popular exercise in the literature. As a matter of fact, the debate on the sustainability of huge and increasing deficits if the current account has a long but also unsatisfying history. A majority of writers treat the United States like any other economy assuming that at the end the United States has to pay back what they borrowed and therefore see a definite limit for its current account deficit[1] (Mann 1999; Mann 2000; see also Millesi-Ferretti and Razin 1996). Others are more relaxed and see no final limits

1 More simplistic interpretations not even try to present theoretical arguments but do take refuge to anecdotal evidence: "America will not be able to continue this borrowing binge. As an economic advisor to Richard Nixon once said: 'Things that can't go on forever, don't'. Today, the question is timing, not whether this trend will be sustainable" (Dieter 2005: 74). A sophisticated version of the same type of argument gives a more sophisticated and refined version (Gray 2004).

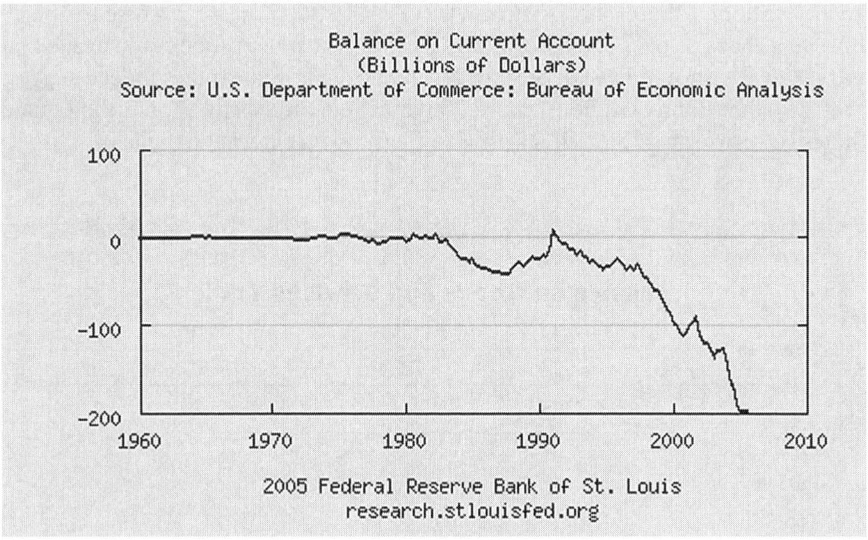

Figure 4.3 Balance on Current Account

Source: US Bureau of Economic Analysis.

for external borrowing on the side of the United States but threats for a further continuation of external indebtedness in case of a coming chronic inflation of the US dollar that would undermine its monetary stability (McKinnon 2001). In the perspective of the majority camp, the depreciation of the US dollar does not come as a real surprise. However, proponents of this view still fight with the problem of why large (albeit smaller) external deficits in the United States during the second half of the 1990s came with a strongly appreciating US dollar. The external deficit variable still is at odds with the requirement for a logical explanation of the direction of exchange rates.

There is another problem to mention. Arguing that the depreciation of the US dollar solely is the market's response to those huge deficits obviously does not solve the appreciation puzzle of the euro. The logic of this argument would require that the economy's currency with the biggest surplus against the United States would experience the largest appreciation. The economies of the eurozone certainly do contribute to the deficit in the trade balance of the United States but not in a stronger way than Japan does. In 2005, for example, the United States suffered their biggest deficits in the trade with goods and services with China ($201.7 billion) and with Japan ($82.7 billion), while the eurozone economies followed close to Japan's surplus. Unlike Japan, and not to mention China, the eurozone economies do have to carry a much stronger appreciation burden. As Figure 4.4 shows, the economies of the eurozone have experienced a much stronger nominal appreciation than the Japanese yen and even than the Canadian dollar.

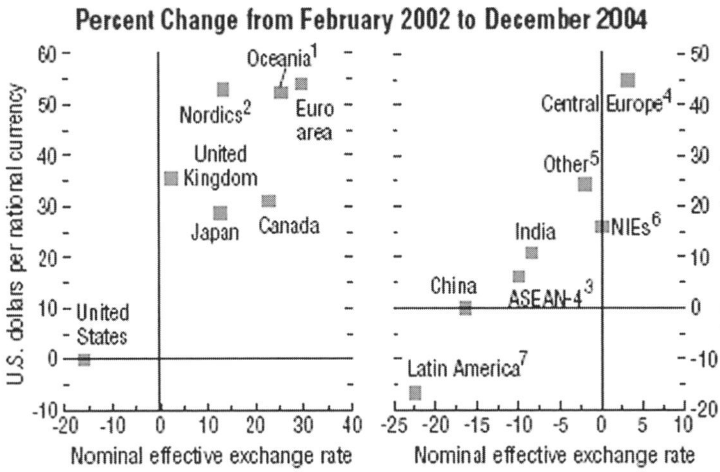

Figure 4.4 Nominal Effective Exchange Rate

Source: IMF (2005).

If one looks at this angle of the puzzle, the natures of the different exchange rate regimes of the various currencies come into the play in explaining the different exchange rate outcomes. Out of the group of three currencies (yen, yuan, euro) it is only the euro that comes with a kind of pure float towards the US dollar. China pegs its yuan to the US dollar; the slight appreciation in summer 2005 and the move towards a currency basket peg has not changed the nature of this arrangement. Other Asian economies, Hong Kong for example, follow a similar strategy to make sure that their cross-rate with the Chinese currency does not hamper their international price competitiveness. Japan favors a managed float by intervening heavily, directly and indirectly, in the foreign exchange markets to secure the price competitiveness of its export sectors. It is only the ECB that follows a pure float on the global exchange markets. In the Annual Report for 2004, for example, the Bank reports that they have not made any interventions in the foreign exchange markets for policy reasons.

Strategically, the various central banks follow different exchange rate policies. Japan and China follow strict mercantilist policies by using the exchange rate as a policy tool. In the case of Japan, the steering of the yen exchange rate towards the US dollar was driven by the need to strengthen the export sectors as the only motors of economic growth. Without this motor, the Japanese economy would have sunk even deeper into the deflationary trap. China uses its politically controlled exchange rate as a tool for its developmental model that tries to integrate China as a relatively low-cost economy into the global economy. The United States has opted, since late in 2001, for a unilateral policy driven by national preference formation towards reducing their external deficits by using the exchange rate as a deliberate policy tool. The depreciation of the US dollar was instrumental in so far as the United States was not forced to get their domestic policy agenda, in particular their fiscal deficit, cleared. The European Central Bank, by contrast, opted for a benign neglect position that seems to accept the foreign exchange market outcome as a given (see Figure 4.5).

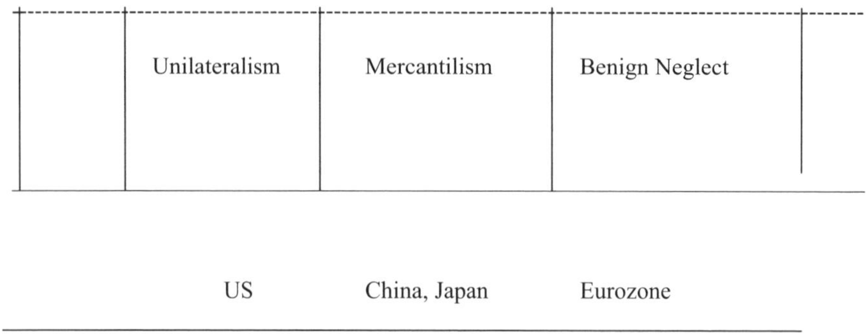

Figure 4.5 Exchange Rate Policies in Comparison

Appreciation of a currency comes with costs. First, it undermines the price competitiveness of the export sectors. Fighting such an effect requires the acceptance of a shrinking of profit margins at foreign markets, leading to increasing downward pressures of direct and indirect wages, forcing cost-cutting measures on the side of the private business sector and providing an incentive for cost-oriented outsourcing policies. Second, an appreciation makes foreign goods and services, calculated in the home currency, relatively cheaper and thus puts producers for the domestic markets under competition pressure. Third, appreciations have, in general, dampening effects on the inflation rate and thus allow more room for monetary policy to maneuver. Appreciations have different effects on the various sectors of an economy. Fourth, s stronger currency obviously nourishes the financial industry by attracting capital inflows driven by appreciation-expectations. Fifth, appreciation generates price and cost pressures and thus helps to keep inflation down. Depreciation of a currency, on the other hand, has the main advantage that it buys time for political as well as for economic actors as the price competitiveness is still kept up and adjustment processes can be delayed. The ability to make a currency depreciate, furthermore, helps to externalize adjustment costs toward third parties.[2]

Given those effects it is no wonder that exchange rate policies are a feature of the International Political Economy (IPE) that needs closer scholarly attention.

2 A similar argument is provided by Cohen (2004) who tries to avoid the strong and loaded term "authority" in an earlier contribution by the weaker term of "influence" but still argues that money carries power and that the United States tries to use its power to influence exchange rates.

The US Depreciation Game

For this purpose, let me turn briefly to the story of the recent depreciation of the US dollar. In particular, in the International Political Economy literature it is usually argued that the US has the undisputed power to use the dollar exchange rate in its own favor. Scholars like Gowan (1999) who argued that the end of Bretton Woods, with its fixed exchange rate system, has freed the United States from constraints and opened up the possibility to use its power for accommodating exchange rate policies in its own favor were instrumental in making such an interpretation popular. According to this analysis the establishment of a Dollar–Wall Street–Regime (DWSR) allowed the US government to leverage on its ties with the financial markets and to move the exchange rate in accordance to its changing strategic objectives. Such an argument is neither convincing in empirical nor in theoretical terms.

Empirically, it does not take into consideration the mechanisms of different exchange rate regimes. Given the nature of a pegged exchange rate regime like the Chinese one and the practice of a managed float like the one followed by Japan, the US government had no real means to go on for a depreciation of its currency. Gowan's argument that verbal signals from US policy makers would bring immediate changes of private financial actors' views on the adequate exchange rate does not hold under such circumstances. Verbal signals cannot work under circumstances of both capital controls and controlled foreign exchange markets, nor under the condition that a central bank tries hard to counter verbal signals from the United States. In both cases, the United States used means of political interference to get what they were looking for. The outcome with Japan was mixed, as the Japanese yen did appreciate but not as strong by far as the bilateral external account positions would have required. The outcome with China has been so far disappointing as the Chinese government's decision to switch from a dollar peg towards a currency basket only led to a tiny appreciation of the yuan despite strong language and threats from the United States. Currently about fifteen bills and amendments are pending in Congress that threaten new tariffs or tighter restrictions.[3] It goes without saying that both cases do not help to verify the structural power argument favored in IPE.

The outcome in regard to the euro was totally different. As shown, the euro appreciated strongly against the US dollar. In the tradition of the DWSR approach it could be argued that the United States enjoys a kind of particular power over the eurozone authorities to make them accept appreciation of their currency. Instead of walking on such a conspiracy path, I prefer to have a closer

3 Five of the most prominent are: (1) the threat of a 27.5 per cent tariff on Chinese imports if China does not substantially appreciate the yuan; (2) easier possibilities for US companies to seek higher protective tariffs on Chinese imports; (3) Treasury inquiry for determining whether China's currency practice distorts international trade; (4) bringing the China case to WTO; (5) establishing a system to monitor China's compliance with specific WTO commitments. All the bills and amendments are driven by the goal of forcing China to appreciate its yuan (*Wall Street Journal*, February 22, 2006).

look at the workings of foreign exchange markets at the first place. Starting from the thesis that in Baker's words, the United States "cannot simply wish exchange rate outcomes into existence" (Baker 2006: 24), neither do I argue that the United States would act as a passive price-taker on foreign exchange markets. Instead, the argument holds that the United States uses existing market power to influence foreign exchange markets to get the exchange rates they prefer. The market power of the United States is not executed foremost by direct interventions into the foreign exchange (forex) markets but by orchestrated efforts to change sentiments in those markets. This market power, however, is not without limits but can be highly contested.

In a pure regime of free float it is foremost the foreign exchange markets that decide about the exchange rates. If economic fundamentals do not drive the decisions of foreign exchange market makers, we have to turn to other factors that help to explain the sentiments of those critical actors. From a theoretical point of view, it is not very convincing to argue that the US government has structural power over private foreign exchange market actors. The determination of exchange rates is more complex than usually assumed in the IPE literature. My own research in this respect is informed by the emerging micro-structural literature that focuses on the formation of expectations of the main foreign exchange market actors. Instead of analyzing order flows between market makers and different kinds of customers,[4] my research emphasizes the formation of expectations on the side of foreign exchange market makers. In a situation where academic exchange rate models fail, actors have to search for alternative tools to generate profit-bringing predictions about the future exchange rates of currencies. Figure 4.6 depicts a brief overview on foreign exchange markets and their environment. The main role is played by so-called market makers,in other words, actors who accept, direct and generate order flows with different economic actors and finally determine with their actions the exchange rate for a given point in time. Market makers use a broad range of information provided by think tanks, consultants, research institutes, central banks, governments, supranational institutions and private business sectors. That information is extracted selectively and is forming a patchwork of explanations and causal relationships. This patchwork is not a sophisticated theory but a middle range approach that is being used to ground decisions and give them some medium sustainability. Aykens (2002) argues in his case study of the ERM crisis of 1992–1993 that foreign exchange markets are governed by technical authority, which is primarily a function of whether groups of actors do or do not believe the truthfulness and correctness of statements and actions by a specialized group of foreign exchange market actors.[5] This technical authority is being executed by special financial market actors who are able to turn their beliefs into temporary social norms that then condition the expectations and actions of broader groups of economic actors. My own research chose a broader

4 See Marsh and O'Rourke (2005) for an overview as well as an empirical testing of different variants.

5 A more refined version of this argument uses the approach of embedded networks to explain the governance structure of foreign exchange markets.

approach by analyzing some elements of the formation of "technical authority" by looking at the communication process between the media and the environment of foreign exchange markets.

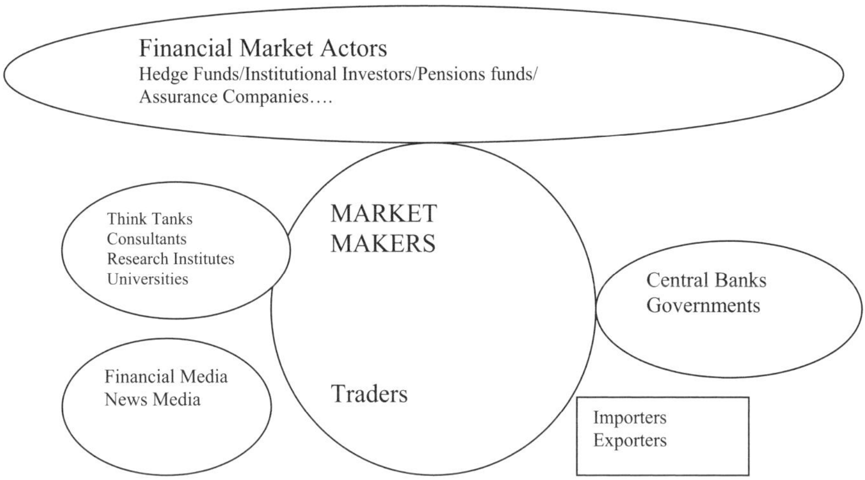

Figure 4.6 Forex Actors and the Forex Environment

Starting late in 2001 and then gaining momentum in 2002, the US government started to distance itself from its previous "strong dollar policy". in order to provide some evidence for this thesis, my research team did some computer-assisted quantitative work by analyzing two leading financial papers (*Wall Street Journal* and *Financial Times*) for the period 2001 until the first quarter of 2005. The research was driven by the hypothesis that market makers will be influenced in their expectation formation process by public discussions and analyses provided and reflected by media. Figure 4.7 outlines the main idea that drove this research.

We added to this quantitative-oriented research a more traditional qualitative analysis of policy statements of the Federal Reserve as well as of speeches by main representatives of the Fed. Far from reclaiming any causal relationship, we got strong empirical illustrative support for our working hypothesis that the US government in combination with the Federal Reserve turned at the end of 2001 to a deliberate exchange rate policy that externalizes the adjustment costs to other actors in the global economy (see Figure 4.8). Market actors changed their medium-range expectations towards the need of the United States for a lower exchange rate of the US dollar. Our frequency analysis of buzzwords used in the media since 2001 could show that the sentiments towards the sustainability of the existing exchange rate in combination with the external deficits would needs some corrections. The change in market sentiments was strong enough to send the US dollar on a steady slide. At the same time, the change of sentiments was never out of control; it never sent the US dollar on a downward slide that

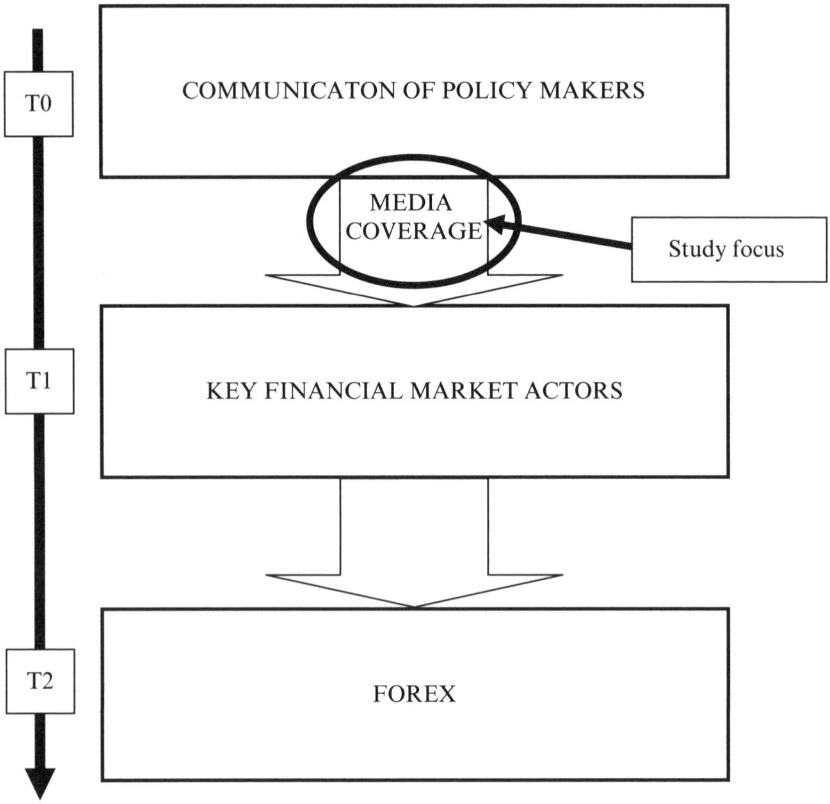

Figure 4.7 Quantitative Research Outline

would produce a hard landing for the United States. As will be argued below, this balanced depreciation is the outcome of politically driven interventions of other actors to keep the US dollar on a level that helps follow up national interests.

Benign Neglect as Consequence of Institutional Flaws

One of the critical arguments against the common currency in Europe referred to the danger of undermining a potentially optimal policy mix due to (1) the ceiling of fiscal deficits by the Stability and Growth Pact and (2) the transfer of monetary policy from the national to the supranational level (see Herr and Hübner 2006). I share this argument but contend that this description of the policy mix is incomplete. As the example of the United States demonstrated, a successful policy mix not only comprises mutual supportive combination of fiscal and monetary policy but also an accommodating exchange rate policy. The launch of the euro not only produced the one-size-fits-all problem in the arena of monetary policy but also the one-rate fits-all problem of the common exchange rate. The same exchange rate towards the US dollar for all eurozone economies creates regional

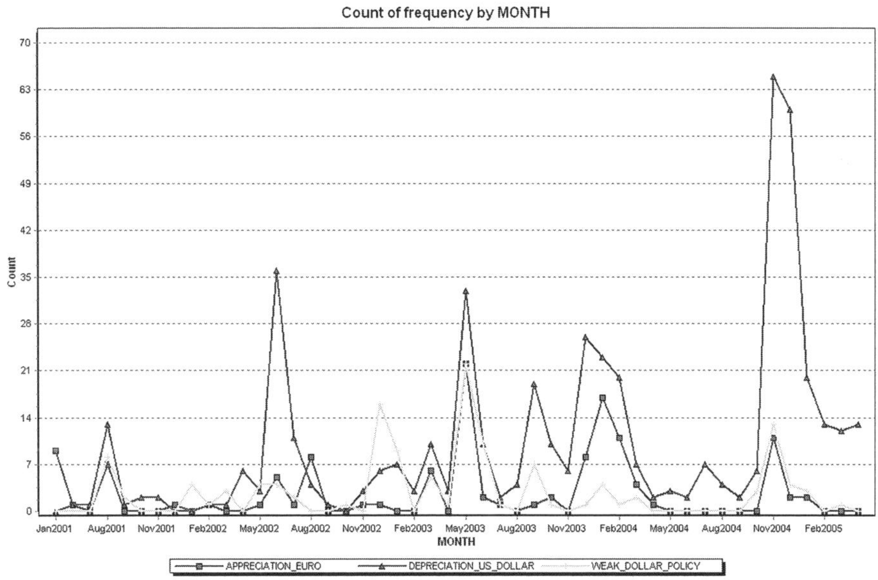

Figure 4.8 News Frequency

imbalances expressed by current account deficits and surpluses for the member states of the eurozone. Portugal's current account deficit as a share of GDP, for example, is slightly higher than the current account share of the United States. Spain's deficit also is coming close to 6 per cent of its GDP. Italy and Greece are two more economies with severe deficits. The overall current account surplus of the eurozone is mainly backed by the enormous surplus of Germany. The same exchange rate for all member economies of the eurozone does not fit their different interactions with the global economy (ECB 2006).

The highly uneven distribution of deficits and surpluses in the group of eurozone economies demonstrates some uneasiness with the one-rate-fits-all situation generated by the common currency. It could be argued that this distribution provides a further argument for an active exchange rate strategy by the ECB. Such an argument, however, assumes that there is sensitivity to and, more important, institutional room for exchange rate policies at all on the side of the ECB. Given the institutional architecture of the euro and its interpretation by the representatives of the ECB, it seems that there is not ample space for an adequate exchange rate policy in the ECB. Nominally, monetary policy-making is based on two pillars. The first pillar (ECB 1999: 47) argues that "inflation is ultimately a monetary phenomenon ... To signal the prominent role it has assigned to money, the Governing Council has announced a quantitative reference value for monetary growth as one pillar of the overall stability-oriented strategy". The second pillar is more opaque: "In parallel with the analysis of monetary growth in relation to the reference value, a broadly based assessment of the outlook for price developments and risks to price stability in the euro area will play a major role in the Eurosystem's strategy. This assessment will be made using a wide range of economic indicators" (ECB 1999: 49). One of the many indicators is the exchange rate. Unlike the practice in the United States, not to mention the highly politicized currency strategies of China and Japan, the designers of the ECB were not overly eager to introduce a discretionary exchange rate policy.[6] The tool kit is very much restricted to its interest rate policy, which addresses the highly ambitious inflation target. Interest rate policy and exchange rate policy are not totally disconnected. It can be argued that the ECB keenly designed its interest rate policy to avoid a further depreciation of the euro against the US dollar. The same argument does not hold, however, for the period of an appreciating euro.

Unlike other central banks, the ECB is not only equipped with a pretty narrow catalogue of policy goals but also with a rather unique hierarchy of goals that puts the fighting of inflation at the very top and downgrades other targets of economic policy to mere by-products. It is this single-minded orientation of the ECB that is characteristic of the technocratic policy approach of the ECB. Instead of entering a "war of words" with the United States, the representatives of the ECB do not openly try to talk the euro up towards a level that would be supportive for stimulating economic growth. The reason for this unassertive attitude may be that ECB representatives fear ruining their fragile reputation in case their efforts are not successful (Hübner 2002). Their need to build up a positive reputation can't sufficiently explain the asymmetric reaction of the ECB. The reason the ECB did not use its exchange rate policy tool in the period of an appreciating euro has much to do with the complementarity of an appreciating euro and the policy goal of the ECB. The strong euro helps to fulfill its main policy target by decreasing the costs of foreign inputs and by keeping competition pressure high. Furthermore, a high exchange rate helps narrow unions' wage demands. Given the "new kid on the block" position of the ECB, the central bankers of the eurozone are very reluctant to exercise an offensive exchange rate policy that is driven by domestic economic interests. Instead they use the strong euro to make an argument for far-reaching reforms of the labor market and welfare regimes of its member economies. Furthermore, a strong euro is instrumental in the bank's fight against inflation as it keeps import prices down and at the same time keeps cost-pressure for the export sectors up. Those effects may also explain the asymmetrical response of the ECB towards the euro exchange rate: intervening with the exchange rate in case of a depreciating euro and following a benign neglect attitude in case of an appreciating euro.

Between Bretton Woods Two and Plaza Two

The depreciation strategy of the United States is supported by the widespread conviction that, in United States, external deficits are not sustainable and urgently need correction. Even if more and more observers agree that such a

6 The differences in the policy approaches reflect differences in the political and institutional set-up of various central banks. In this respect, the ECB represents probably the most orthodox version of central bank independence (Watson 2002).

correction cannot come solely by a further depreciation of the US dollar but needs fundamental changes in the fiscal policy arena of the United States, there seems to be a joint understanding in many sectors of the public in the recent past that any serious corrections need to be accompanied by bringing the US currency down to a lower level. Curbing the external deficits of the United States needs a further substantial depreciation of the US dollar to make US exports more price competitive and therefore more attractive for foreigners and to make foreign products less attractive for US consumers and producers. It also needs a drastic shift in the fiscal deficit of the United States that would create some space for shifting domestic production towards exports. As argued in this paper, the United States has so far only pushed for a downward movement of the exchange rate and let the fiscal deficit mainly untouched.

It seems logical to expect that economies with relative big surpluses against the United States need larger currency appreciation than economies with relative small surpluses or even deficits. Using calculations provided by Cline (2005) about "optimal" real appreciation rates against the US dollar in order to reduce those surpluses, it is obvious that the group of Asian economies is most far away from any optimal appreciation rate. China would need a real appreciation of 43 per cent from its 2002 level; Hong Kong's remaining appreciation rate would be 74.5 per cent; Singapore's missing appreciation rate would be 90 per cent. And even the euro would need a further appreciation of 20 per cent from its 2002 level to kick-start a significant turn in the US external deficit towards the eurozone.

Such calculations should not be taken for granted. However, they make the case that the exchange rate arena should be prepared for further conflicts. From the perspective of global financial stability, a unilateral depreciation strategy by the United States can be seen as potentially damaging. It may even lead to a "hard landing" scenario that has been discussed for a couple of years. This possibility provides the case for a "Plaza Two Agreement". Compare the situation today with the situation in mid-1985 when the US dollar, despite its decline from peak value in February of that year, was widely seen as overvalued. To avoid a market sentiment–driven avalanche, representatives of the five largest industrial countries met at the Plaza Hotel in New York and came up with a plan to bring the dollar down in a controlled manner. They agreed upon joint and concerted exchange rate interventions combined with a detailed policy program that agreed upon a tightening of fiscal policy in the United States and pushing private demand through tax reforms in Japan and Germany in order to make both economies growth locomotives of the world economy (Klein, Mizrach and Murphy 1991).

Supporters of a Plaza Two Agreement argue that such an approach needs to be revived, although no longer as a G-5 project but as a joint political project that brings economies like China, Brazil and India to the table of the OECD countries. In terms of exchange rate policies this group should agree upon measures to depreciate the US dollar in selective ways by sales of dollar reserves, and respectively by purchases of currencies on the side of the United States. At the same time the United States should commit to significant and sustainable corrections of its domestic deficits. The proposal of a Plaza Two Agreement provoked criticism reaching from the argument that exchange rate movements should be left to markets to the argument that any combination of shrinking US fiscal deficits and a depreciating US currency would lead to global economic chaos. The main problem with such a proposal is political. As long as important actors use the exchange rate as a policy tool driven by national interest formations, there is no common ground for a global concerted political project that will contradict those national interests.

Proponents of a Bretton Woods Two approach[7] not only do not endorse a Plaza approach but furthermore completely disagree with such an interpretation of the global condition. According to this analysis, there is no urgent need for any fundamental changes on the side of the United States nor on the side of existing exchange rate policies of other actors. The situation of high and even rising external deficits of the United States meets exactly the needs of emerging market economies, in particular the group of Asian economies, which are willing to finance the US deficits as long as the United States keeps its markets open for products and services of the Asian economies. In this view, the United States and the Asian economies have complementary economic interests and mutually complimentary policy tools that make the overall situation nearly a pareto-optimum. In such a scenario the ECB is degraded to a minor player that should follow its exchange rate policy abstinence by accepting potential adjustment costs in case of a further depreciation of the US dollar. Given the current accumulation of currency reserves around the globe, there is no doubt that this game could indeed continue: Asian central banks can continue to purchase US government bonds. Between 1992 and 2004 the holdings of US Treasury Securities by the foreign official sectors has risen from 10.5 per cent of the total outstanding to 27.9 per cent. Assuming that the current account surpluses of the Asian economies continue, then this share will further increase, making the US even more vulnerable. A recent Banque de France report argues that Asian central banks, in order to keep their currencies from rising against the US dollar, probably will have acquired even higher amounts of Treasury Securities as those figures show, and that this strategy will probably continue.

Even if one accepts this Bretton Woods view and buys into the functionality of such an arrangement for the global economy, it still raises the problem how other actors will deal with the uneven distribution of the costs of this arrangement. Following the logic of this paper, such an arrangement could only work successfully as long as the ECB was willing to accept the distribution of adjustment burdens. To put it bluntly: A change of the ECB's policy stance would undermine this functional arrangement fundamentally. However, currently there is no cogent reason to expect a fundamental change of this attitude on side of the ECB. Given the positive effects of a strong euro for its inflation target, Bretton Woods Two produces some complementarity with the ECB's policy target. This only will change if the ECB received negative political pressure for its single-minded policy approach.

7 This debate has been started with Dooley, Folkerts-Landau and Garber (2003) with their essay on a revived Bretton Woods System. The debate has not yet ended. For an instructive critique of this approach see Eichengreen (2004).

Let me assume, for a moment, that this happens and the ECB joins its brethren, the other central banks that do their jobs differently, in a pro-active exchange rate policy. Undertaking individual exchange rate market interventions by selling US dollars would empty its coffers but produce no serious results, as private markets would not be convinced that such interventions could change market sentiments. Starting a war of words with the United States would probably produce the same negative results, as the ECB could not live up to any serious threats in a tit-for-tat game with the United States. The only way to deal with the given problem would be a joint strategy of all significant global players towards a long-term band of exchange rates based on mutually compatible national economic interests. Such a strategy would have to be more encompassing than a Plaza Two Agreement and would have to be more formal than a Bretton Woods Two by (1) bringing China and other emerging market economies on board of a exchange rate band project and by (2) fixing clear rules of responsibilities to make such a project work without shifting adjustment burdens to third parties. Getting support for such an initiative is beyond the official policy horizon of the ECB. It would help, however, if the ECB would finally rise to the challenge created by its brethren and take a more active policy stance towards the exchange rate of the euro.

References

Arestis, P., Brown, A., Mouratidis, K. and Sawyer, M. (2002), "The Euro: Reflections on the First Three Years", in *International Review of Applied Economics*, vol. 16, no. 1, 1–17.

Aykens, P. (2002), "Conflicting Authorities: States, Currency Markets and the ERM Crisis of 1992–93", in *Review of International Studies*, vol. 28, no. 2, 359–80.

Aykens, P. (2005), "(Mis)Trusting Authorities: A Social Theory of Currency Crises", in *Review of International Political Economy*, vol. 12, no. 2, 310–33.

Baker, A. (2006), "American Power and the Dollar: The Constraints of Technical Authority and Declaratory Policy in the 1990s", in *New Political Economy*, vol. 11, no. 1, 23–45.

Campanella, M.L. (2006), "Is The Euro Ready to Play the Global Currency Role?", paper for the Euro conference in Miami, April 2006.

Cline, W.R. (2005), "The Case for a New Plaza Agreement", *Policy Briefs in International Economics*, Number PB05–4.

Cohen, B.J. (2004), "The Macrofoundation of Monetary Power", unpublished paper.

De Grauwe, P. and Grimaldi, M. (2004), "Exchanger Rate Puzzles: A Tale of Switching Attractors", Sveriges Riksbank Working Paper Series No. 163.

Dieter, H. (2005), "The US Economy and the Sustainability of Bretton Woods II", in *Journal of Australian Political Economy*, no. 55, 48–76.

Dooley, M.P., Folkerts-Landau, D. and Garber, P. (2003), "An Essay on the Revived Bretton Woods System", NBER Working Paper No. 9971.

Eichengreen, B. (2004), "Global Imbalances and the Lessons of Bretton Woods", NBER Working Paper No. 10497.

European Central Bank (January 1999), *Monthly Bulletin*, Frankfurt.

European Central Bank (February 2006), "Monetary Bulletin".

Feldstein, M. (2000), "The European Central Bank and the Euro: The First Year", NBER Working Paper No. 7517.

Gowan, P. (1999), "The Global Gamble: Washington's Faustian Bid for Global Dominance" (London: Brill Academic Publishers).

Gray, H.P. (2004), "The Exhaustion of the Dollar: Its Implications for Global Prosperity" (London).

Hau, H., Killeen, W. and Moore, M. (April 2002), How Has the Euro Changed the Foreign Exchange Market?", in *Economic Policy*, 151–91.

Herr, H. and Hübner, K. (2005), "Währung und Unsicherheit in der globalen Ökonomie. Eine geldwirtschaftliche Theorie der Globalisierung" (Berlin).

Hübner, K. (2002), "Reputation Failure: The Economic and Monetary Union and its Institutional Flaws", Working Paper 3, CCGES, York University.

Hübner, K. (2005), "Can Money Ground Identity? The Case of the Euro", in Eurostudia. *Transatlantic Journal for European Studies*, vol. 1, no. 1.

Jansen, D-J. and de Haan, J. (2005), "Were Verbal Efforts to Support the Euro Effective? A High-Frequency Analysis of ECB Statements", DNB Working Paper No. 33.

Klein, M., Mizrach, B. and Murphy, R.G. (1991), "Managing the Dollar: Has the Plaza Agreement Mattered?", in *Journal of Money, Credit and Banking*, vol. 23, no. 4, 742–51.

Mann, C.L. (1999), "Is the US Trade Deficit Sustainable?", Washington DC.

Mann, C.L. (2000), "Is the US Current Account Deficit Sustainable?", in *Finance and Development*, vol. 37, no. 1.

Marsh, I.W. and O'Rourke, C. (2005), "Customer Order Flow and Exchange Rate Movements: Is There Really Information Content?", unpublished paper.

McKinnon, R. (2001), "The International Dollar Standard and the Sustainability of the US Current Account Deficit", in *Brookings Papers on Economic Activity*, 1, 227–39.

Milesi-Ferretti, G.M. and Razin, A. (1996), "Current-Account Sustainability", *Princeton Studies in International Finance*, no. 81.

Schroeder, J. (2003), "The European Central Bank (ECB) and the International Role of the Euro", in *Journal of Asian Economics*, 14, 209–18.

Sinn, H.-W. and Westermann, F. (2001), "Why Has the Euro Been Falling?", CESinfo Working Paper No. 493.

Watson, M. (2002), "The Institutional Paradoxes of Monetary Orthodoxy: Reflections on the Political Economy of Central Bank Independence", in *Review of International Political Economy*, vol. 9, no. 1, 183–196.

Chapter 5

Euro–Dollar: An Holistic View of the Economy

Hans Martens

Introduction

In the relatively short period from March 2002 to early 2005, the euro moved from an exchange rate of 0.88 against the US dollar to around 1.35. This dramatic development took place against the backdrop of a euro which had previously been weakening vis-à-vis the dollar since its birth in 1999. However, since it peaked in 2005, the euro has maintained its strong position at a level of around 20 per cent above the dollar (see Figure 5.1).

Figure 5.1 Euro–Dollar Exchange Rate

The discussion about whether this was due to a "strong euro" or a "weak dollar" has not really shed much light on understanding why this happened. It is, nevertheless, worth noting that the euro has also strengthened in relation to other currencies as well (see Figures 5.2 and 5.3).

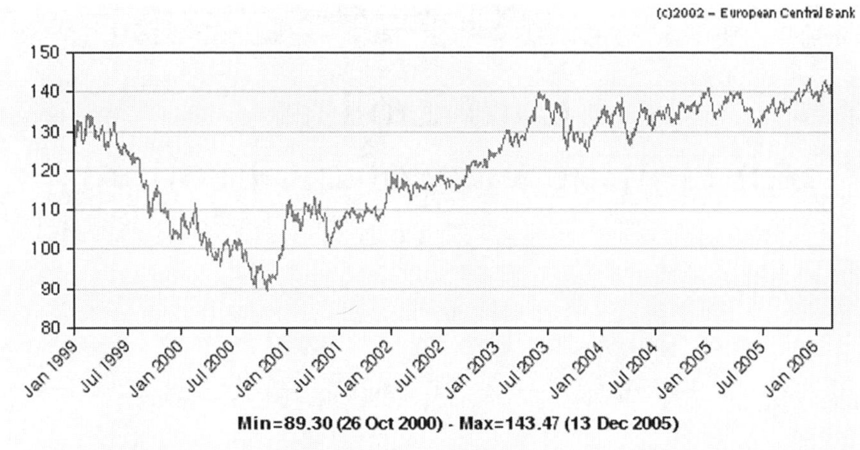

Figure 5.2 Euro–Yen Exchange Rate

Figure 5.3 Euro–Sterling Exchange Rate

This development may have surprised many who argued that since the United States' macroeconomic performance has been better than Europe's, the dollar should have become the stronger of the two currencies. It is true that the US economy has delivered better growth rates and higher employment than Europe, which has been developing rather slowly in recent years. However, this chapter argues that looking at economic growth and job creation alone will not explain why exchange rates change in the way they do. What is required is a holistic view that takes into account the fiscal performance of the economy.

Thus this chapter distinguishes between the "real economy" (mainly economic growth and employment) and the "fiscal economy" (mainly the current account and government budgets).

Spend or Save

This debate is particularly relevant in the European context, as Europe's Growth and Stability Pact set out the basic rules for balancing the real and the fiscal economies within the eurozone.

Against this backdrop, a government budget can only provide a macroeconomic stimulus if the government acts within the limits set by the Pact. Some argue that this has restricted European economic growth and job creation. They maintain that if Europe had gone down the US route, with its "Keynesian-style" fiscal policies, it would be in better macroeconomic shape today.

The fathers of the Growth and Stability Pact were influenced by rather traditional monetarist thinking, and were not convinced that the short-term gains to be had from an expansive fiscal policy would be of longer-term macroeconomic benefit. This is probably the nub of the issue: if fiscal stimuli do not generate substantially higher economic growth quickly, the pain of repaying the subsequent debt overshadows the short-term benefits.

At the same time, while twelve different EU countries' monetary policies were merged into one in the eurozone, this was not the case for fiscal policies. However, the Growth and Stability Pact was also seen as a necessary framework to guide fiscal policies, since a large deficit in one country would affect all the countries in the eurozone countries.

Historically, the United States and Europe have experienced rather similar government deficits.

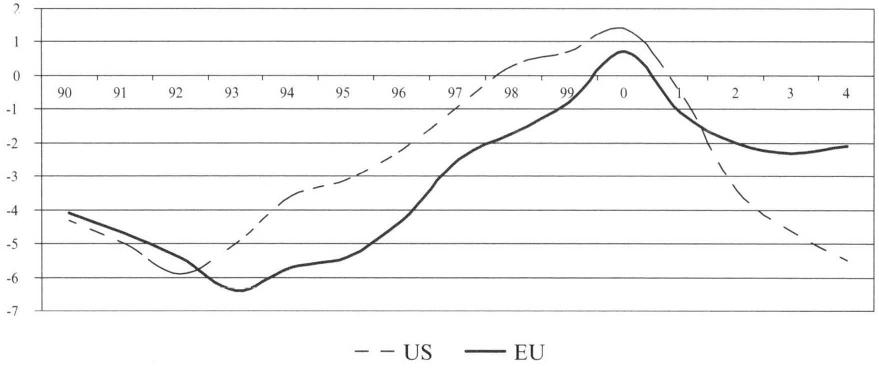

Figure 5.4 Government Budget Deficits in the US and in the EU

Source: OECD.

Before 2000, with the emergence of the euro and the Growth and Stability Pact, the two economies were very similar in this respect. The existence of the pact has clearly changed this and although some eurozone members have had difficulties in applying its terms strictly, the eurozone has more or less stayed in line with its requirements. US fiscal policy, on the other hand, has completely changed from the Clinton years of fiscal consolidation to the expansive fiscal policies of the Bush administration.

Another important deficit also has a significant effect on exchange-rate developments: namely, the current account. The present US current account deficit is the largest ever since records began in 1989. This probably has more impact on exchange rates than the government budget deficit, and probably also provides a more precise explanation of euro–dollar movements since 1999.

The euro's change of direction in relation to the dollar started in March 2002, prompting a warning from Federal Reserve Chairman Alan Greenspan in the same month to the financial community, which was reported as follows:

> Greenspan noted that over the past six years, about 40 per cent of growth in U.S. capital stock has been financed by foreign investment, increasing America's reliance on others and running up mounting deficits that need to be controlled because it means a growing share of interest payments are sent abroad. "Countries that have gone down this path invariably run into trouble and so would we," he said. "Eventually, the current account deficit will have to be restrained. Because of the near certainty of a major rise in the retiree-to-worker ratio in the next few decades, we now face the pressing need to set policies for the enhanced productivity growth that will be necessary. "Boosting savings is essential even though it does not affect the number of people in the workforce. "But it surely affects capital investment, which it finances, and the productivity that it engenders," Greenspan noted. (Federal Reserve Board, March 13, 2002, http://www.federalreserve.gov/boarddocs/speeches/2002/20020313/default.htm)

This appears to have been the first (but not the last) time that Greenspan issued a serious warning about the current account deficit and its important implications for the US economy – not only in relation to financing the deficit, but also the question of American dependence on foreign investors, as an increasing proportion of the future wealth created in the United States would have to be paid to investors who had helped finance the deficit.

Since Greenspan's speech in 2002, the financial markets' attention has been focused on the US deficit and this, more than anything else, seems to have steered the exchange rate in the euro's favor, although references are also made from time to time to the United States' "double deficits" or even "triple deficits" (the latter also refers to private debt levels in the United States).

Thus trade deficit figures, current account figures and the level of capital imports into the United States have been crucial for currency dealers. It seems very likely that they have "discounted" the US currency because they are not entirely convinced that it will be possible to finance the current account deficit.

Consumer spending also remains very important to the macro economy in the United States and, while positive signals may lead to an upturn in the stock market, this can often result in the dollar being downgraded, as concern mounts over increased imports and the consequent worsening of the current account.

The question of how to finance the US deficit is a relatively new issue: firstly, because the current account deficit has reached new heights; and secondly, because the US dollar is no longer the world's only real reserve currency. Although the euro cannot yet match the universality and global use of the dollar, it is a valid alternative as a global reserve currency. Its strength may also influence US decision-makers' choices – something that might not yet have been fully been understood.

The Policy Mix

The optimum policy mix would, of course, be economic growth coupled with low unemployment at the same time as fiscal balance, but neither the US economy nor the eurozone have managed to achieve this. In Europe, only the Nordic countries have enjoyed a situation close to this ideal over the last five to ten years.

When we look at the economy as a whole, there are significant differences in the situation in the United States and in the eurozone: the United States is doing quite well in terms of growth and jobs, but not on the current account and government budget balance, while the eurozone is doing quite well in terms of fiscal balances, but rather poorly on growth and jobs. While the Nordic example shows that there does not need to be such a trade-off, neither the United States nor the eurozone seem to have got the balance right: this may very well be down to poor political leadership rather than basic economics.

To a very large extent, the US economy is dependent on consumer spending. It has also developed a low-tax culture. Any proposal to raise taxes would be tantamount to political suicide, given that consumer spending rather than collective spending via the government – is king.

However, the combination of increased government demands for public spending – to finance the fight against terrorism, war and other policy goals – and tax cuts does not look like prudent fiscal policy. As there is still a high demand for investment in the economy, a current account deficit is bound to arise alongside the fiscal deficit. While balancing the government budget would obviously help to address both deficits, this is not a political option today or in the immediate future. This puts the burden on monetary policy, but as the deficit is not being addressed, interest rates go up and the economy gradually slows down.

This could help to address the current account deficit through lower imports, which could substantially reduce the deficit and create a trade balance surplus that could help to balance the current account. However, it is equally likely that increased interest rates will make the debt problem even worse, since, although higher interest rates would attract more capital, they could also slow down the economy and reduce the incentive to invest in the US stock market or directly in American businesses.

A strong fiscal policy that aims to create a surplus in the government budget, or at least a balanced budget, would send a stronger signal to the markets and could help to achieve a soft landing instead of the hard landing which could be the result of too much emphasis on monetary policy. For Europe, this balance seems equally hard or perhaps even more difficult to achieve, not least because some policies are still decentralized and determined by twelve independent countries and governments. It is also important to understand the political instruments at Europe's disposal.

Focus on Structural Reforms

European political leaders still appear to be wedded to traditional fiscal and monetary polices, even though these now have very limited impact in Europe. Although monetary policy has been centralized, the "one size" determined by the European Central Bank is expected to "fit all". For most countries in the eurozone, the terms of the Growth and Stability Pact mean that using fiscal policies is either not an option or they are reduced to trying to control public finances in order to meet the Pact's requirements. If public deficits are at three per cent of GDP or above – the limit set by the pact – then the fiscal policy instrument is of very limited use. Europe needs to focus on structural reforms. The world in which stable, industrially dominated central European economies thrived no longer exists. Global competition requires much greater flexibility in companies and in the labor market – and this requires structural reforms that politicians are reluctant to implement because they require changes that tend to be unpopular with voters, take away "acquired rights" and take a long time to produce results – some of which will not be visible until after the next election!

Some claim that whether a country is a member of the eurozone or not is the defining difference between the successful and unsuccessful parts of Europe, but this is not supported by empirical evidence. Ireland and Finland, which are both eurozone members, are among the most successful and competitive economies in Europe, while Italy, which is also in the eurozone, is among the weakest. The real dividing line is between those countries that have understood the need for structural reform, such as Ireland, Finland and others in northern Europe, and those that have not.

European Models

The debate is still raging over whether there is a "European" economic and social model. However, one thing clearly characterizes Europe: a willingness to pay taxes at a level of 40–55 per cent of GDP, which are then spent on collective action. There are no other major economies in the world that share this preference for collective action (see Figure 5.5).

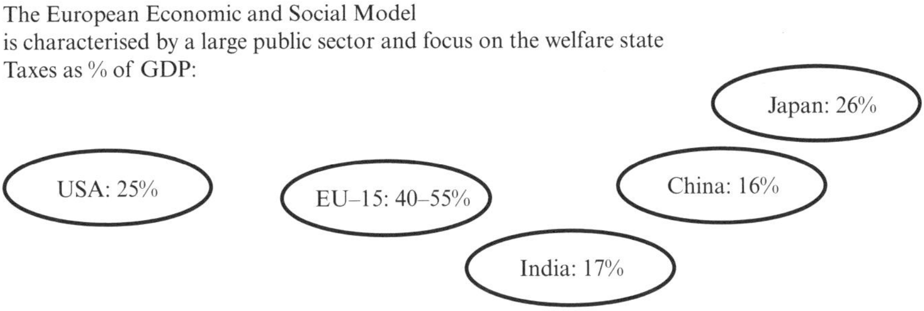

Figure 5.5 Taxes as Percentage of GDP

While there are many socio-economic sub-models in Europe, there appear to be three main, fairly well-defined overarching ones, as shown in Figure 5.6: the Nordic, the Anglo-Saxon and the Continental models. (Southern European countries are dominated by the key features of the Continental model, while eastern European countries that are emerging from the period of Communist planned economies are adopting elements of existing European models.)

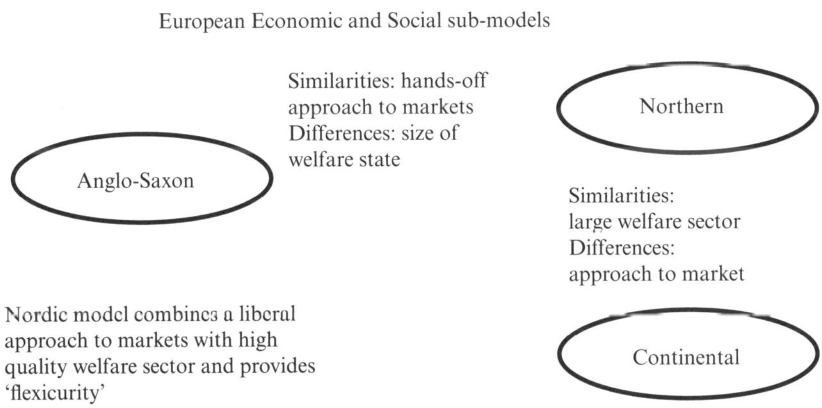

Figure 5.6 European Economic and Social Sub-Models

The Anglo-Saxon and the Nordic models are generally characterized by governments that take a "hands-off" approach to labor, product, service and capital markets. The Continental countries are still characterized by a high degree of state intervention in markets: in the labor market, for example, this means that workers are well protected by national legislation. This is a policy that might have fitted the requirements of an industrial society, but its high degree of rigidity is a disadvantage in today's rapidly changing globalized world, which requires an agile and flexible workforce. Government intervention to protect key industries is another example of state intervention in markets (see Figure 5.7).

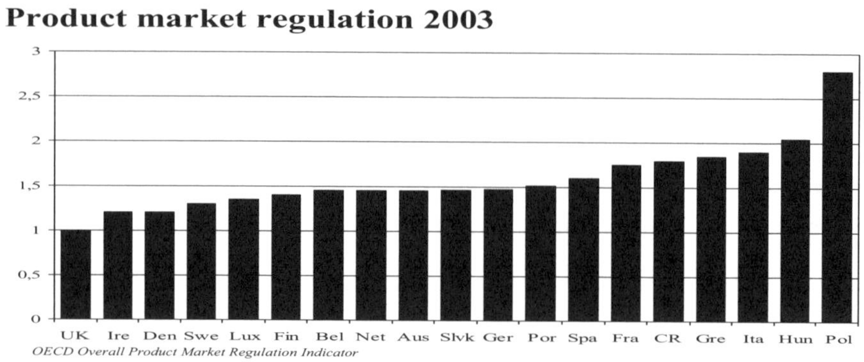

Figure 5.7 European Product Market Regulation 2003

While the Northern economies have a more liberal economic and social regime that appears better able to meet current demands, they are organized quite differently. The Nordic countries have the highest taxes of all and the Anglo-Saxons the lowest. The Nordic countries have maintained a high degree of competitiveness through an efficient, well-performing public sector and they (alongside the United States) always top the *World Economic Forum*'s list of the most competitive economies.

Is this because they are small economies? Perhaps, but this is clearly not the only explanation, since, if it were, why are other small European economies not particularly competitive? The explanation lies in other factors, but this does not necessarily mean that they can be replicated to boost competitiveness elsewhere.

The Nordic countries also stand out as the only Western economies that have been able to perform well on all the economic indicators over the last decade. They have achieved stable growth and high levels of job creation while maintaining a fiscal balance or even generating surpluses.

As the key representative of the Anglo-Saxon model in Europe, the United Kingdom is often portrayed as an economic success. However, this is truer for the "real economy" than for the "fiscal economy".

The UK suffers from a slightly milder version of the US economic disease. Increasing triple deficits also threaten the UK economy, for reasons similar to those in the United States: the illusion of a low-tax society with a preference for private consumption combined with a high level of public services. This will eventually lead to "boom and bust", as more restrictive monetary policies are introduced to cope with increasing debt burdens in the vacuum left by a weak fiscal policy.

Viewing the economy in a holistic way – looking at the real and fiscal economies at the same time – provides a better understanding of how economies perform, particularly in the longer term. It also shows that it is difficult for larger economies to achieve really robust economic performance and a balanced fiscal economy.

PART III
The International Role of the Euro

Chapter 6

Living up to Expectations? Taking Stock of the International Role of the Euro

J. Onno de Beaufort Wijnholds and Julie McKay

Introduction

It was well recognized in the run up to the introduction of the euro that the new currency would be the first serious rival to the US dollar since the dollar's displacement of the pound as the major international currency. There was much debate about the extent to which the euro would be accepted as a strong currency, the opportunity it offered for portfolio diversification, and whether it would precipitate a shift away from the dollar as an invoicing currency. The euro has now been in existence since 1999. It quickly assumed second place in international financial markets behind the US dollar (formerly occupied by the deutschmark) and continues to consolidate its position. Is this better or worse than neutral observers predicted? When will the euro's international importance in financial markets stabilize and at what level? This chapter takes stock of the international stature that the euro has reached and compares it to the original expectations of academic researchers and commentators.

Prior to the introduction of the euro, there was a general consensus that the rise of the euro's international role would be slow, although views diverged on how smooth or bumpy this rise would be. The switch from sterling to the US dollar as the major international currency occurred gradually over the course of the interwar period, culminating in the definitive supremacy of the dollar in the aftermath of World War II. Only in 1973 with the breakdown of the Bretton Woods system did the first signs of a weakening role for the dollar emerge. With the end of the dollar peg system, the need for dollar reserves declined. As countries chose alternative anchors, reserves shifted to new anchor currencies. In particular, the establishment of the Exchange Rate Mechanism in Europe raised the international profile of the deutschmark. Yet this re-evaluation of the dollar by the official sector has sometimes been overestimated. Many countries continued to peg to the dollar either *de jure* or *de facto*, and the rapid growth in global trade and financial markets as a result of globalization, de-regulation, liberalization and innovation in the late twentieth century deepened and extended the use of the dollar in foreign exchange markets. The rise of the international role of the euro and its impact on the US dollar is therefore an interesting subject for study, both from a positive and normative perspective. This chapter offers insights into the expectations for the euro prior to its inception and the extent to which it has met those expectations since 1999.

Of course, to speak of the "international role" of a currency is somewhat misleading, since a currency fulfills several international roles depending on whether it is used by the official or private sector, and in line with its functions as a unit of account, means of payment and store of value. One would not expect the various international roles of the euro to proceed at exactly the same pace, but what is of interest is the relative growth of the different functions and the relationship between them, and these issues are revisited in the course of this chapter.

The discussion begins with a review of the anticipated role of the euro. It explores the desirability of a strong international role for a currency, the policy stance of the European Central Bank (ECB) towards the euro's international role, the factors that influence the rise of an international currency and on this basis, the prospects for the euro that were anticipated upon its introduction in 1999. Next we take stock of the extent of the use of the euro internationally, in financial markets, for trade, as a parallel currency and by the official sector. Finally, we offer some remarks on the future development of the euro's international role.

By way of qualification it should be noted that the discussion focuses solely on the rise of the euro by the non-resident official and private sectors. It deals neither with the political implications for international co-operation, nor the course of the euro–dollar exchange rate.

The Anticipated International Role of the Euro Post-Introduction

As the plans for a new European currency took shape, there was increasing speculation about the impact it would have internationally. In order to gauge its rise internationally, attention was focused on the factors that determine the rise of an international currency and how the euro would measure up. This section investigates more closely the relevant considerations, but begins with the more fundamental question of whether a significant international dimension is at all desirable.

Is a Strong International Dimension Desirable?

Much of the discussion about major currencies betrays an implicit assumption that a strong international dimension is inherently desirable. At the same time, some countries, such as Germany and Japan, purposely discouraged an international role for their currency (particularly as a reserve currency), which suggests the issue is not so clear cut.[1] Pertinent issues to consider are possible financial advantages and the impact on financial markets, asset prices and monetary policy.

---

1 Henning (1994) remarks that both countries shared a concern that capital flows may influence monetary policy and thus impair monetary control, both under fixed and

Possible financial advantages are thought to accrue from two sources. Firstly, the higher trading volumes of an international currency imply lower transaction costs in foreign exchange and financial markets. Since this implies lower total costs for traded goods, services and financial instruments, there are thought to be positive repercussions for demand. However, although evidence is hard to come by, the net direct benefits accruing to the country from this source are thought to be small.[2] Secondly, countries stand to gain from the seigniorage arising from foreign demand for the international currency. Here too, the few studies that have been undertaken into this issue suggest that the sums involved are rather modest.[3]

Related to this, debt issuers in key currency countries, both private and public, potentially enjoy lower costs of financing as a result of international demand for their bonds. Portes and Rey (1998) refer to this as a liquidity discount and estimated that this has saved the US government 25–50 basis points on debt. (These savings can be expected to be higher today on account of the large US current account deficit, if not in basis points, then in the absolute magnitude of interest payment savings.)

It is often noted that a country with a major international currency is able to finance current account deficits with liabilities denominated in its own currency, since other countries are ready to accept very large amounts of debt and at low cost to the issuer. This "exorbitant privilege" is cited as one reason why the current account deficit of the US has been able to widen without the emergence of strong corrective pressures. Yet to the degree that this "privilege" weakens policy discipline and allows imbalances to accumulate, it cannot only be seen as a blessing, at least not beyond the short run.

A strong international dimension clearly enhances the breadth and efficiency of domestic financial markets, and this is also cited as a key advantage to an international currency. At the same time, international acceptance of a currency presupposes deep and well-functioning domestic financial markets, and hence it is not easy to disentangle the benefit arising solely from the currency's international usage. Rather, there is a virtuous cycle.

To the extent that the international usage contributes to capital market efficiency, it may enhance the transmission of monetary policy and shorten the lags. At the same time, this advantage needs to be weighed against the greater analytical challenge that international usage poses for monetary policy in assessing exchange rate developments and money demand. Non-resident demand for a currency is potentially more volatile and less meaningful for monetary policy purposes than resident demand, and not only influences the aggregate demand for money (via banknotes held abroad), but also the exchange rate. Insofar, monetary authorities need to accurately gauge and evaluate developments in non-resident

flexible regimes. This could lead to a conflict between maintaining confidence and providing liquidity.

2 See Wyplosz (1997).

3 Rogoff (1998) and Alogoskoufis and Portes (1991) estimate that for the United States, annual revenue from seigniorage amounts to around 0.2 per cent of gross domestic product per year. This should be considerably less for the euro area.

demand for the physical currency in order to properly inform monetary policy. (In terms of the ECB's two-pillar analytical framework, this requires developing a keen understanding of the international aspects of money demand for both the exchange rate element of pillar I and monetary growth element of pillar II.[4])

If the pecuniary advantages are considered small, the impact on financial markets unclear and the implications for monetary policy formulation mixed, international currencies do at least appear to enjoy symbolic importance. As Mundell (1993) put it: "great powers have great currencies", and by the same token, great currencies are perceived as the manifestation of a great power. With respect to the euro, such symbolism is arguably of great importance, though it should be stressed that this was not the rationale for the introduction of the euro. As a currency shared by many countries, the euro lifts consciousness above the nation-state and serves to foster a super-national identity, a European identity. Conversely, it unites euro area member countries in the eyes of the rest of the world. The value of this shift in mindset is beyond the realm of quantitative evaluation.[5]

The ECB's Policy Stance towards the International Role of the Euro

Notwithstanding the euro's symbolic value, little consideration was given to the euro's international role upon its introduction. At the time, some observers maintained that one of the main motives behind economic and monetary union in Europe was the creation of a major international role for the euro, and that fostering such a role would be an important objective for the European Central Bank.[6] Both assertions are wrong. The euro was introduced to promote economic integration and economic welfare in the member states. To this end, the mandate of the European System of Central Banks (in the event, the Eurosystem) is defined as maintaining price stability in the euro area. As for the euro's international role, the Eurosystem takes a neutral stance. The ECB holds the view that it would be neither feasible nor desirable to directly promote or hinder the international role of the euro. This role is, and should remain, the outcome of market forces acting on economic and financial developments and policies inside and outside the euro area. Of course, to the extent that the Eurosystem is successful in fulfilling its mandate and maintaining price stability in the euro area, it will *indirectly* foster the use of the euro as an international currency.

---

4 For detail, see Hartmann and Issing (2002).

5 Some observers at the time warned that the introduction of the common currency could lead to severe political tension between participating countries. Feldstein (1997/8) even suggested that it could eventually lead to a new war in Europe.

6 See for example, Wyplosz (1997: 1): "The international role of the euro is the hidden agenda of Europe's long-planned adoption of a single currency."

Factors Affecting the Rise of a Major International Currency

This brings us to the question of what determines the rise of a major international currency. Here we focus on four key factors.[7]

Firstly, the *strength of the underlying economy and the stability of the currency* play an important role in supporting the emergence of an international currency. To the extent that a currency is expected to hold its value or even rise, it becomes attractive as a *store of value*. But it will also be attractive as a *unit of account* and a *medium of exchange* if its value can be expected to remain stable. Consequently, internal stability of the currency (that is, a low and stable inflation rate) as well as external stability (a reliable rate of exchange) are paramount. Therefore, the soundness and credibility of economic policies are key determinants in the emergence of an international currency.

Yet sound policies are not sufficient *per se* to ensure the rise of a major international currency. Since an exchange rate is a function of the relative attractiveness of two currencies, the attractiveness of one currency over another for foreign residents depends not least on the *relative* performance, and performance prospects, of the underlying economy. A crucial aspect of the strength of a currency is its vulnerability to external shocks. All open economies with convertible currencies are exposed to external shocks, but the potential impact decreases, the smaller the relative size of the traded goods sector. For this reason, the currencies of the largest open economies are the best candidates to become major international currencies. Hence, the second key factor behind the rise of an international currency is the *size of the underlying economy.*

Size also confers other advantages besides reduced sensitivity to external shocks. The larger the economy, the larger the *absolute* flows of private investment, government debt issuance and gross trade. These volumes confer economies of scale and scope in transactions in the domestic currency and exert an implicit pressure for international transactions to be denominated in the domestic currency. This has spillover effects raising the currency's international role: if trade is largely invoiced in a particular foreign currency, a country may choose to peg to that currency and hold reserves in that currency.[8] (It should be added that the US dollar has become entrenched as the main invoicing currency of primary commodity trade. Since primary commodities are traded on centralized exchanges, the dollar was the most efficient choice given that it was the most widely known and accepted, and had the lowest transaction costs.)

Yet economic size alone is not enough, as the example of China illustrates. The currency of the world's fourth largest economy is far from becoming an international currency. A key reason is the weakness and immaturity of domestic financial markets, and hence the lack of capital account convertibility. For

---

7 See, for instance, Duisenberg (1996).

8 Eichengreen (1997) found that a one percentage point increase in the share of world GDP by a major currency country was associated with a 0.9 per cent increase in that currency's share of global central bank reserves, taking into account the difficulties in overcoming inertia to change currencies.

widespread international acceptance of a currency, foreign residents must be able to easily acquire, hold and dispose of financial instruments denominated in it. This presupposes deep, well-functioning and accessible capital and money markets. So the third key criterion is a *broad, deep, sound and well-regulated domestic financial system*.

Finally, even with a stable value, a large economy and sophisticated financial markets, it may still be a long time before a currency is accepted as a major international currency. It took many years for the US dollar to displace sterling as the leading international currency. Part of the explanation lies in the fact that the internationalization of a currency is unlikely to proceed at the same pace in all its different functions. Often the "store of value" function expands first, since the alternative currency offers diversification possibilities. Only with a lag does a currency become used for other functions. This is because of both the switching costs and the effort needed to overcome inertia and change common practices in view of network externalities and the related functional synergies.

Network externalities refer to the strong convenience and cost incentives of using the currency that is widely used by others, and hence the more a currency is used, the more attractive – and entrenched – its use becomes. On the demand side, the high liquidity in one currency market attracts more market participants, since traders can be matched more quickly and at lower margins, resulting in more trades. Increased trade leads to lower transaction costs, and better hedging instruments, reinforcing the attractiveness of the currency. *Functional synergies* refer to the gains from using a currency already employed in one function for a related function. For example, when a currency is accepted as a means of payment, it increases the incentive to use it, for example, as a store of value. As in the example above, if trade is denominated in a given currency, this strengthens the case for holding reserves in the same currency.

In view of these factors, a major international currency is neither easily nor quickly toppled. However, once a critical threshold, or tipping point, has been reached, the change can come rapidly. Such a switch may be triggered by a policy error by the lead currency country.

How do the four elements – stability, size, financial market sophistication and network densities – rank in terms of importance in the rise of a currency's international role? Although views diverge, most observers tend to place greatest weight on the incumbent's network advantages and believe that an equally well-qualified newcomer currency is unlikely to unseat the incumbent without the erosion of existing network externalities and functional spillovers. Incumbent error rather than newcomer virtue is considered to be the decisive factor, though the incumbent's position could also be gradually undermined by financial innovation reducing currency conversion costs and leveling the playing field.

Prospects for the Euro Prior to Its Inception

In terms of the four criteria mentioned above, the consensus view was for a slow climb for the euro in international standing, albeit at differentiated speeds for the different functions.

Based on currency stability and relative economic performance, Schieber (1998) remarked that "there is no doubt that the euro has great potential as an international currency". The euro was expected to be well received internationally but not to rival the US dollar (see, for example, McCauley 1997). While the euro was yet to establish a track record on stability, the independence and mandate given to the ECB to safeguard price stability suggested that the internal value was likely to be strongly safeguarded. Nevertheless, prospects of strength are no substitute for evidence, and on this count most commentators expected a relatively cautious adoption by international users during the period of credibility building. The common assertion that the euro area was not, *ex ante*, an optimal currency area fuelled concerns there would be tensions among members in the conduct of monetary policy.

In an analysis of the consequences for the international monetary system of the coming EMU, de Beaufort Wijnholds (1997) focused on the possible strength or weakness of the euro,[9] its role as an international reserve currency and its position within the IMF, suggesting that in the long run, important changes could take place in the configuration of its Executive Board. Wijnholds foresaw a potentially important, though not dominant role for the euro as a reserve currency, a fall in total reserves of EMU members as the deutschmark became a domestic currency, and a reduction in the need for international reserves of the euro area. Looking forward, we can observe a reduction in the euro area's foreign exchange reserves from €200 billion at end 1998 to €142 billion at end 2005.

In terms of economic growth, in the five years to the introduction of the euro on January 1, 1999, the United States had outpaced the euro area, and US unemployment was lower (see Figure 6.1). At that time, the United States also appeared to have brighter growth prospects. Bergsten (1997) warned that a key risk to euro area performance was that structural reforms necessary to support growth may not be implemented in a timely manner. On the other hand, the euro area was expected to maintain a much more sound external position than the United States. Rising US external debt and a widening current account deficit were considered to raise doubts about the stability of the dollar.

The size of the underlying economy was considered a key criterion favoring the continued dominance of the US dollar. In 1998, euro area GDP was 76 per cent of the size of US GDP. At the same time, the trade openness of the euro area (26 per cent in 1999) was higher than for the US (20 per cent), with potential implications for increased sensitivity to external shocks. It should also be noted that greater trade does not necessarily translate into noticeably greater international usage of the larger trader's currency. For one thing, some key goods, especially energy and primary commodities are, by convention, priced in US dollars. For another, capital flows outweigh trade flows, especially for industrial countries.

This highlights the importance of broad, deep and liquid financial markets for the international currency. In this respect, those of the United States were – and

9 He observed: "It cannot be excluded that the euro will be relatively weak in the initial phase, especially if EMU participation is large from the beginning (twelve or more countries) and there exists doubt about the strength of the stability pact" (205).

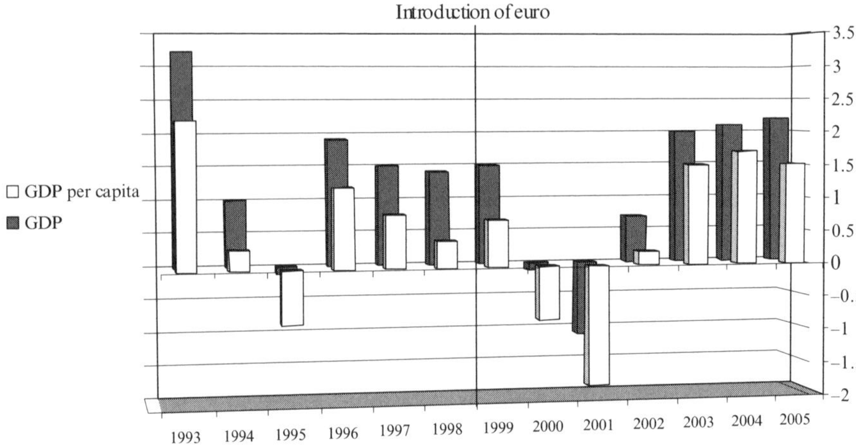

Figure 6.1 Growth Rate Differential between the US and the Euro Area, 1993–2005

Note: US growth rate minus euro area growth rate, in percentage points.

mostly still are – more developed than those of the euro area. For example, the size of the market for domestic securities in 1997 was twice the size of all EU markets combined. This is essential for liquidity and as a result, US Treasury bills were expected to remain the preferred money market instrument: the market is deep, liquid and operates around the clock.

At the same time, some researchers expressed confidence that parity in international stature was likely to occur "eventually" (for example, Bergsten 1997). This view was based on the fact that the total value of government bond markets in the EU was larger than in the United States; the EU issues more international bonds and equities than the United States; and there is more futures trading in the EU than in the United States. These augur well for further development.

Inertia is perhaps the main factor working against a speedy rise of the euro as an international currency. However, Bénassy-Quéré *et al.* (1998) posited that the shock to global financial markets from the appearance of a major new currency (specifically, the introduction of a new currency with deep financial markets, no intra zone exchange rate risk and an independent central bank) may provide a positive jolt. Other commentators predicted that a triggering factor for faster euro take-up could occur on the side of the US dollar, for example, from the effects of prolonged inflation, escalating public debt or spiraling external debt.[10] In the meantime, the euro was considered most likely to overcome inertia first in its usage as a store of value (on account of the portfolio diversification possibilities that it offers), with greater usage made of other functions more slowly over time.

In sum, the euro was expected to be well received internationally, but to develop its international dimension only gradually and pose no threat to the US dollar's

10 See, for example, Wyplosz (1997) and Bergsten (1997).

dominant role. McCauley (1997) suggested that the euro would outweigh the deutschmark's international role, but not that of all its constituent currencies, in part because of the mechanical adjustments eliminating intra-area exchange rates, trade and reserves.

The Euro's Stature as an International Currency Today

Moving from the general to the specific, this section lays out the inroads made by the euro into its various roles as an international currency. The main arena for international currencies remains financial markets, where volumes traded are many multiples of those required for trade in goods and services. As a rule, the official use of an international currency is normally dictated by private sector usage. Following this schematic, this section explores euro usage by financial market participants, exporters and importers, residents of foreign currencies as a parallel currency, and the official sector.

Developments in Domestic Financial Markets

For the euro to realize its full potential in financial markets, European financial markets need to be properly integrated. Upon the introduction of the euro, it was recognized that financial markets were still quite fragmented, but that the euro itself would exert pressure for improvement. Since then integration has proceeded at a strong, albeit non-uniform pace. Money markets have been fully integrated since the introduction of the euro in 1999. Debt markets have flourished. Since euro area governments began issuing in a small number of different maturities, liquidity in government bond markets has increased significantly, thereby overcoming the disadvantage associated with the plurality of issuers. Corporate and mortgage bond markets have also thrived – though not to the same extent as public debt markets. While they have been assisted by the introduction of Eurobor and Eonia as reference interest rates for financial market operations, they are impeded by differing national legal systems. Nevertheless, a survey of central bank asset managers (Pringle and Carver 2005) found that the quality of euro area financial markets matched US markets in terms of liquidity and availability of money market and debt instruments. Rather, it is in equity markets and at the retail level (banking, insurance) that progress has been slowest and markets remain fragmented along national lines. In time, these areas will benefit from the Financial Services Action Plan launched in 1999. This plan, a legislative program to remove impediments to financial market integration, was completed in 2004 and is now in the implementation phase. Although slowed by pockets of resistance, progress is gradually being made.

Developments in International Financial Markets

Foreign exchange markets

In foreign exchange markets, the most actively traded currencies are those that serve as vehicle currencies, that is, as a means of exchanging one relatively illiquid currency into another. Since bilateral trades in illiquid currencies are subject to relatively high transaction costs and more volatile exchange rates, it is more cost efficient to employ as a medium of exchange a currency with low transaction costs, especially in the interbank market, which in turn "thickens" trading networks in that currency. Owing to the United States' sophisticated domestic financial markets and freely mobile capital, the US dollar has long been the most widely used vehicle currency, and consequently has the highest turnover on foreign exchange markets. Data from the Continuous Linked Settlement system show that 90 per cent of all daily transactions on foreign exchange markets globally in the year to July 2005 involved the US dollar, compared to 43 per cent for the euro.[11]

Less recent but more broadly-based data from the BIS Triennial Central Bank Survey of Foreign Exchange and Derivatives Market Activity of April 2004 also show that the euro is the second most actively traded currency in foreign exchange markets worldwide, accounting for around 37 per cent of all transactions. This share stabilized after foreign exchange transactions between euro area countries ceased to exist. (Legacy currencies of the euro accounted for 53 per cent of the global foreign exchange turnover in 1998.) Unsurprisingly, most trades with the euro involved the US dollar (76 per cent of all euro foreign exchange transactions), and the euro/dollar currency pair was the most actively traded in 2004 (28 per cent of total global turnover).

International debt markets

International debt is defined here narrowly as issues in a currency other than that of the country in which the borrower resides. On that basis, of the stock of international debt outstanding at end 2005 Q2, figures show that almost one-third (31.5 per cent) was denominated in euros, up from 20 per cent in 1999 on a slowing trend (see Figure 6.2). This ranks second after US dollar issues (44 per cent) and ahead of the yen (8 per cent). Large issuers include non-euro area EU governments and financial institutions, and US corporates and financial institutions.

A cross-country comparison of international bond issues denominated in euros confirms the strong geographic concentration of issuers among non-euro area European countries. Figure 6.3 shows that euro-denominated international debt issues accounted for 75 per cent of total issues by the new member states, and 56 per cent of UK issues (compared to 14 per cent and 34 per cent in US dollars respectively). For other regions, the share is considerably lower, with the US dollar being the preferred currency of issue. For the US, most international bonds are denominated in euros (66 per cent), with the yen a distant 12 per cent.

---

11 Note that the sum of all percentages of currencies traded equals 200 per cent on account of the two-sided nature of foreign exchange transactions.

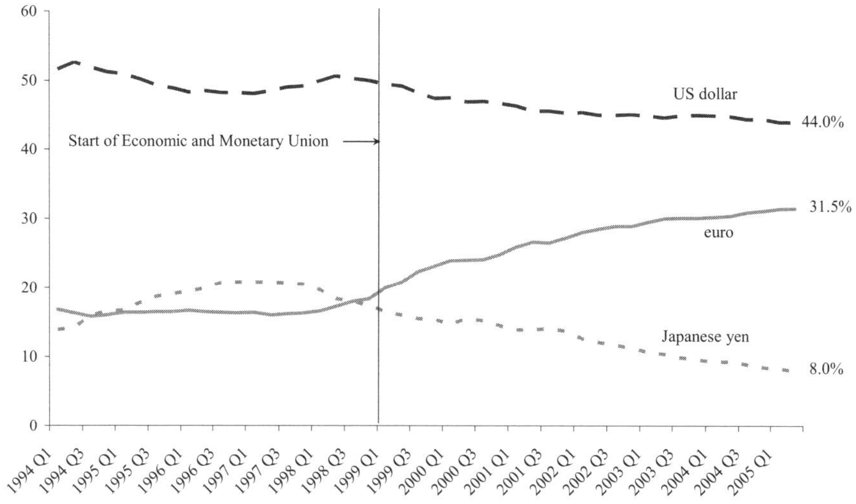

Figure 6.2 Stock of International Debt Securities: Currency Shares

Note: Bonds and notes and money market instruments, excluding home currency issuance, as per cent of the total amount outstanding and at 1994 Q1 exchange rates.

Sources: BIS and ECB.

In the main, euro-denominated international debt is targeted at euro area investors. At end 2004, more than one-half of international euro-denominated securities were held by euro area residents. However, there has been increasing interest by Asian and to a lesser extent US investors since 1999. By June 2005, Asian investors held around 35 per cent and the US just over 20 per cent of euro-denominated international debt. At the same time, of total US bond holdings, the share in euros is negligible. (Survey data by Lipper, a financial information provider, suggests that the euro's share is around 0.7 per cent. A low figure is not surprising in view of the fact that most US-based investors manage their portfolios invested in euro from the City of London.[12])

International loan and deposit markets
Since 1999, there has been little variation in the shares of major currencies in international loans and deposits. Where one of the parties to a loan or a deposit is located in the euro area, the euro features prominently, but not if both parties are outside the euro area. As might be expected, the UK is the main originator of euro-denominated international loans and recipient of euro-denominated international deposits.

12 ECB, *Review of the International Role of the Euro*, December 2005.

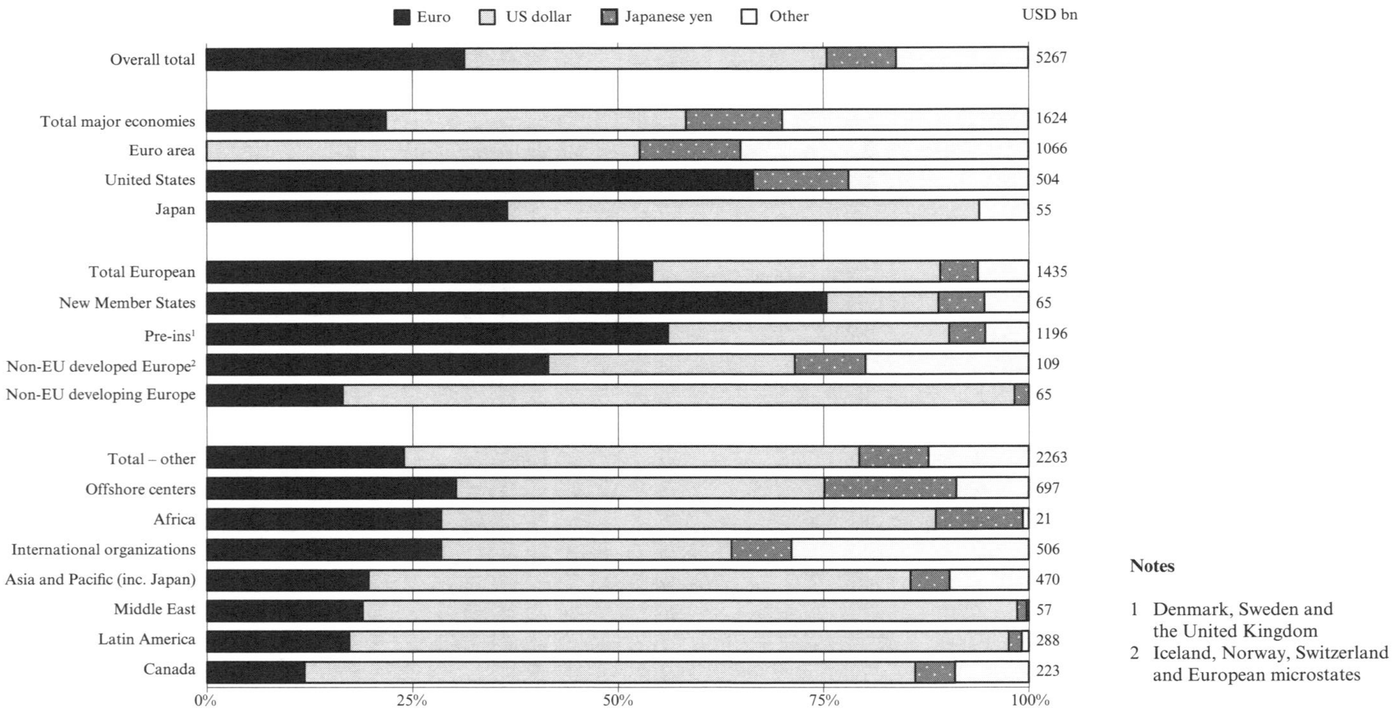

Figure 6.3 Currencies' Shares in the Stock of Outstanding International Debt Securities in Selected Regions

Note: Narrow measure; that is, excluding home currency issuance, as a percentage of the total amount outstanding and at constant 1994 Q1 exchange rates.

Sources: BIS, ECB calculations.

Loans Data from the BIS provide an insight into the relative role of the euro in international loan markets. There are three types of euro-denominated international loans: loans by banks in the euro area to borrowers outside the euro area; loans from banks outside the euro area to borrowers inside the euro area; and loans transacted entirely outside the euro area. (The data reported here are for *bank* lenders and *non-bank* borrowers.) The euro-denominated share of all three types has barely changed since 1999. Firstly, of the stock of loans made by euro area banks to "external" borrowers (that is, non-bank borrowers outside the euro area), around 40 per cent are denominated in euros (compared to 44 per cent for the US dollar). Figure 6.4 provides details. Most of these loans are extended to developed country borrowers (mainly in the UK: 46 per cent[13]). By contrast, euro area bank loans to emerging markets are mainly denominated in US dollars for borrowers in Latin America and offshore financial centers. (Loans to Africa and the Middle East, Asian and the Pacific and Europe are, however, mainly in euros.)

Secondly, of loans extended by "external" banks to euro area borrowers, a larger percentage (56 per cent) is in euros (compared to 27 per cent in dollars). Again, the UK is the main non-euro area counterparty; its banks accounted for 69 per cent of loans outstanding at end 2005 Q1.

Finally, of total loans transacted entirely outside the euro area, only 7 per cent were in euros (2005 Q1), compared to 70 per cent in US dollars. UK banks accounted for the largest proportion (over 77 per cent) of euro-denominated lending.

Deposits As with international loans in euros, there are three types of international euro deposits. Deposits originating outside the euro area to banks in the euro area are mainly in euro (51 per cent for 2005 Q1). Of the stock of euro denominated international deposits, around half emanate from the UK, 18 per cent from offshore financial centers and only 9 per cent from the US. The picture is roughly similar for deposits from euro area residents in "external" banks: 54 per cent are in euro and 73 per cent of these are held in UK banks. Finally, and in stark contrast, of deposits in banks outside the euro area made by depositors also outside the euro area, a mere 9 per cent are denominated in euros. However, here too, UK banks attract the lion's share (48 per cent), followed by banks in offshore financial centers (25 per cent) and Switzerland (21 per cent).

Usage in International Trade

According to "Grassman's law", which states that trade tends to be invoiced in the currency of the exporter, the role of the euro as an invoicing or settlement currency should be commensurate with euro area external trade. However, several more recent studies have shown that Grassman's law no longer holds. Instead, the use of the euro for invoicing was expected to be determined, for primary commodity

13 A significant share of these loans may be lent on to borrowers outside the UK, given London's predominant role in international financial intermediation.

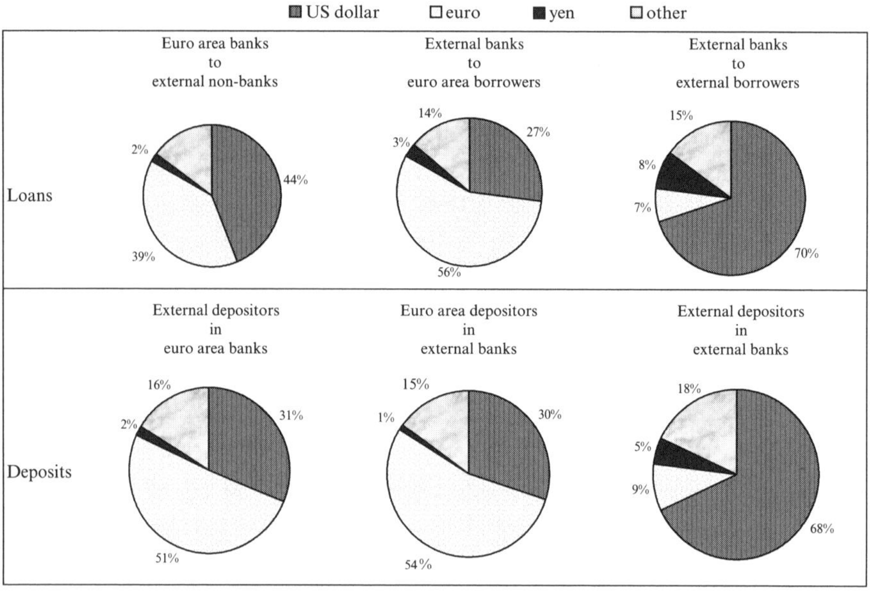

Figure 6.4 Cross-Border Loans and Deposits Between Euro Area and Non-euro Area Entities

Source: European Central Bank (December 2005), *Review of the International Role of the Euro* (Frankfurt), BIS and ECB calculations.

trade, by the transaction costs associated with the euro, and for differentiated manufactures, by the variability of the euro against other key currencies and switching costs from the usage of the dollar as a vehicle currency. While the idea has been floated by some oil exporting countries to change the invoicing of oil sales from dollars to euros, it is unclear whether these notions are to be considered as more than alternatives in a general discussion of pricing strategies.

In terms of concrete figures, Hartmann (1998) expected the share of the euro in extra–euro area exports to be around 58 per cent after EMU. This was based on the invoicing practices of five EU member states in the early 1990s. Indeed, by 2004, the euro's share had reached this percentage. The use of the euro has risen for imports too but remains somewhat lower than for exports. Currency denominations of trade in goods are shown in Figure 6.5. Although lagging initially, the use of the euro in services trade is gradually catching up with usage in goods trade. The exception is Greece. Its euro-invoiced services exports are anomalously low, probably on account of its exports in the maritime transport sector, which traditionally uses the US dollar.

Among non-euro area countries, the new EU member states have increased their use of the euro as an invoicing currency to such an extent that it exceeds the value of their trade with the euro area. This is as could be expected. Some trade with other new EU member states is likely to be conducted in euro since

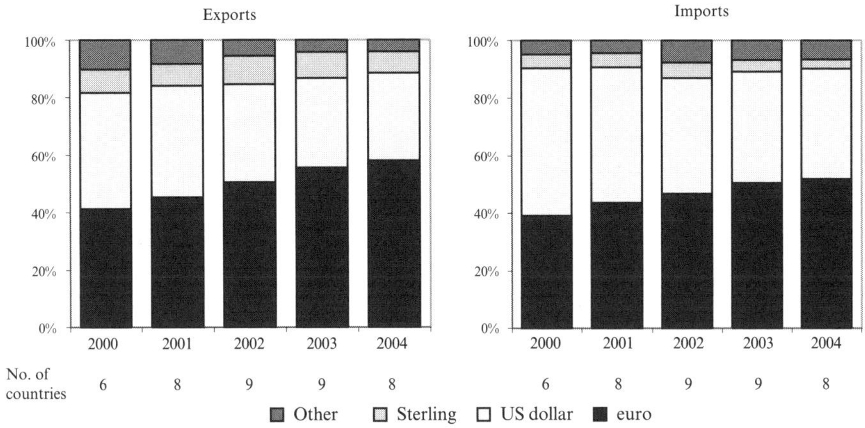

Figure 6.5 Euro Area Trade: Average Share of Currencies Used in Exports and Imports

Source: European Central Bank (December 2005), *Review of the International Role of the Euro* (Frankfurt).

it will serve as a vehicle currency between the currencies of the two countries. As such, the transaction costs are equally borne by both parties, and neither is exposed to the currency variability of the other. Outside Europe, use of the euro as an invoicing currency is most prevalent in Asia, but remains minor. Figure 6.6 illustrates.

Usage as a Parallel Currency in Third Countries

Finally, another international use of a currency is as a parallel currency in a foreign country where it is valued for its strength. Residents of many developing, emerging market and transition economies hold a significant share of their financial assets in the form of foreign cash or foreign currency-denominated bank deposits.

Information on non-resident demand for euro banknotes can be derived only indirectly and with considerable uncertainty. Upon the introduction of the euro, euro area monetary and financial institutions shipped large quantities of euro banknotes to destinations outside the euro area. Thereafter, net shipments started to stabilize and increasingly exhibit a seasonal pattern (Figure 6.7). In June 2005, the stock of euro banknotes outside the euro area amounted to around €55 billion. This is likely to be an underestimation of the true figure since there are many other channels through which euro banknotes are transferred, such as tourism, worker remittances and activity in the grey economy.

The ECB (2005) reports on a study estimating that in central south-eastern and eastern Europe, the quantity of US dollars circulating in those countries declined by about 23 per cent between 2003 and 2005, while the amount of euros rose around 60 per cent. Today, a far larger proportion of the population holds euros than dollars.

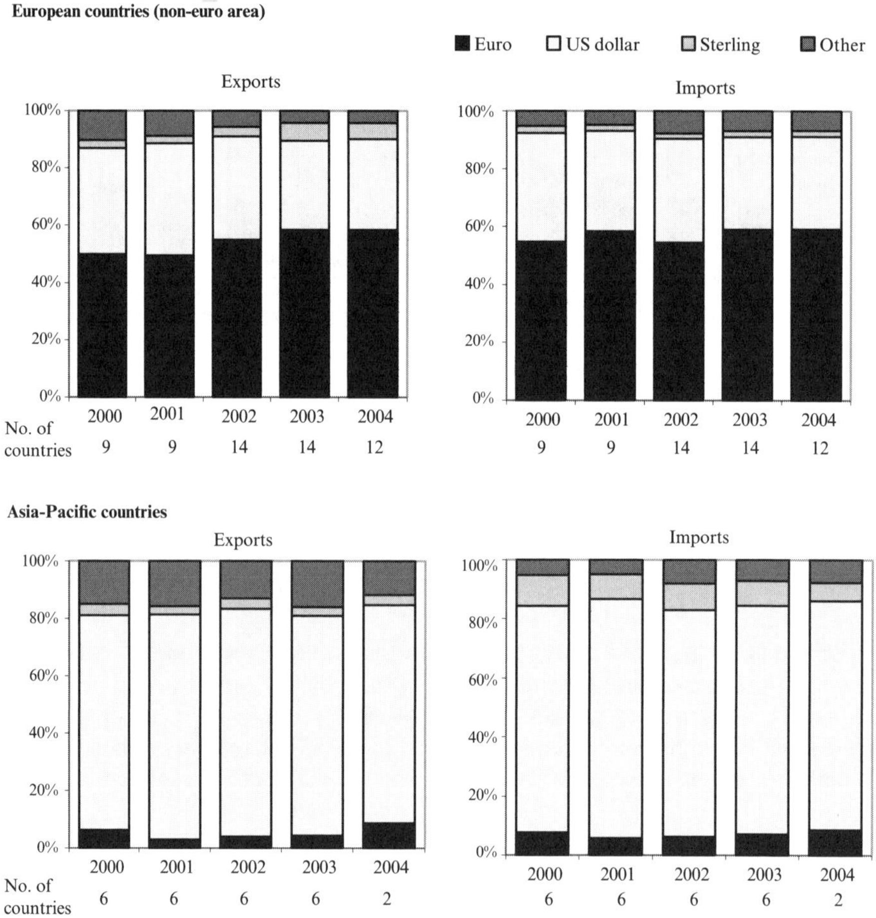

Figure 6.6 Average Share of Currencies Used in Exports and Imports by Region

Source: European Central Bank (December 2005), *Review of the International Role of the Euro* (Frankfurt).

Information on bank deposits denominated in euros also shows strong demand following the cash changeover – probably reflecting in part a substitution of euro legacy currency banknotes with euro-denominated deposits. In mature economies, the share of euro-denominated deposits has remained relatively stable, but it is on an upward trend in most new EU member states, EU acceding and candidate countries, and some countries in the CIS (Commonwealth of Independent States) and Middle East.

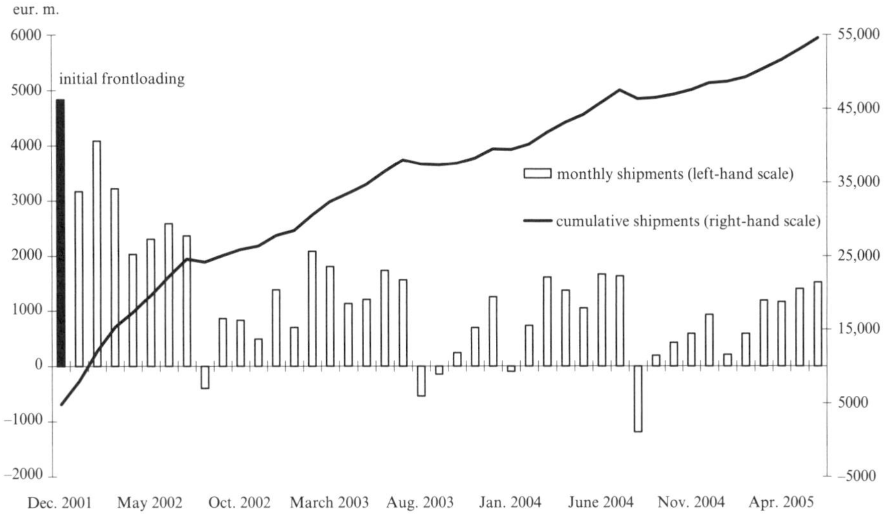

Figure 6.7 Shipments of Euro Banknotes to Destinations Outside the Euro Area

Sources: European Central Bank (December 2005), Review of the International Role of the Euro (Frankfurt).

Usage by the Official Sector

The contribution of the official sector to the international usage of a foreign currency may be through its choice of an anchor currency, denomination of foreign exchange reserves and intervention currency. These three roles are closely interlinked and, for the euro, show a strong geographic concentration in non-euro area European countries.

An anchor currency

The selection of a particular currency to serve as an anchor is significant in that it has strong spillover functional effects on the use of the same currency for foreign exchange reserves (store of value) and as an intervention currency (means of payment). The pegging of the domestic currency to another currency reduces the costs and risks of using the other currency, and hence acts a fillip to its international usage.

For countries of Central and Eastern Europe looking for a suitable peg, a euro anchor was considered "natural" based on the well-known optimum currency area criteria.[14] By contrast, it was clear that the euro would not be of interest as an anchor for pegged regimes in Asia, principally because the euro area is not the main trading partner and the use of the dollar for this purpose is well entrenched.

14 See Mundell (1961) and McKinnon (1963).

Table 6.1 Countries with Exchange Rate Regimes Linked to the Euro (as at December 1, 2005)

Region	Exchange Rate Regimes	Countries
European Union (non-euro area)	ERM II	Cyprus, Denmark, Estonia,[1] Lativa,[2] Lituania,[1] Malta,[3] Slovenia, Slovakia
	Peg arrangements based on the euro	Hungary
	Managed floating with the euro as reference currency	Czech Republic, Romania
	Pro memoria: Independent floating	Sweden, United Kingdom, Poland
Acceding, accession and potential candidate countries	Unilateral euroization	Kosovo, Montenegro
	Euro-based currency boards	Bulgaria, Bosnia and Herzegovina
	Peg arrangements or managed floating with the euro as reference currency	Croatia, FYR Macedonia, Serbia
	Pro memoria: Independent floating	Albania, Turkey
Others	Euroization	European microstates,[4] French territorial communities[5]
	Peg arrangements based on the euro	CFA Franc zone,[6] French overseas territories,[7] Cape Verde, Comoros
	Peg arrangements and managed floats based on the SDR and other currency baskets involving the euro (share of the euro)	Seychelles (37.7%), Russian Federation (35%),[8] Libya, Botswana,[9] Morocco,[10] Tunisia,[11] Vanuatu[12]

Notes

1 Unilateral commitment to a currency board.

2 Unilateral commitment to an exchange rate fluctuation band of +/–1%.

3 Unilateral commitment to maintain a fixed rate exchange.

4 Republic of San Marino, Vatican City, Principality of Monaco, Andorra. In the case of Andorra: unilateral euroization. The other countries and jurisdictions are entitled to use the euro as their official currency.

5 Saint-Pierre-et-Miquelon, Mayotte.

6 WAEMU (Benin, Burkina Faso, Côte d'Ivoire, Guinea-Bissau, Mali, Niger, Senegal, Togo) and CAEMC (Cameroon, Central African Republic, Chad, Republic of Congo, Equatorial Guinea, Gabon).

7 French Polynesia, New Caledonia, Wallis and Futuna.

8 Trade-weighted currency basket for monitoring and setting ceilings for real appreciation (euro share of 36.4%); since February 2005 dollar–euro basket for daily exchange rate management (since August 2005 euro share of 35%).

9 Weighted basket of currencies comprising the SDR and the South African rand.

10 Weighted basket in accordance with the distribution of Morocco's foreign trade and the pattern of currencies of settlement.

11 Real effective exchange rate target.

12 Weighted (trade and tourism receipts) basket of currencies of Vanuatu's major trading partners.

Sources: IMF and European Central Bank compilation; European Central Bank (December 2005), *Review of the International Role of the Euro* (Frankfurt), 50.

Indeed, there is a strong geographic bias to the countries pegging in whole or in part to the euro. As of December 2005, 40 of the 150 countries that have some sort of peg used the euro as the sole or a partial anchor, and of these, 18 are in Europe, and a further 14 belong to the CFA Franc Zone. Table 6.1 provides details. For countries outside ERM II, the adoption of the euro as a peg is a unilateral decision and involves no commitment by the Eurosystem. For ERM II countries by contrast, pegged currencies are kept within the prescribed fluctuation bands of ±15 per cent around the agreed central parity to the euro with assistance from the ECB at the margins of the band. Two ERM II countries – namely Latvia and Malta – voluntarily and unilaterally maintain narrower bands of ±1 per cent and 0 per cent respectively.

The euro as an anchor has also been considered by two large emerging market economies, Russia and China. Russia's currency is pegged to a trade-weighted currency basket, which includes the euro. By December 2005, the weight of euro had risen to 35 per cent in line with the euro area's share in Russia's total trade. China announced a regime shift to managed floating based on a basket of currencies in July 2005. A later announcement listed the currencies, but not the weights, in the basket, and the euro was among them. Despite this, the reform has so far resulted primarily in only a one-off revaluation against the US dollar, with an otherwise tightly managed renminbi/US dollar exchange rate.

Reserves

Regarding the use of the euro for reserves, the decision is a function of the choice of exchange rate regime (and anchor), the direction and invoicing currency of trade flows, the currency denomination of debt, risk diversification strategies and possibly political considerations. Clearly, Asian countries were less likely to move heavily into euros, while central and eastern European countries were far more likely.

At the end of 2004, total world reserves stood at SDR 2.4 trillion (USD 3.7 trillion). Full data on the currency breakdown of reserves are not available. Data collected by the IMF are the most comprehensive but do not include major reserve holders in Asia, which comprise 50 per cent of the reserves of emerging market and developing countries. Keeping this in mind, the data indicate that at the end December of 2004, around 25 per cent of reserves were denominated in euros, up from around 18 per cent in 1999 (see Table 6.2). Although not strictly comparable, this is more than the sum of legacy currencies despite the elimination of intra-euro area reserves of legacy currencies, and is quite remarkable given the large increase in global reserves over the same period driven in large part by US current account deficits. As Figure 6.8 shows, it is partly due to valuation effects.

Across groups of countries, it should be noted that the euro is more popular in developing countries (29 per cent of reserves) than advanced countries (21 per cent of reserves). As with the choice of an anchor currency – and for similar reasons – there is a regional bias in favor of the euro in eastern European countries. Russia is thought to be among the largest holders of euro-denominated foreign exchange reserves. One third of Russia's total foreign exchange reserves are in euro (around USD 50bn), according to the authorities, reflecting the fact that

Table 6.2 Official Foreign Exchange Reserves: Currency Shares (as a percentage of total identified holdings, end-of-year values)

	1999	2000	2001	2002	2003	2004
All countries						
Total (SDR bln)	1300	1490	1633	1771	2037	2407
US dollar	71.0	70.5	70.7	66.5	65.8	65.9
Euro	17.9	18.8	19.8	24.2	25.3	24.9
Other currencies	11.1	10.7	9.5	9.3	8.9	9.2
Industrialized countries						
US dollar	73.5	72.5	72.7	68.9	70.5	71.5
Euro	16.1	17.1	18.0	22.4	22.1	20.9
Other currencies	10.4	10.4	9.3	8.7	7.4	7.6
Emerging markets and developing countries						
US dollar	68.2	68.2	68.6	64.0	60.7	59.9
Euro	19.9	20.6	21.8	26.1	28.9	29.2
Other currencies	11.9	11.2	9.6	9.9	10.4	10.9

Source: IMF (2005). European Central Bank (December 2005), *Review of the International Role of the Euro* (Frankfurt), 52.

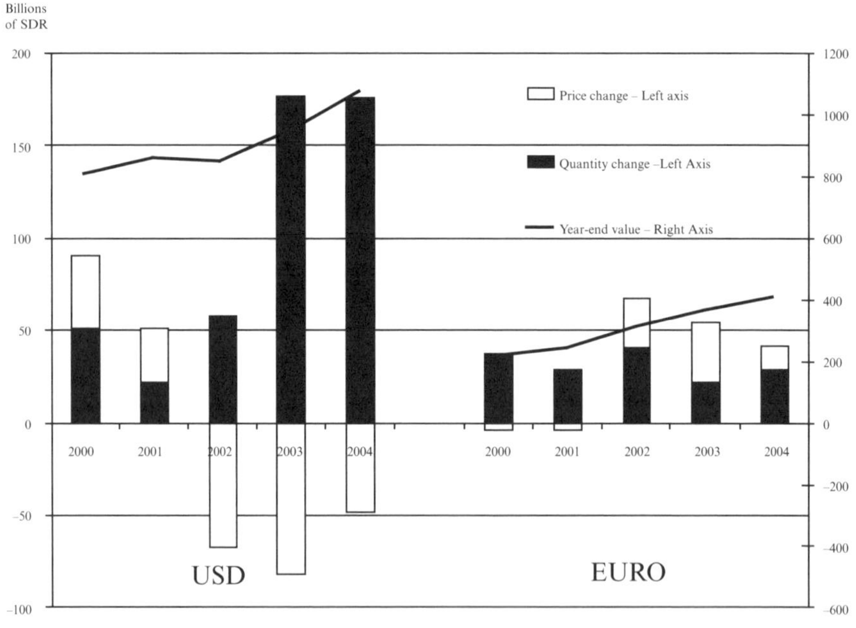

Figure 6.8 Currency Composition of Official Holdings of Foreign Exchange, End of Year

Source: European Central Bank (December 2005), *Review of the International Role of the Euro* (Frankfurt).

one-third of its trade is with the euro area, and 35 per cent of the anchor basket is accorded the euro. It is also noteworthy that some South American countries hold a significant share of their reserves in euros. Their sizable trade and financial links with Europe help explain this choice. As to the oil-exporting countries of the Middle East, the share of euros in their reserves is believed to be modest, although there are some indications of a wish for more diversification. Least is known of euro holdings of central banks in emerging Asia.

Intervention currency

The functions of anchor and reserve currency are closely intertwined with that of intervention currency. While few central banks disclose intervention currencies, press reports and statements by authorities appear to confirm that the euro is mostly used to intervene in the exchange rate by European countries, such as the new EU member states (notably, the ERM II members Latvia, Slovakia and Slovenia, as well as the Czech Republic and Hungary) and those neighboring the EU, particularly those with euro-based currency boards. This is consistent with the geographic trade and financial linkages of these countries.

The Future for the International Role of the Euro

Summing up, how far has the euro come? The euro was expected to become the second most important international currency after the dollar and it has firmly established itself in this position. It is widely used in international debt, loan and deposit markets, and its role as reserve and invoicing currency is gradually growing. While its introduction did not provide a sufficient shock – as speculated by Bénassy-Quéré *et al.* (1998) – to displace the US dollar as the world's dominant international currency, it has nevertheless exceeded the role of the deutschmark and in many instances also the legacy currencies combined. Its influence is most pronounced in the region around the euro area – in line with optimal currency area theory.

Hence, the prediction that the euro would not constitute a challenge to the US dollar is so far correct. At the same time, this does not invalidate prognoses (by, for example, Portes and Rey 1998 and Mundell 1998) that the euro will draw equal to the dollar at some point in the future. Bergsten (1997) envisaged a five to ten year transition phase for the euro to establish its international stature, after which it would settle into a long term structural position vis-à-vis other leading currencies. He suggested an equilibrium where the dollar and the euro each command around 40 per cent of world finance, conditional on some "serious policy lapse by the US". Indeed, Chinn and Frankel (2005) speculate that under certain conditions (UK entry to the euro area, or persistent depreciation of the dollar), the euro could eclipse the dollar as a leading international reserve currency by 2022.

The future role of the euro continues to be dependent on the four core factors already identified. A crucial element is the speed of progress in financial market integration in Europe. Also, an expansion of the euro area with the accession of new members, particularly the UK, could have an important bearing. While mechanically the immediate impact would be a fall in international usage (since previously international transactions would be classified at domestic), it could further boost the euro's international standing, for example as a reserve currency.

Not least, increased international usage of the euro depends on an improvement in the economic performance of the euro area relative to the United States. The euro area needs to raise its growth rate through increased structural flexibility as foreseen under the Lisbon Agenda. Alternatively, the perception of a sustained internal and external weakening of the dollar relative to the euro could favor greater international use of the euro. Such a perception may arise from a slowing of growth in the US economy owing to falling consumption (as the housing market slows), rising interest rates, rising inflation, a worsening current account deficit or rising debt levels. Finally, some (for example, Stark, 2000) believe that for the euro to challenge the dollar it will need more cohesive external representation on all related matters.

The benefits to the issuing economy from international dominance by its currency are the topic of ongoing debate. For the euro area, perhaps the most obvious benefit is symbolic. Nevertheless, for the Eurosystem, competition between the euro and the dollar is a non-issue since both currencies have important roles to play. The contribution of the ECB is to safeguard the internal stability of the euro and it has established a track record in maintaining price stability. The ECB will continue to refrain from directly promoting or hindering the usage of the euro abroad. The international role of the euro is for the markets to determine.

References

Alogoskoufis, G. and Portes, R. (1991), "International Costs and Benefits of EMU", in *The Economics of EMU*, European Economy, Special Edition, no. 1, 231.

Alogoskoufis, G. and Portes, R. (1992), "European Monetary Union and International Currencies in a Tripolar World", in *Establishing a Central Bank for Europe*, ed. Canzoneri, M. *et al.* (Cambridge University Press), 273.

de Beaufort Wijnholds, J.A.H. (1997), "The EMU and the International Monetary System" (in Dutch) *Economisch Statistische Berichten*, no. 82, March 12.

Bénassy-Quéré, A., Mojon, B. and Schor, A.-D. (July 1998), "The International Role of the Euro" *CEPII 3.*

Bergsten, C.F. (July/August 1997), "The Dollar and the Euro", *Foreign Affairs*, 83.

Bergsten, C.F. (2005), "The Euro and the World Economy", ECB Colloquim held in Honour of Tommaso Padoa-Schioppa, 27 April (Frankfurt).

Chinn, M. and Frankel, J. (December 2005), "Will the Euro Eventually Surpass the Dollar as Leading International Reserve Currency?", *John F. Kennedy School of Government Faculty Research Working Paper Series* RWP05–0641.

Deutsche Bank Research (2005), "The Euro: Well Established as a Reserve Currency", *Reports on European Integration*, EU Monitor 28, September 8.

Duisenberg, W. (1996), "The Euro as a Reserve Currency", De Nederlandsche Bank, Quarterly Bulletin, December 13.

Eichengreen, B. (1997), "Comments on Bergsten", in Masson, P., Krueger, T.H. and Turtleboom, B.G., eds, *EMU and the International Monetary System.*

European Central Bank (2001), *Review of the International Role of the Euro* (Frankfurt).

European Central Bank (December 2002), *Review of the International Role of the Euro* (Frankfurt).

European Central Bank (December 2003), *Review of the International Role of the Euro* (Frankfurt).

European Central Bank (January 2004), *Review of the International Role of the Euro* (Frankfurt).

European Central Bank (December 2005), *Review of the International Role of the Euro* (Frankfurt).

Feldstein, M. (1997–1998), "EMU and International Conflict", *Foreign Affairs.*

Hartmann, P. (1998), "The Currency Denomination of World Trade after European Monetary Union", *Journal of the Japanese and International Economics*, 12, no. 4-424.

Hartmann, P. and Issing, O. (2002), "The International Role of the Euro", *Journal of Policy Modeling*, 24, 315.

Henning, R. (1994), *Currencies and Politics in the United States, Germany and Japan*, (Washington, DC: Institute for International Economics).

Lim, E. (2006), "The Euro's Challenge to the Dollar: Different Views from Economists and Evidence from COFER (Currency Composition of Foreign Exchange Reserves) and Other Data", *IMF Working Paper*, forthcoming.

McCauley, R. (November 1997), "The Euro and the Dollar", *BIS Working Papers*, no. 50.

McKinnon, R.I. (1963), "Optimum Currency Areas", *American Economic Review*, vol. 53, 717–724.

Mundell, R. (November 1961), "A Theory of Optimum Currency Areas," *American Economic Review*, LI, no. 4, 509–517.

Mundell, R. (1993), "EMU and the International Monetary System", in de la Dehesa, G., Giovannini, A., Guitián, M. and Portes, R. (eds), *The Monetary Future of Europe* (London: Centre for Economic Policy Research).

Mundell, R. (1998), "The Case for the Euro – I and II", *Wall Street Journal*, March 24 and 25.

Portes, R. and Rey, H. (1998), "The Emergence of the Euro as an International Currency", *Economic Policy*, April 26, 305.

Pringle, R. and Carver, N. (2005), "Trends in Reserve Management – Survey Results" (London: Central Banking Publications).

Rogoff, K. (1998), "Foreign and Underground Demand for Euro Notes: Blessing or a Curse?", *Economic Policy*, April 26, 263.

Schieber, H. (1998), "The International Role of the Euro", Intervention at the "Euromoney" conference, September 21.

Stark, J. (2000), "The Role of the Euro in the World – Past Developments and Future Perspectives", joint Bundesbank/BIS conference on "Recent Developments in Financial Systems and the Challenges for Economic Policy", speech, September 28–29, Frankfurt.

Wyplosz, C. (1997), "An International Role for the Euro?", report prepared for the European Capital Market Institute.

Chapter 7

Is the Euro Ready to Play the Global Currency Role?

Miriam L. Campanella

Introduction: The US Current Account Deficit and Global Imbalances

Financial integration, the driver of contemporary globalization, has accelerated considerably since the early 1990s and shows in the trend toward larger external assets and liabilities, which is especially relevant for industrial countries where, relative to output, both average external assets and liabilities about tripled between 1990 and 2003, reaching levels of more than 200 per cent by the end of the period (IMF 2005: 110).

In a list of determinants of financial globalization, information technologies have played a big part in contributing to the decline in information processing and dissemination costs and have fostered cross-border trade in expanding financial instruments through decreasing transaction costs. Opportunities for international diversification have increased and obstacles, such as high-cross border transactions and information costs or regulatory barriers, have been reduced. Speedy and less costly technologies and enhanced opportunities for financial diversification have weakened the "home bias", turning investors into risk-takers. The home bias is crucial to the "external imbalances and their adjustment because it determines the extent to which desired current account balances … are accommodated by international financial markets" (IMF 2005: 112–113). If home bias is strong, global demand for foreign assets will be low and price-inelastic. Large issuers of foreign liabilities will thus face high yields; this will discourage net external borrowing, and actual current account balances will likely be smaller than desired ones. On the other hand if home bias is small, demand for foreign assets will be higher and more price-elastic, and larger net external liabilities will be less costly. Over the past two decades, for countries belonging to the Organization for Economic Cooperation and Development, the GDP-weighted correlation between domestic saving rates and domestic investment rates (a standard measure of home bias) fell from 0.96 in 1992 to less than 0.8 in 2002 (Greenspan 2003). The home bias decline points to easing restrictions on net external borrowing.

- Portfolio holdings of foreign bonds have increased compared with domestic capitalization.

- External current account deficits or surpluses have on average increased, as has their dispersion in industrial countries; less so in emerging countries.

Though risk diversification is an important motive for investors, it is unevenly spread across markets. European countries are the example where forces of "gravity"[1] are also relevant. Despite growing US net external liabilities, European countries tend to hold less US equity than implied by the international capital asset pricing model benchmark.

The Savings Glut and the Three Global Imbalances

On the whole, financial globalization has created an environment where net external borrowing and lending are less restricted, and where maintaining larger net foreign liabilities appears to involve relatively lower costs. The United States, where the financial globalization of the 1990s shows its upper limit, is the perfect case.

After the slowdown in 2000 and the 9/11 tragedy, US output growth returned to healthy levels, the labor market strengthened, and inflation was brought well under control. However, one aspect of US economic performance, the US current account deficit, has steadily climbed in recent years. Corresponding to that deficit, US citizens, businesses and governments on net would have raised about $666 billion on international capital markets. The deficit upward trajectory started from a modest $120 billion (1.5 per cent of US GDP) in 1996 to $414 billion (4.2 per cent of GDP) in 2000 on its way to 6.5 per cent at the end of 2005. In less than ten years (between 1996–2005), the US current account deficit grew up from 2.4 per cent of GDP ($210 billion), to 6.5 per cent at the end of 2005, with net external liabilities amounting to 22 per cent of GDP at the end of 2004. Evidence that Mundell's prediction that the United States was set to turn from the "world's biggest creditor to its biggest debtor" is accurate.

But: "Why is that the United States, with the largest world's economy, is borrowing heavily on international capital markets, rather than lending, as would seem more natural?" Challenging a vast literature stressing economic policies and other economic developments within the United States as the source of the build-up of US current account deficit, Bernanke points at events outside the United States as holding a primary role in the US deficit. In the last decade, for a combination of events and forces in Europe and Asia, financial economy has featured an increase in the global supply of saving, "a global saving glut". An excess of saving has flown towards the United States for investment and asset allocation, a phenomenon helping " to explain both the increase in the US current account deficit and the relatively low level of long-term real interest rates"

1 The so-called gravity model of international trade suggests that, everything else being equal, neighboring countries tend to have closer trade linkages than more distant countries. The model is found to perform well in explaining bilateral investment patterns.

(Bernanke 2005: 1). This saving glut is the result of a number of developments that started to surface in the global economy in the mid-1990s. A first source of savings comes from the rich and aging countries of Europe and Japan, hedging against an impending sharp increase in the number of retirees relative to the number of workers. "With slowly growing or declining workforces as well as high-capital ratios many advanced economies outside the United States also face an apparent dearth of domestic investment opportunities. As a consequence mature economies as a group seek to run current account surpluses and thus to lend abroad" (Bernanke 2005: 3). A second flow of saving originates from developing countries, which are used to being borrowers rather than suppliers to international capital markets. In Table7.1 figures on the global current account balances in 1996, 2000 and 2004 show the shift in the global supply of and demand for saving

Table 7.1 Global Current Account Balances, 1996, 2000, 2004 (Billions of US Dollars)

Countries	1996	2000	2004
Industrial	**41.5**	**–331.4**	**–400.3**
United States	–120.2	–413.4	–665.9
Japan	65.7	119.6	171.8
Euro area	**78.5**	**–71.7**	**53.0**
France	20.5	18.3	–5.1
Germany	–14.1	–29.3	104.3
Italy	39.6	–5.7	–13.7
Spain	0.5	–19.3	–49.4
Other			
Australia	–15.8	–15.4	–39.6
Switzerland	21.3	30.6	46.0
United Kingdom	–10.8	–36.2	–46.9
Developing	**–90.4**	**131.2**	**326.4**
Asia	–40.6	86.8	179.5
China	7.2	20.5	55.5
Hong Kong	–2.6	7.1	16.0
Korea	–23.1	12.3	27.6
Taiwan	10.9	8.9	19.0
Thailand	–14.4	9.3	7.3
Latin America			
Argentina	–6.8	–9.0	3.0
Brazil	–23.2	–24.2	11.7
Mexico	–2.5	–18.5	–8.6
Middle East and Africa	1.1	74.5	116.4
Eastern Europe and former USSR	–13.5	16.8	12.0
Statistical discrepancy	48.9	200.2	73.9

Source: From Bernanke (2005).

The sharp increase in the US current account deficit between 1996 and 2004, amounting to $546 billion, must have been matched by a shift toward surplus of equal magnitude in other countries. This change has not been experienced by the group of mature economies, which increased surpluses only by $106 billion. The bulk of the increase in the US current account deficit was balanced by changes in the current account positions of developing countries, which moved from a collective deficit of $90 billion to a surplus of 326 billion – a net change of $416 billion between 1996 and 2004. A change of such magnitude has been the result of a succession of financial crises experienced by developing countries in the 1990s: the Mexico crisis in 1994, the East Asian countries in 1997–1998, Russia in 1998, Brazil in 1999 and Argentina in 2002. From these countries capital outflows were triggered by a sharp decline in domestic assets prices, weakened banking system, and loss of credibility for domestic institutions. For those countries not affected, for example China, building up reserves, the war chests of foreign reserves, to buffer capital outflows, was an unavoidable imperative. Further, foreign reserves were instrumental in pursuing export-led growth by preventing exchange rate appreciation (Dooley, Folkerts-Landau and Garber 2004). In practice, those countries issuing debts to their high-saving citizens use the profits to buy US Treasury securities and other assets. Bernanke sees those governments acting as "financial intermediaries, channelling domestic saving away from local uses and into international markets". Another factor that contributed to the swing to current account surplus among the non-industrialized countries is the sharp rise in oil prices. Surpluses are recorded not only for Middle East, but also for Nigeria, Russia and Venezuela, for a collective figure of more than $115 billion between 1996 and 2004.

Whose Turn is It to Adjust?

As accounted by Bernanke, the three imbalances of the global economy feature an apparently global economy, which is in a transitional state, growing on a lopsided pattern. Domestic demand – specifically consumer and business spending – fuel the US expansion, while exports drive growth in the rest of the world, including the Japanese and eurozone economies. Larry Summers' definition of the United States as the "importer of last resort" is shown clearly in Figure 7.1, where trade clearly drives the external deficit.

The US current account deficit starts to widen from less than 2.0 per cent of GDP in 1997 to a then-record of over 6.5 in 2005. Still, in 2000, at the start of the downturn, the demand for US assets, especially high-tech equities, was still strong enough that there was no problem financing the shortfall, while the dollar trend rose steadily higher.

To fix global imbalances, textbook economics offer a well-known recipe: In the United States, measures decelerating growth of consumer and business spending by running more restrictive monetary and fiscal policies; in the rest of the world, Japan and the eurozone, central banks stimulate consumer and business spending by running more accommodative macroeconomic policies. The general consensus

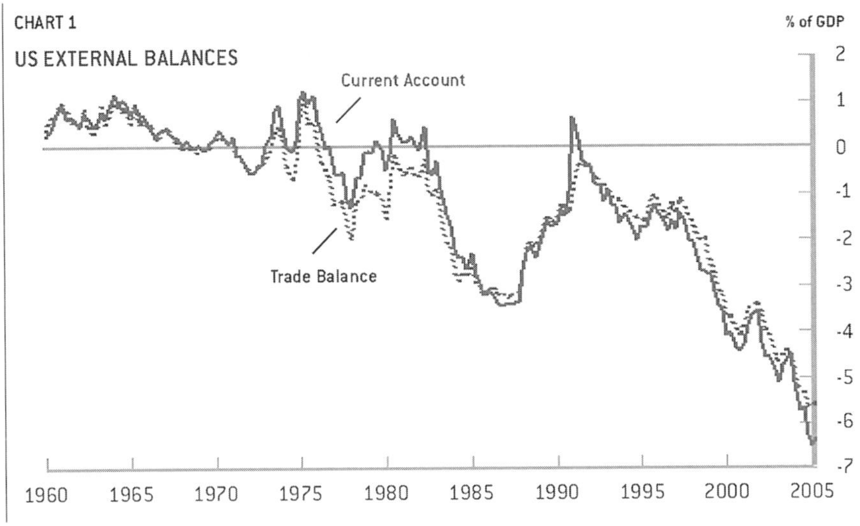

Figure 7.1 US External Balances

Source: Bureau of Economic Analysis (BEA).

is that with a lower dollar, US exports would turn more competitive abroad and US imports less competitive at home.

However, in the real world, things run differently. The 2000–2001 recession made these choices difficult. In the United States, the Bush administration weighed in with three tax cuts, and the Federal Reserve eased aggressively to hold up consumption and housing in the wake of a business spending collapse. Meanwhile, the Japanese had little ammunition to use, as the Bank of Japan already had lowered interest rates close to zero and the budget deficit in excess of 7.0 per cent of GDP. The Europeans had more room to maneuvre and the European Central Bank (ECB) did slash interest rate by 275 basis points, but EMU fiscal discipline, entrusted into the Stability and Growth Pact (GSP) prohibited governments from reducing level of taxation or approving spending packages. As an economist in the market comments: "… the recession sent policy mixes in altogether the wrong direction, compounding the imbalances – as manifested in the further deterioration of the US current account deficit to over 6 per cent of GDP by the end of last year" (Probyn 2005).

In the United States, the weakening of the dollar followed by a combination of the bursting of the NASDAQ bubble (2000), extraordinarily low US interest rates (2001), and the chronic current account deficit ended to reduce private-sector demand for US assets. The euro rose from a low of 84 cents in July 2001 to a high of $1.36 in December 2004 while the dollar fell from around ¥125 to ¥103 over the same period. The dollar, however, remained unchanged at 8.28 Chinese renminbi because of the Chinese pegging to the dollar. The third global imbalance originates from the currency inflexibility in Asia, and has far-reaching implications given the current pattern of world trade and capital flows. Running a sizeable ($150 billion) bilateral trade surplus with the United States, China also is net recipient of capital investment from US corporations setting up production facilities (direct investment) and from dollar-based investors purchasing securities of one type or another (portfolio investment). Trade, inflow of capital for direct investment, and portfolio investments imply a demand for renminbi and corresponding supply of dollars on the foreign exchange market. Under a flexible exchange rate regime, the renminbi would simply rise against the dollar, but the People's Bank of China stops that from happening by selling the required quantity of renminbi to the market at the given rate. The other side of this transaction is the offsetting purchase of dollars, which end up as Chinese foreign exchange reserves. The story does not even end there. As the Chinese authorities seek to earn a market return on their assets, the reserves are "recycled" back to the US, mainly in the form of demand for Treasury securities. While estimates vary on the exact impact, the explosive growth of Chinese reserves and associated demand for Treasuries clearly goes some way to explaining Greenspan's "conundrum", that is, the unusually low level of longer-term yields given relatively robust growth, accelerating inflation and rising short-term interest rates in the United States. Ultra-pessimists see this a "ticking" time bomb capable of destroying the global recovery. China, they argue, will eventually tire of accumulating greenbacks, or seek to diversify its reserve holdings, leading to both a dollar crash and US interest rate spike – a combination that would propel both the US and global economies into recession. Probyn questions the "ticking time bomb" argument on the basis of China's necessary economic gradualism: "China is forced to continue its export policy to the United States, and is still not ready or able to abandon its currency peg in favour of a freely floating exchange rate" (2005: 2). For these two "facts", Chinese accumulation of dollar reserves is obligatory, not optional. As China needs to grow rapidly – so that labor shed from the decaying state-owned enterprises can be absorbed into the private sector – the Chinese authorities appear unlikely to revalue substantially any time soon. Accordingly, the People's Bank of China has clearly spelled out that a policy of gradualism, initiated in July 2005 when the bank suspended the dollar peg to move into a managed floating regime based on a basket of currencies, is more appropriate. In the bank's quarterly survey of the economy, the Chinese authorities are clearly telling they would maintain a basically stable renminbi (as it presently stands after a tiny 2.1 per cent revaluation and the introduction of a tightly managed float (McGregor 2006: 4).

On a similar note, Richard N. Cooper of Harvard and Vincenzo Quadrini (*et al.*) of the University of Southern California challenge the argument of unsustainable deficit, and the consequence of US decline. They explain that the US deficit is not only sustainable, it is logical as the continuing current account deficit reflects a deficiency of savings in the United States relative to investment there, and it also reflects an excess of savings in the rest of the world relative to investment in the rest of the world. Any attempt to reduce the US deficit abruptly, other than through a spontaneous but unlikely surge in domestic investment in many other countries, would undoubtedly produce a world recession (Cooper 2005: 3). The best way to reduce the ongoing imbalances is through an improvement in the financial structure of countries with growing foreign asset positions (Quadrini *et al.* 2007: 9).

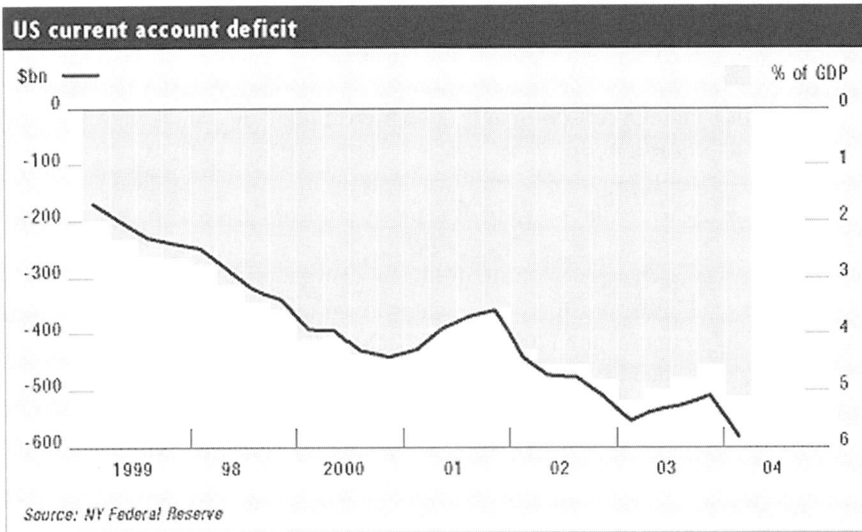

Figure 7.2 US Current Account Deficit

Source: NY Federal Reserve.

However, this optimism may go too far. Despite the depreciation of the dollar that has already taken place, the US current account deficit[2] shows no sign of shrinking. The deficit is likely to grow substantially in the next several years, absent a major change in economic fundamentals. As a result, the United States has become a net debtor in the strict sense of the term – after excluding foreign direct investments from both sides of its balance sheet. At the end of 2003, foreign claims on the United States exceeded US claims on foreigners by $2.94 trillion, and foreign official dollar holdings held in the United States rose from $1.21 trillion in December 2002 to $1.65 trillion in June 2004 (Kenen 2005). A gradual deterioration in the US reserve position comes from foreign central banks,[3] which seem to have reduced their purchases of American Treasuries: official holdings of those rose by only $2 billion in the first seven months of

2 In the period 1895–1980 the US current account was typically in surplus, averaging about 1 per cent of GDP and peaking at about 6 per cent in 1917 (Cline 2005).

3 Matthew Higgings and Thomas Klitgaaed note "the predominance of dollar reserve holdings has made foreign central banks important players in U.S. financial markets … at the end-2003, central banks holdings of dollar assets, at roughly $2.1 trillion, were equivalent to more than half of marketable Treasury debt outstanding" (quoted by James D. Sidaway 2005: 74).

2005, against $295 billion in (the whole of) 2004 and $175 billion in 2003. "If this trend continues, other currencies could one day challenge the dollar's dominance" (*Economist* 2005). The US large net foreign liabilities, though sustainable in the long run at a lower cost than twenty years ago, will eventually adjust by means of a sharp fall of the dollar value. According to Bergsten, a devaluation of the greenback by 20–25 per cent would reduce the current account deficit to the level around 2–2.50 per cent of GDP.[4] The problem is whether the fall is triggered by a deterioration of market sentiment against the dollar, or will be managed by exchange rate co-ordination.

Estimating the Size and the Likely Consequences of the US Current Account Adjustment

How far can the US current account deficit go? Estimates by Cline (2005), Roubini and Sester (2004) and Mann (2003) with unchanged policies and exchange show current account deficit by 2010 respectively of about 8 per cent, 10 per cent and 12 per cent of GDP. According to Cline's projections by 2010 US external liabilities are likely to rise to about 55 per cent of GDP (2005). "This trajectory", Cline observes, "is highly undesirable" (2005). Delayed adjustments are potentially much more disruptive. Projections indicate that with the dollar at the level of January–May 2005, the baseline current account deficit reaches 14 per cent of GDP by twenty years from now and net foreign liabilities reach 135 per cent of GDP. "Though some crisis would intervene, forcing a cutback in the deficit and curbing the build-up of external debt, it is a matter of prudence to limit long-term liabilities" (Cline 2005). To avert such crisis, net foreign liabilities should be held to no more than 50 per cent of GDP, which translates into a long-term current account deficit by only 3 per cent of GDP. The problem depends on whether the adjustment comes early or later. An early adjustment in domestic demand for investment, consumption and the fiscal deficit would be only 4 per cent of GDP; if delayed until a decade from now it would amount to 9 per cent of GDP (Cline 2005: 1). First, a later adjustment would risk not being achieved smoothly, the required exchange rate would be much larger and a loss of confidence by foreign investors would likely lead to a larger run-up in interest rates and greater risk of recession. Second, as the US external deficit rises, so does the risk of hard landing for the dollar, the US economy and the world economy. Third, it is fundamentally perverse for capital to be flowing from developing countries to the United States, instead of the other way around. Fourth, an overvalued currency prompts protectionism, which is happening in the United States with increased protection against China. In a few words, for the US current account adjustment to rebalance, Cline sees that two key economic changes would be required:

- A substantial depreciation of the US dollar to make US exports more attractive, and imports less attractive, to US buyers.

---

4 On record, the US dollar has devalued about once per decade by the 1970s, triggered by external imbalances that never reached 4 per cent of GDP (Bergsten 2002: 1).

- A fiscal restraint, which will affect US domestic demand (Cline 2005).

These are two changes that imply costs for all concerned parties, especially Asian economies and EU economies. In a few words: when the US adjustment occurs, it will be accompanied by slower global growth; the only question is how much slower.

In a more optimistic outlook, the US deficit can and will be recycled until the incipient Japanese and European recoveries broaden out to include domestic demand. In that case, steps could be taken by the US government to gently rein in domestic demand while other Asian economies cool down their growth, letting wages to rise. This is a scenario, however, too good to be true. Firstly, few believe that the US trade shortfall is sustainable in the long term, and that Asian nations progressively revalue their currencies and ultimately move to flexible exchange-rate regimes. Indeed, the ECB has until now tolerated a super-strong euro and not intervening in markets to hold it down, it has accepted the "logic of post-Bretton Woods regime to support the US adjustment process" (Padoa-Schioppa 2005: 173). This is not the case for United States' major trading partners and lenders in Asia and Latin America, especially China and Mexico, which are not as cooperative. "Asian governments, for the most part, are playing a more mercantilist game by selling their currencies for dollars to artificially suppress their exchange rates" (Garten 2005: 1–2). On the historical record, in the last two occasions when the pattern of international capital flows proved unstable – in the late 1920s and the late 1960s – the ensuing breakdown caused some degree of economic dislocation.

The Euro: A Regional Currency Turning Global?

The Euro's Strong Regional Focus

In Europe, the build-up of the large current account deficit in the United States, matched by an increasing current account surplus, in particular in East and the Middle East, raises concerns over the possible effects of the US deficit shrinking on the eurozone economic growth. In Washington observers at IMF have expressed concern that corrections to sustainable levels will likely require large exchange rate adjustments, especially against the US dollar, with possibly disruptive effects on global financial markets and economic activity (IMF 2004: 109). In Brussels, the European Commission warns "the unprecedented scale of these imbalances has led to fears that their eventual correction could give rise to disruptive exchange rate realignments, with significant global implications". The euro area, in sharp contrast to the United States and its East Asian and Middle Eastern lenders, enjoys a roughly balanced current account, though "it could find itself at the heart of the economic disruption caused by a possible disorderly correction of global imbalances" (European Commission 2005: 7). A consequence can be, Bergsten argues, that when private and official holders reach between $500 billion and $1 trillion, the euro can become a major competitor for the dollar (2005: 35).

Though, its venue does bear some risks. At the Meeting of American Economists Association (January 2005), Peter B. Kenen warned: "We thus face the rising risk of a disorderly shift from the present dollar-based monetary system to a multiple-currency monetary system based on the dollar and the euro. Some of my European friends would welcome the ultimate outcome, a large international role for the euro, but they should be worried about getting there quickly". The potential for the euro to replace the US dollar as the world's premier currency is one of the understated motivations of EMU. In part, the desire is a symbolic one; it is the belief that "great powers have great currencies". In part, it is a hope to reap seigniorage, although US benefits from seigniorage are worth only about 0.2 per cent of GDP. The usual criteria for becoming the world's lead currency are measures like size (GDP or the share of world trade). By these measures, the prospects for the euro to challenge the US dollar are favorable, but not overwhelming.

ECB policy makers have, indeed, taken a more cautious approach. For the Euro the prospect is to go "spontaneously, slowly, but inexorably" (Padoa-Schioppa 1999) at the appointment of a global currency along a steadily regional development, rather than jumping abruptly on the global stage. The regional roles of the euro have three facets. First, its use by non-euro area residents continues to show a significant degree of stability. Second, an increasing use in euro area countries' trade with non-euro area countries, as well as in the foreign trade of a number of the countries which joined the EU on May 2004 and EU candidate countries. Third, the international use of the euro is most prominent in regions neighboring the euro area and has been driven, to some extent, by euro area investors, who have purchased significant amounts of euro-denominated international bonds. There are about 50 countries with an exchange rate regime linked to the euro, including those EU member states that have not yet joined the euro area. Non-EU countries that use the euro as an anchor currency are mainly located in the EU's neighboring regions or are countries that have established special institutional arrangements with the EU or some of the EU member states, like the CFA zone in Africa. In most of these countries, the euro is also the main or the sole intervention currency used by the authorities to stabilize the exchange rates of their respective currencies. Additionally, in these countries euro-denominated assets account for a substantial share of the foreign exchange reserves held by the respective authorities. Globally, at the end of 2002, the euro's share in foreign exchange reserve assets was close to one-fifth (Padoa-Schioppa 2005: 171–174).

Turning to private users, the internationalization of the euro has been most visible in global capital markets, in particular when it comes to the role of the euro as an international financing currency. Since the start of Stage Three of EMU, the stock of euro-denominated debt securities issued by non-euro area residents has risen by around €800 billion. This represents an increase in the share of the euro in the stock of international bonds from around 20 per cent in 1999 to more than 30 per cent in 2003, while the share of dollar-denominated bonds has remained stable at around 45 per cent. A significant share of euro-denominated securities have been targeted at, and purchased by, euro area investors. In using the euro as an issuance currency, financial institutions and corporations, mainly from mature economies, most notably the United States and the United Kingdom, have taken advantage of the greater size and liquidity provided by the increasingly integrated euro-denominated bond markets. Between 2002 and 2003, the share of the euro in the flow of net issuance of *international debt* securities has been the same as the dollar's, with the share in the outstanding stock reaching 31 per cent now only 13 per cent less than the dollar's share, and with a rising interests from Asian and Middle Eastern investors.

Besides the international financial markets, there is also evidence that the euro is increasingly being used as a settlement or invoicing currency in euro area countries' trade with non-euro area residents (Bruni, Pepe 2004). The use of the euro as a *currency of invoicing* for international trade keeps increasing. In 2002 the euro's share in the invoicing of exports and imports of European goods increased by 5 to 6 percentage points, reaching more than 50 per cent on the export side. Japanese exports to the EU invoiced in euros were 44 per cent in 2000 and grew to 54 per cent in 2002. On the import side, the figure grew from 17 to 31 per cent.

However, there is also evidence of inertia in some of the facets of the euro's international role. The share of the euro in foreign exchange transactions today has not significantly augmented in comparison with the previous national currencies, accounting for about one-fifth to one-quarter of all daily transactions. By way of comparison, the US dollar is used in more than 40 per cent of foreign exchange transactions. There are several factors explaining why some of the facets of a currency's international use are characterized by a high degree of stability or inertia rather than gradual change. The most prominent ones are what economists usually call "dynamic economies of scale" and "network externalities", which tend to freeze existing situations into steady states. Hence, as Eichengreen explains, any shift from the use of one currency to another currency would require a significant and exogenous shock. Movement on foreign exchange markets or the invoicing of raw materials, such as oil, can deliver to such a shock.

For now, the most successful story about the euro is its strong regional focus. By granting monetary stability to an economic area that is by far the largest trading partner of our neighbors, the euro's central bank has helped anchor policies in the region. It has prevented a mismatch between trade and financial links and provided clear guidance to one of the most profound processes of economic transformation. The anchoring effect has been most pronounced with regard to the ten new member states that joined the Union on May 1, 2004. EU's links with the Western Balkans, the Mediterranean countries and the countries of the Commonwealth of Independent States, notably Russia, have strengthened as well. In line with this, we have also observed significant use of the euro by public authorities and private agents in these countries. The major success story of the euro as an international currency is in Eastern Europe. In the case of using the euro as a pegging currency, approximately 30 countries outside the euro area currently have exchange rate regimes involving the euro to a greater or lesser extent.[5]

5 These exchange rate regimes are currency boards (Bosnia-Herzegovina, Bulgaria, Estonia); currencies pegged to the euro (Cyprus, the Former Yugoslav Republic of Macedonia and fourteen African countries in which the CFA franc is the legal tender); currencies pegged to a basket of currencies including the Euro, in some cases with a

Is the Euro Institutional Structure Appropriate?

By considering institutional structure, literature (Eichengreen 1997; Wachtel 2006) signals in-built limits to playing a global currency role. First, the euro obviously lacks the advantages of incumbency. In the Eichengreen definition: "An incumbent international currency, like an incumbent politician, has a built-in advantage when competing to retain its status. It pays for central banks to hold their foreign exchange reserves in a currency that is widely used for settling international financial transactions, that is in a currency the markets in which are liquid and stable. It follows that it will pay for them to hold their reserves in the same currencies held by other international investors, including (but not limited to) other central banks. This network externality lends inertia and an element of path dependence to the development of reserve-currency status". Though the incumbency's handicap can be surmounted by a big potential advantage of the euro over the dollar: its greater price stability policy. The ECB constitution makes the euro policy makers more independent and more focused on price stability than the US Federal Reserve so, Eichengreen admits, incumbency's advantages are not for ever. "[S]ystematic economic mismanagement by a reserve-currency country, like a politician's systematic failure to show up for roll-call votes, can quickly alienate its constituency" (1997: 2). A counter-argument might be that the board of the European Central Bank is composed of representatives of all member countries, so that some creeping inflation bias can emerge. A second potential advantage of the euro, the depth and cost-efficiency of financial markets, is in fact only virtual. The market for the euro and euro-denominated assets could be the world's largest if the City of London did shift to the eurozone, but this event is unlikely to occur at any time soon.

Further, the euro faces two structural impediments to its becoming an alternative reserve currency. The first involves the "lender-of-last-resort standard". As Wachtel remarks, "The ECB has no authority to be a lender-of-last-resort. National central banks in the Euro zone retain this authority and responsibility but only within their own countries. The Euro zone has not faced this problem across its jurisdiction and neither the ECB nor national central banks have this authority outside either their own countries or the euro zone. Absent this capacity, the euro at best can only be a limited alternative reserve currency in global markets" (2006: 8).

The second impediment relates to ECB institution-building as laid down in the Maastricht Treaty. Though granted the highest degree of independence in running monetary policy, the ECB lacks supervisory and regulatory functions, which still rest with national authorities. As Eichengreen observes, "The Maastricht

fluctuation band (Hungary, Iceland, Poland, Turkey and so on); systems of managed floating in which the euro is used informally as the reference currency (Czech Republic, Slovakia and Slovenia) and, last but not least, European Union currencies pegged to the euro through a co-operative arrangement, namely ERM II. As is well known, Denmark and Greece joined ERM II on January1, 1999, with a ±2.25 per cent fluctuation band for the Danish krone and a ±15 per cent fluctuation band for the Greek drachma.

Treaty had the Bundesbank in mind when it made the ECB subordinate to the relevant national supervisory authorities". The provision rests on the rationale to insulate the Central Bank from lobbying by large, politically influential financial institutions, and is consistent with the bank-based financial systems prevailing in the euro area where there is less need for the central bank to inject liquidity to prevent financial markets from packing up. Accordingly, a lacking financial-sector policy apparatus, crucial function in the prevention and resolution of financial problems, makes it difficult to see the euro reaching its full potential to either catalyze the creation of deep, liquid and efficient pan-European markets or serve as an international vehicle for finance (Wihlborg 1999, Schinasi 2005).

Summing up, in order for the euro to be credited global currency standing, it must pass at least five criteria, as listed by Bergsten (Box 7.1).

Box 7.1 Bergsten's Five Criteria

The economy that supports the currency must have significant weight in world trade and product.
With a population of 309.7 million, the euro area share of world GDP amounts to 15.3 per cent; the United States, with a population 294.0 million, accounts for a GDP world share of 20.9 per cent. The euro area share of world trade (imports and exports) amounts to 48.9 per cent against the United States' 24.4.per cent. The euro area goods and services exports amount to 34.3 per cent against the United States' 16.7 per cent.

There must be no significant external constraints, that is, lasting current account imbalances.
The eurozone current account runs on balance, at 2004 with a tiny surplus of 0.6 per cent of GDP against the United States' 5.7 per cent (2004).

Capital must enjoy full freedom of movement.
All restrictions to capital movements were eliminated under the Single European Act regime (1985). This step made a move to monetary union unavoidable.

Financial markets should be deep and liquid.
Under the Maastricht regime, the ECB lacks policy instruments for prevention and resolution of financial crises (no bail-out clause). The lack of "the lender of last resort" instruments makes the euro unfit to counter financial crises

The economy must be strong and stable.
The ECB has established a eurozone GDP non-inflationary potential growth rate between 1.8 to 2.0 per cent, half that of the United States

The euro passes just two out of five criteria. It is especially the failure to meet the fourth criterion which hit its ambition to become a global currency. As Wachtel put it:

> What if dollar holding countries decide to move out of the dollar and into euro bonds because of the projected exchange rate risk associated with U.S. current account deficits, its budget deficits, and a general waning of confidence writ large in America's global leadership. And what if some of this movement away from the dollar will manifest itself in euro denominated debt in vulnerable third world or transition economies outside of the euro zone? Or transition economies outside of the euro zone? In other words, what if the scenario of the euro rivaling the dollar as a reserve currency outside of the EU becomes reality? Further what if the next debt crisis implicates the euro, to whom do the debt holders place a phone call? To the ECB? To the Bundesbank? To the central bank of France? Absent a lender-of-last-resort capacity of the ECB, at a minimum confusion would prevail in the midst of a financial challenge that demands flexibility, alacrity of response, and steadiness in leadership. There is not much time to buy in the midst of a debt crisis and time becomes very expensive to both the debtor and the creditor. I suspect the managers of dollar reserves know this and, whatever their political posturing about moving out of the dollar into euros for public consumption, they will not take such steps in any significant way until the lender-of-last-resort conundrum is resolved (2006: 8).

The Global Euro: A Mess or a Blessing?

Though calling for vigorous action to address global imbalances, the G-7 EU members rest on the idea the United States' adjustment need not be disruptive to financial markets, and especially not to euro area economies as their collective external surplus is roughly on balance. Warnings to policy makers in the United States, Europe and Japan to design their policies on the assumption that over the next three to five years the US current account deficit will likely narrow to about 3 per cent of GDP have not received too much attention (Truman 2005, Ahearne and von Hagen 2005). Truman calculates the growth of US domestic demand will slow by at least a percentage point from its recent rate and probably much more. "Most U.S. consumers will feel this effect, and they will also suffer a substantial terms-of-trade loss" (2005: 32). The growth stimulus the US economy has been supplying for more than a decade will be reversed (Brook *et al.* 2004: 3). It is up to the euro and yen policy makers to minimize the risks of reserve diversification, which translates in propelling their own currencies on a global stage. The impact of a falling US dollar, as part of the US adjustment on the euro economy, finds an early assessment in the *Quarterly Report on the Euro Area 2005* (European Commission 2005). Some six channels will act as the pass-through of dollar depreciation into the euro economy (Box 7.2).

The trade channel is, among the most sensitive of the eurozone economies. Despite being a large and relative closed economy in comparison to its individual member countries, the euro-area economy is more open than larger economies. Its exports of goods and services to the rest of the world are equivalent to around 19.5 per cent of nominal GDP compared with about 10 per cent and 13 per cent for the United States and Japan respectively (see Figure 7.3).

Box 7.2 Channels Affecting Euro Area Economies

Trade channel

An appreciation of the euro increases the price of exports and lowers the price of imports. Over the medium term, this relative loss in European price competitiveness will have a negative impact on the trade balance, the magnitude of which depends on:

- the extent of the pass-through of the exchange rate to import prices;
- the degree to which exporters reduce their profit margins and cut their prices to maintain market shares;
- the relative elasticity of export and import substitution;
- the starting position;
- the exchange rate's movement relative to lag times: the timing of trade orders and receiving the products.

Purchasing power channel

While a euro appreciation leads to a loss of competitiveness for producers of tradable goods and services, consumers might actually benefit. A rising euro means lower import prices and, hence, an increase in purchasing power.

Asset price channel

A dollar devaluation leads to a proportional reduction in the value of dollar-denominated assets. This in turn reduces the value of euro area companies with US assets, and might limit their capacity to borrow and invest. On the other hand, these companies may benefit from the increased competitiveness of their foreign subsidiaries.

Interest rate channel

A fall in the dollar triggered by reduced demand or an increased risk-premium for US-held assets would lead to higher interest rates in the United States and lower interests rates in Europe through increased demand for euro-denominated assets. This channel could benefit the euro area unless the demand for higher-risk premium also spilled from the United States to the eurozone, with the effect of reducing investment.

Relative price channel

A change in exchange rates will not affect all sectors equally. Tradable goods and services will fall visibly, while non-tradable goods and services will remain practically unchanged. In the tradable sectors, this effect would vary depending on market structure, import and exports ratio, relative exposure to the dollar and so on.

Confidence channel

An euro appreciation would also affect consumer and producer confidence. Much depends on whether the euro appreciation is the result of an improved outlook and hence capital inflows for the euro area or the result of a dollar deterioration in the United States. In the latter case, private sector, private sector confidence is likely to fall, in the light of strong linkages between American and European financial markets. If falling confidence leads to lower spending, and hence lower imports, the contractionary effect of lower exports to the United States might be aggravated. A countervailing effect would be a rise in consumer confidence as a result of lower import prices.

Source: European Commission, Directorate-General for Economic and Financial Affairs, Quarterly Report, Vol. 4, no. 3, 200.

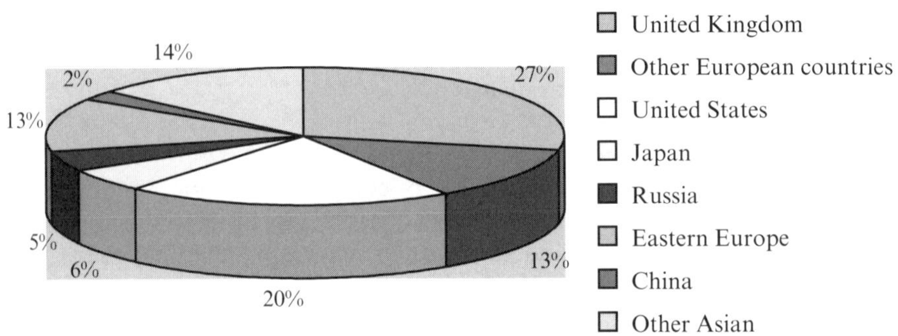

Figure 7.3 Shares of World Exports

Source: ECB database 1999.

Even more significant is the fact that exports of goods and services represent around 17 per cent of the euro area's GDP, compared with just over 11 per cent for the United States and 9 per cent for Japan, while imports are equivalent to around 15 per cent of its GDP, compared with circa 13 per cent and 8 per cent for the United States and Japan respectively. Hence, in terms of exports, the euro area is approximately 50 per cent more open than the United States; a feature which, given its persistant weak internal demand, explains the vulnerability of the eurozone to export performance. Data relating to 2001 show domestic demand and investment were at the root of Germany's problems. Although household disposable income rose by 3.6 per cent in 2001, up from 2.8 per cent in 2000, Germans put much of their extra money into savings. The savings rate went up in 2001 for a first time in the last decade to 10.1 per cent of disposable income from 9.8 per cent in 2000. Between 1999 and 2001, the weak euro has continued to be, in spite of global trade recession, the very positive factor of German exports growing at annual rate of 5.1 per cent, well below 13.2 per cent, but enough to ensure that overall gross domestic product was positive at its 0.6 for 2001(Campanella 2003: 200). As reported by the Federal Statistical Office (2005), in the period 2000 to 2004, German exports rose from 83 to 96 and hence by 16 per cent.

The eccentricity of eurozone economy shows in its persisting dependency on export performance (ECB 2005). Following the entrance of new world players – most notably Asian emerging economies as well new EU member states – developed economies have lost export market shares since the early 1990s, at times substantially. In this respect, the losses for the euro area as a whole were smaller in comparison to the decline in export market shares experienced by some of its major competitors, namely the United States and particularly Japan (ECB 2005: 8). It is still more surprising that the eurozone outsourcing of production to new EU member states by countries such as Germany has been export-enhancing for the euro area in a completely opposite direction than in Japan, which by using South Asian countries as export platforms, has experienced export-diverting effects.

The euro countries' export performance remains highly vulnerable to developments at the country level. Germany's export performance, which has excelled relatively to the other euro countries in recent years, took place during a period of particularly weak domestic demand in Germany and is partly the result of a spillover of substantial FDI activity, particularly in the new EU member states, as well as successful ongoing industrial restructuring. There are, however, clear cases such as Italy whose exports suffered from fierce and direct competition from both the new EU member states and Asia, combined with weak technological competitiveness. Structural weaknesses, common to several eurozone economies, can undermine the Eurozone's export performance. Technological competitiveness is clearly a major weak point. in Japan it is 50 per cent higher than in the euro area. Both patenting and R&D data show that most of the euro area's innovation occurs in medium-technology-intensive sectors, while the share of the high-tech sectors is substantially below that of the United States and Japan. With respect to structural competitiveness, the eurozone shows a source of disadvantage in educational attainment, business environment, labor regulations, relatively high taxation, both of households and businesses.

The ECB (2005) warns to avoid complacency regarding euro area exports and sends signals that euro area "exports remain vulnerable" (2005: 8). Similarly, Ahearne and von Hagen caution European policy makers who "seem to have watched the growing imbalances without much concern, in the hope that the EU will be largely unaffected by the inevitable correction of the US external" (2005: 2). Developments can indeed go in the wrong direction. If the US adjustment should occur by a trade contraction narrowing the deficit to about zero, this would imply a loss of US net exports of roughly $700 billion at an annual rate. "The flip side of this adjustment is that the rest of the world's trade surplus would necessarily shrink by $700 billion", with a loss of euro's exports to the US dollar area by $96 billion per year" (Ahearne, von Hagen 2005: 5–6). In a few words, if not offset by increased internal demand and an appropriate anti-deflationary monetary policy, eurozone economies can blow up. The magnitude of euro area casualties depends on how much of US adjustment will be born by Asian policy makers.

Box 7.3 The Eurozone Share of US Adjustment Depends on Asian Economies

1 If the Asian economies will stick pegging their currencies to the dollar, the euro will appreciate, and therefore will generate greater deterioration in the European trade balance.
2 If the Asian economies instead are prepared to tolerate appreciation of their currencies, Asia's trade surplus will decline and euro economies will bear little weight.
3 A surge in investment and a decline in saving in Asia would reduce Asia's demand for U.S. assets and induce the U.S. government to reduce budget deficit and private citizens to save more.
4 A shift of Asia from a dollar-dominated portfolio policy to a euro-denominated portfolio policy would see a heavy burden of the U.S. adjustment falling on euro economies.

Source: Adapted from Ahearne and von Hagen (2005), 6.

Under these circumstances, Asian countries' exchange rate policies, that is, exchange rate level and exchange rate regime, especially the Chinese one, would affect the eurozone's export performance in a minor or major way, depending on Asia's choices. For example, if the renminbi exchange rate level, is revalued against the US dollar, the larger the part of the US current account adjustment that falls on trade would flow between China and the United States, and the less need there would be for adjustment between the United States and Europe. Considering the exchange rate regime, "the more the Chinese peg shifts from dollar to euro, the more China will become a net buyer of euro assets. This is likely to result in a euro area current account deficit vis-à-vis China, and an appreciation of the euro exchange rate, thereby weakening euro area exports. This apparent complacency is completely unwarranted. Europe may be not part of the global current account problem, but it is bound to be part of the solution" (2005: 1).

Is it all a mess? No: The euro going global can reverse into a blessing, too. Not so much because of its seigniorage revenues, as the euro can also be exposed to large and volatile shifts (a consequence the German Bundesbank was always reluctant to accept). The blessing can arrive from net capital inflows and lower interest rates, spurring additional investment in more innovative services and industry sectors. In order for this to happen, a shift in euro macroeconomics is also needed. Fiscal and monetary policy should be ready to change their present paths. The ECB should be ready to prevent risks of deflationary expectations following a sharp depreciation of the US dollar and shrinking US demand, and fiscal policy should head for an expansionary path. To turn the US sharp adjustment into a blessing, euro policy makers should act preventively and pro-actively. Will they be as prudent as the situation necessitates?

Conclusions

The euro, a tailor-made regional currency, can be prompted on the global stage not by choice, but by chance, as a consequence of US current account adjustment and Asia's reserve shift. As structural reforms are on hold, euro member economies seem unprepared to cope with the consequences and related structural adjustments a global currency entails. A global euro ahead of time can trigger loss of exports, a driver of euro economies, and unpleasant consequences in terms of current account rising deficits, volatile exchange rates, and so on. On the positive side, more pleasant things can follow from a global euro. Structural reforms, solicited by the European Commission and the ECB and so often shelved by members' governments, could eventually enter national governments' agendas. Although Europe may be only part of the global current account problem, a global euro can eventually resolve the euro's own problems.

References

Ahearne, A. and von Hagen, J. (December 2005), *Global Current Imbalances: How to Manage the Risk for Europe.* Bruegel Policy Brief, Issue 2005/02 (Brussels).

Bergsten, F. (2002), *The Dollar and the US Economy*, Institute for International Economics (Washington, DC), 1.

Bergsten, F. (April 27, 2005), "The Euro and the World Economy", European Central Bank (Frankfurt am Main).

Bernanke, B. (2005), *The Global Saving Glut and the US Current Account Deficit*, Remarks by Governor Ben S. Bernanke at the Homer Jones Lecture, April 14 (St. Louis, Missouri).

Brook A., Francois, S. and Ollivaud, P. (2004), "Channels for Narrowing the US Current Account Deficit and Implications for Other Countries", Paris: OECD Economic Department, Paper no. 390.

Bruni, F. and Pepe, F. (2004), "On Transatlantic Financial Relations: Competition, Cooperation or Conflict?" www.documents/ispisonlinc.it/it/bruni.pdf (Milan: ISPI).

Campanella, M. (2001), "The Battle between ECOFIN–11 and the European Central Bank: A Strategic Interaction Perspective", *The State of the European Union*, ed. Green Cowles, M. and Smith, M., vol. 5 (Oxford, Oxford University Press), 110–126.

Campanella, M. (2003), "Euro Weakness and the ECB Economic Governance: A Strategic Institutionalist Perspective", in Campanella, M. and Eijffinger, S.C.W., eds, *EU Economic Governance and Globalization* (Aldershot: Edward Elgar), 171–203.

Cline, W. (2005), *The United States as a Debtor Nation.* Institute for International Economics and Center for Global Development (Washington, DC).

Cooper, R. (November 2005), *Living with Global Imbalances*, Policy Briefs in International Economy. Institute for International Economics (Washington, DC).

Dooley, M., Folkerts-Landau D. and Garber, P. (July 2004), *Direct Investment, Rising Real Wages, and the Absorption of Excess Labor in the Periphery.* NBER.

Economist (2005), "How the Dollar Might Lose its Status as the World's Main Reserve Currency", *Economics Focus. Currency Competition*, September 29.

Eichengreen, B. (1997), "The Euro as a Reserve Currency", unpublished paper (Berkeley).

European Commission (2005), *Quarterly Report on the Euro Area 2005* (Brussels).

European Central Bank (January 2005), *Review of the International Role of the Euro* (Frankfurt).

European Central Bank (June 2005), *Competitiveness and Export Performance of the Euro Area*, Occasional Paper Series, no. 30. See http://www.ecb.int.

Federal Statistical Office Germany (2005), "German Export Performance on the Rise Again Since the Year 2000", Press Release, October 17.

Garten, J. (January/February 2005), "The Global Economic Challenge", *Foreign Affairs*.

Gilpin, R. (1987), *The Political Economy of International Relations* (Princeton, NJ: Princeton University Press).

Greenspan, A. (2003), *Remarks at the 21st Annual Monetary Conference*, cosponsored by the Cato Institute and the *Economist* (Washington, DC).

IMF (April 2004), *World Economic Outlook* (Washington, DC).

IMF (April 2005), *World Economic Outlook* (Washington, DC).

Kenen, P. (2005), *Stabilizing the International Monetary System*, Contribution to the Roundtable on "The Dollar, the Euro, and the International Monetary System" at the Annual Meetings of the American Economic Association, Philadelphia.

Mann, C. (2003), "How Long the Strong Dollar?", in Bergsten, C.F. and Williamson, J., eds, *Dollar Overvaluation and the World Economy*, Institute for International Economics (Washington, DC).

McGregor R. (2006), "Beijing Sticks with Policy of 'Gradualism' on Renminbi", *Financial Times*, February 22, 4.

Padoa-Schioppa, T. (1999), *Eurosystem: New Challenges for Old Missions* www.ecb.int (April 15).

Padoa-Schioppa, T. (2005), "Building on Euro's Success", in Posen, A.S., ed., *The Euro at Five*. Institute for International Economics (Washington, DC), 171–178.

Probyn, C. (2005), *An Unbalanced World*. State Street Global Advisers (July 1).

Quadrini V., Mendoza E.G. and Rios-Rull, J.-V. (February 2007), "Financial Integration, Financial Deepness and Global Imbalances", NBER Working Paper No. 12909.

Raghuram, R. (2006), *Perspectives on Global Imbalances* (London).

Roubini, N. and Sester, B. (2004), *The US as a Debtor: The Sustainability of the US External Imbalances*. See www.rgemonitor.com/Roubini-Setser-US external-imbalances.pdf (New York: New York University).

Sidaway, J.D. (December 2005), "Asia-Europe-United States: The Geoeconomics of Uncertainty", *Area*, vol. 37, 374.

Truman, E. (2005), *Postponing Global Adjustment: An Analysis of the Pending Adjustment of Global Imbalances*. Working Paper No. WP 05–6, Institute for International Economics (Washington, DC).

Wachtel, H. (2006), "Euro–Dollar Currency Competition". Paper presented at the Conference "The Political Economy of Currency Unions in a Globalizing World", April 30–May 1. The Leonard Davis Institute for International Relations (Jerusalem: The Hebrew University of Jerusalem).

Wihlborg, C. (1999), "Supervision of Banks after EMU", European Investment Bank 1999, 4, 1.

Chapter 8

Enlargement and the International Role of the Euro

Benjamin J. Cohen

Introduction

How will enlargement of the European Union (EU) affect prospects for the euro as an international currency? Will the eventual addition of ten or more new members to the Economic and Monetary Union (EMU) enhance the euro's ability to challenge the US dollar for global monetary supremacy? Previously, I have argued that Europe's joint currency is fated to remain a distant second to America's greenback long into the foreseeable future (Cohen 2003). In this chapter I extend my earlier analysis to consider the impact of enlargement on the euro's international role. My conclusion now is, if anything, even more skeptical than before. Enlargement, I submit, will diminish, not expand, the euro's attractiveness as a rival to the greenback.

To date, progress in building a global role for the euro has been underwhelming. To some extent, this might be due simply to the inertia that is inherent in all monetary behavior – a well documented stickiness in currency preferences. Since the adoption of a new money is costly, involving an expensive process of adaptation, an already popular currency like the dollar enjoys a certain natural advantage of incumbency. My previous work, however, suggests that there are also more fundamental forces at work. Three factors, all structural in character, have been largely responsible for the euro's slow start as an international currency: relatively high transactions costs, due to inefficiencies in Europe's financial markets; a serious anti-growth bias built into the institutions of EMU; and, most importantly, ambiguities at the heart of the monetary union's governance structure. The analysis offered here suggests that adding new members to EMU will, if anything, simply make matters worse. Larger numbers will aggravate the negative impact of all three factors.

Of particular salience is the impact of enlargement on the governance structure of EMU. From the start, internationalization of the euro has been retarded by a lack of clarity about the delegation of monetary authority among governments and EU institutions. The addition of a diverse collection of new members, with significantly different interests and priorities, can only make the challenge of governance worse, exacerbating ambiguity at the expense of transparency and accountability.

The organization of the chapter is as follows: The first two sections set the stage for analysis. The first section reviews the story of the euro's internationalization to date, while the second outlines prospects for enlargement of EMU and what the addition of new members could mean for the currency's future. The main analysis then follows in three subsequent sections, addressing in turn the impact of enlargement on each of the three structural factors identified in my previous work. The results and implications of the analysis are summarized in a concluding section.

Dream Delayed

At its birth, the euro's future as an international currency seemed assured. Yet since the new money's introduction in 1999, acceptance beyond EMU itself has actually been quite slow, limited mainly to the euro's natural hinterland in and around Europe – "the euro's turf", as economist Charles Wyplosz calls the nearby region (Wyplosz 1999: 89). In many respects, Europe's monetary union has been a resounding success. But in terms of its anticipated challenge to the dollar, performance to date can only be described as disappointing. In the global marketplace, the greenback remains as dominant as ever.

Grand Ambitions

Europe's ambitions for the euro have always been grand. Internally, the joint currency was expected to help promote the EU's long-standing goal of an "ever closer union among the peoples of Europe". Externally, EMU was meant to enhance Europe's role on the world stage by creating a potent rival to the dollar, the leading international money of our era. Resentment has long simmered among Europeans sensitive to the inordinate power that the greenback's popularity gives to the United States – America's "exorbitant privilege", in Charles de Gaulle's memorable phrase. Europe is the equal of the United States in output and trade. Why should it not be America's equal in monetary matters, too? Though the "old dream of enthusiasts" (Zimmermann 2004: 235) was never formally articulated as such, it was evident from the start. EMU was supposed to challenge the dollar for global supremacy. Wyplosz calls this "the hidden agenda of Europe's long-planned adoption of a single currency" (Wyplosz 1999: 76).

The stakes were clear. Four distinct benefits are derived from widespread international circulation of a currency: (1) a potential for seigniorage (the implicit transfer of resources, equivalent to subsidized or interest-free loans, that goes to the issuer of a money that is used and held abroad); (2) an increased flexibility in macroeconomic policy, afforded by the privilege of being able to rely on one's own currency to help finance foreign deficits; (3) a gain in status and prestige that goes with market dominance, a form of "soft" power; and (4) a gain in influence derived from the monetary dependence of others, a form of "hard" power. America had long enjoyed all four benefits. It is understandable that Europeans might desire a piece of the pie, too.

Few knowledgeable observers questioned the euro's potential. Fundamentally, international currency choice is shaped by three essential attributes. First, at least during the initial stages of a money's cross-border adoption, is widespread confidence in its future value backed by political stability in the economy of origin. No one is apt to be attracted to a currency that does not offer a reasonable promise of stable worth. Second are the qualities of "exchange convenience" and "capital certainty" – a high degree of liquidity and reasonable predictability of asset value – both of which are essential to minimizing transactions costs. The key to each quality is a set of broad and efficient financial markets, exhibiting both depth and resiliency.

Third, a money must promise a broad transactional network, since nothing enhances a currency's acceptability more than the prospect of acceptability by others. Historically, this factor has usually meant an economy that is large in absolute size and well integrated into world markets. The greater the volume of transactions conducted in or with an economy, the greater will be the economies of scale to be derived from use of its currency. Economists describe these gains as a money's "network externalities". Network externalities may be understood as a form of interdependence in which the behavior of one actor depends strategically on the practices adopted by others in the same network of interactions.

Europe's new currency was set to begin life with many of the attributes necessary for competitive success. Together, prospective members would provide an economic base roughly comparable to that of the United States, enjoying extensive trade relations around the world. The potential for network externalities, therefore, was considerable. Likewise, EMU would start with both unquestioned political stability and an enviably low rate of inflation, backed by a joint monetary authority, the European Central Bank (ECB), that was fully committed to preserving confidence in the euro's future value. Much room existed for a successful challenge to the dollar, as frequently predicted.

Typical was the view of Robert Mundell, a Nobel laureate in economics, who expressed no doubt that the euro "will challenge the status of the dollar and alter the power configuration of the system" (Mundell 2000: 57). Similarly, Daniel Gros and Niels Thygesen, two prominent European economists, asserted that "the most visible effect of EMU at the global level will be the emergence of a second global currency" (Gros and Thygesen 1998: 373). The conventional wisdom was unambiguous. The markets would ultimately elevate the euro to a top rank alongside the greenback. In the oft-quoted words of Jacques Delors, when he was head of the European Commission, "*le petit euro deviendra grand*".

In fact, the only question seemed to be: How soon? For many, the answer was equally unambiguous: Very soon. Fred Bergsten, a former US Treasury official, predicted a decade ago that Europe's new currency would achieve "full parity" with the dollar in as little as five to ten years (Bergsten 1997). Economists George Alogoskoufis and Richard Portes were even more enthusiastic, contending that "the fundamentals point toward a potentially large shift in favor of the euro ... The dollar would *immediately* lose its importance as a vehicle currency" (Alogoskoufis and Portes 1997: 63; emphasis added). The old dream did not seem unrealistic.

The Story so Far

So what is the story so far? Viewed purely in exchange-rate terms, the euro's record of performance has been mixed – first embarrassing, more recently a point of some pride. From an opening value of $1.17 the currency initially drifted downward, sinking to a low near $0.83 by mid-2000 and subsequently languishing at well below par for upwards of two years. In mid-2002, however, the euro began an impressive recovery, climbing decisively to a high above $1.35 in 2004 before drifting down again. In 2006 the currency was back to a range very close to where it started in 1999.

Exchange rates, however, are not the issue. A currency's price is at best an imperfect indicator of its international status. What really matters is not price but *use*: the extent to which a money is voluntarily chosen by market actors outside EMU for the standard functions of medium of exchange, unit of account, and store of value. Central banks, of course, may also adopt the euro, as an intervention medium, currency anchor or as part of their foreign reserves. But currency use by state actors understandably tends, for efficiency reasons, to reflect prevailing market practice. In the absence of political pressures, central banks prefer to use a currency that will be most helpful to them in managing their exchange rates and monetary policy. The key issue, therefore, is what happens to the preferences of *private* actors. If the euro is ever truly to challenge the dollar, it will be by displacing the popular greenback for any or all of the traditional roles of money in the broad global marketplace.

Viewed in these terms, there is little evidence yet of any significant progress. The eurozone, as it is commonly known, presently comprises thirteen EU members. A look at the available data suggests that in most categories of use the euro has held its own as compared with the past aggregate shares of EMU's thirteen "legacy" currencies. Hence Europe's new money has easily taken its place as successor to Germany's old deutschmark (DM), which had already attained a rank among international currencies second only to the dollar. But that is about all. As economist Hélène Rey concludes, the euro "has established itself immediately as the second most important currency in the world … It has not, however, displaced in any significant way the dollar as the currency of choice for most international transactions" (Rey 2005: 114). In the euro's first years of existence, the only significant gains have been in the European Union's immediate neighborhood, including the EU's ten newest members, before they joined, as well as other actual or potential candidate countries. In the words of the European Central Bank, a "regional pattern … continues to characterize the internationalization of the euro" (2005: 7). Outside the European region, the dollar remains dominant.

The clearest indicator of a money's international status is the amplitude of its use as a medium of exchange in the foreign-exchange market, where according to the latest survey of the Bank for International Settlements (BIS 2005) average daily turnover in 2004 approximated some $1.9 trillion worldwide. Top currencies are bought and sold not only for direct use in trade and investment but also as a low-cost intermediary – a "vehicle" – for the trading of other currencies. A vehicle role is a direct consequence of high market turnover, which yields substantial economies of scale. Typically, it will be less expensive for a market agent to sell a local money for a vehicle currency and then use the vehicle currency to buy the needed foreign money than it would be to exchange one infrequently traded money directly for another.

No currency has more market turnover than the dollar, reflecting the large size of the US economy and its leading role in world trade. The low transaction costs that result from high market volume explain why the greenback has long been the most favored vehicle for global currency exchanges, appearing on one side or the other of some 89 per cent of all transactions in 2004 (barely changed from its 90 per cent share in the first such survey by the BIS in 1989). The euro, by contrast, entered on one side of just 37 per cent of all transactions in 2004. That was higher than the share of the deutschmark, which had appeared in 30 per cent of transactions in 1998 (its last year of existence) but lower than that of all euro's legacy currencies taken together (53 per cent). Only in trading in the Nordic countries and East-Central Europe is the euro clearly the favored vehicle.

The greenback also remains the most favored vehicle for the invoicing of global trade, which adds the role of unit of account (currency of denomination) to that of medium of exchange (currency of settlement) for international contracts. Overall, the dollar is estimated to account for nearly half of all world exports – more than double the US share of world exports. The DM's share of trade invoicing in its last years, prior to its replacement by the euro, was 15 per cent, roughly equivalent to Germany's proportion of world exports. Evidence from the European Central Bank suggests that this share was maintained by the euro after its introduction in 1999 but has not yet shown any sign of increase except in neighboring European countries (ECB 2005).

Likewise, the dollar remains the most favored store of value in global capital markets, where the euro has yet to catch on significantly as an investment medium for international portfolio managers. There has been some increased use of the euro as a financing currency (a vehicle for borrowing). Non-Europeans have been attracted by the opportunity to tap into the much broader pool of savings created by the consolidation of EMU. Overall, the share of the euro in the stock of international debt securities has risen steadily, from less than 22 per cent in 1999 to some 31.5 per cent in mid-2004, while the US dollar share has modestly declined from 47 per cent to 44 per cent (ECB 2005: 13). But these developments represent an increase only in the *supply* of euro-denominated assets, not *demand*. On the demand side, foreign investors so far have been slower than anticipated to add to their holdings of euro-denominated assets, despite the greater depth and liquidity on offer. Overall, the euro's share of world portfolios has changed little from the previous aggregate of legacy currencies.

So far, therefore, the story is unencouraging – certainly not the happy outcome that so many had predicted. The old dream has been delayed. Other than within the European region itself, use of Europe's new currency has shown little sign of growth and may indeed have already begun to stabilize. Summarizes the ECB: "The euro [has] continued to expand some facets of its role as an international currency, while in other market segments a leveling-off has set in … confirming the geographic focus of the euro's international role" (ECB 2005: 61). All this is a far cry from attaining full parity with the dollar in as little as five to ten years.

Dream Revived?

Yet despite the euro's disappointing performance to date, hope lives on, now buoyed by the prospect of a significant increase of membership. Enlargement of the EU will mean, in time, an expanded EMU, too. Bigger, it is said, will also be better. Greater numbers will enhance the currency's power and prestige, increasing its attractiveness as a rival to the dollar. Europe's grand dream has been revived.

Enlargement

The European Union's enlargement in May 2004 added ten new "accession countries", bringing total membership of the EU to twenty-seven with the addition of two more neighbors, Bulgaria and Romania on January 1, 2007; and yet others, including the successor states of the former Yugoslav Republic and even Turkey, hope to follow in the more or less distant future. All are legally obligated, sooner or later, to adopt the euro. The only question is when.

Upon entering the EU, each accession country is automatically enrolled in EMU with a "derogation". Simply put, derogation means that adoption of the euro is mandatory but only when the country is deemed ready. Several critical conditions must be satisfied first – the same so-called convergence criteria that were demanded of the thirteen present participants before they could join EMU. The convergence criteria were first spelled out in the 1992 Maastricht Treaty (Article 109j), which brought the euro into existence. The four familiar conditions are:

1. Relative price stability – in practical terms, an average rate of consumer price inflation, observed over a one-year period, that does not exceed by more than one and a half percentage points the average rate of inflation in the "three best performing member states in terms of price stability";
2. Interest-rate stability – in practical terms, a year-average nominal interest rate on a ten-year benchmark government bond no more than two percentage points above the average in the three best performing members;
3. Fiscal stability – specifically, a fiscal deficit below 3 per cent of GDP and public debt totaling less than 60 per cent of GDP; and
4. Exchange-rate stability – specifically, participation in the pegging arrangement known as the Exchange Rate Mechanism (ERM) for at least two years while the country's currency trades against the euro without severe tensions, within "normal fluctuation margins". Because the present Exchange Rate Mechanism is a successor to an earlier arrangement that existed before 1999, it is usually referred to as ERM II to distinguish it from its predecessor.

It is not expected that all accession countries will manage to satisfy the necessary conditions at the same pace. Quite the contrary, in fact. Key is the exchange-rate criterion. Only six of the ten new members, to date, have even tried to commit to ERM II. These are Estonia and Lithuania, which carried over their long-standing currency boards anchored on the euro; Cyprus, which already had a firm euro peg; Latvia and Malta, which converted basket pegs to the euro; and Slovenia, which moved from a managed crawl to a stable euro peg. The four largest new members – the Czech Republic, Hungary, Poland and Slovakia – so far have opted to preserve a higher degree of exchange-rate flexibility.

Accordingly, target dates for adoption of the euro vary considerably. The latest to make the move was Slovenia, which joined the zone in January 2007. Estonia and Lithuania had also hoped to join in January 2007 but have been forced to postpone because of excessively high inflation rates. Others will take even longer. Cyprus, Latvia and Malta each aim for January 2008; Slovakia has tentatively penciled in January 2009; while the Czech Republic and Hungary have 2010 in mind. Poland has yet to set a target date. And even these goals may be subject to slippage. As of November 2005, only four of the ten – Estonia, Lithuania, Slovakia and Slovenia – had actually completed formal plans for a changeover to the euro (European Commission 2005). Moreover, in a number of the accession countries, such as Poland, domestic political opposition to the euro is growing, spurred in particular by concerns over the prospective loss of monetary autonomy. In some instances, adoption could be delayed for years.

The status of the ten accession countries at the end of 2005 is summarized in Table 8.1. Much, obviously, remains uncertain. All we know for sure is that, sooner or later, the number of countries in the eurozone will be a lot bigger than it is now.

Size Matters, But …

But will bigger really be better? The case for such a presumption seems clear. Larger numbers will mean an even broader transactional network, increasing exponentially the potential for network externalities. Hence, conclude many, the euro is bound to grow even more attractive as a rival to America's greenback. That is the logic of Robert Mundell, for example, who has argued that "the outlook for the euro is very favorable [because] as the EU expands into the rest of Central Europe, the euro will have a substantially larger transactional domain than the dollar" (Mundell 2000: 60). Likewise, it is the logic of Jacques de Larosière, former managing director of the International Monetary Fund (IMF). "The euro's position as a reserve currency will progress in the future", de Larosière asserts, because "with the monetary integration of candidate countries to the European Union, we see the geographic reach of the euro is likely to expand considerably" (de Larosière 2002: 15–16). Prospects for Europe's money as an international currency are assumed to depend directly on the absolute size of the euro zone.

Nowhere is the logic clearer than in the writing of Fred Bergsten, long one of the euro's biggest boosters. What qualifies a currency for international status?

Table 8.1 Accession Countries: Status at End 2005

	Target date for adopting the euro	ERM2 participants	Current exchange rate regime	Comments
Czech Republic	2010	No	Managed float since 1997	Inflation targeting regime. Public deficits are too high.
Estonia	January 1, 2007 (postponed)	Joined June 2004	Long-standing currency board, pegged to the euro	Rapid growth has increased inflationary pressures, forcing postponement of target date.
Cyprus	January 1, 2008	Joined 2005	Hard peg to the euro	Interest rates unstable. Needs to speed up practical preparations.
Latvia	January 1, 2008	Joined 2005	Re-pegged from a currency basket to the euro	Rapid growth is increasing inflationary pressures.
Lithuania	January 1, 2007 (postponed)	Joined June 2004	Long-standing currency board, pegged to the euro	Excessive inflation has forced a postponement of target date.
Hungary	2010	No	15% fluctuation band around central rate, though the exchange rate moves de facto in a limited range at the upper end	Inflation targeting regime. Public deficits are too high.
Malta	January 1, 2008	Joined May 2005	Re-pegged from a currency basket to the euro	Areas of concern include public finances, inflation, and national debt. Needs to speed up practical preparations.
Poland	No target date	No	Pure float	Inflation targeting regime. Public deficits are of concern, along with a lack of enthusiasm for the euro from political leadership.
Slovenia	January 1, 2007	Joined June 2004	Moved from a tightly managed crawling peg to a euro peg	Application approved by the Commission in May 2006. Adopted the euro in Jan. 2007.
Slovakia	January 1, 2009	No	Managed float	Inflation targeting regime. Public finances are a problem.

"There is good reason", Bergsten contends, "to believe that the relative size of key currency countries' economies and trade flows is of central salience … The sharp increase in the size of the economy and trading unit underlying the European key currency could produce a quantum leap in the international role of that asset" (Bergsten 1997: 25, 27). The old deutschmark had first gained widespread acceptance when Germany accounted for no more than 9 per cent of world output and 12 per cent of world trade. The twelve original members of EMU would more than double both ratios; enlargement would add even more. A dramatic rise in euro use, therefore, should be expected as well. In Bergsten's words: "In the eventual steady state, a rise of 65–250 per cent in the size of the relevant economic base could be expected, which would expand the potential size of the currency's role by 30–335 per cent" (Bergsten 1997: 27).

Arguments like these, however, are far too simplistic to be taken seriously. As economist Barry Eichengreen has noted in a comment on Bergsten: "This argument allows no role for other determinants … One cannot forecast the international role of the euro simply by replacing a Germany that accounts for 9 per cent of world output with an EU that accounts for 31 per cent" (Eichengreen 1997: 50, 52). Size no doubt matters. Economies as small as, say, Norway or Sweden could never realistically hope to see their currency compete for global status. Patently, the network externalities would be too limited. But while a large economic base may be necessary, it is hardly sufficient. For a period in the 1980s, Italy's GDP surpassed that of Britain. No one, however, rushed to substitute lire for sterling as a vehicle for trade or investment. Clearly other factors matter, too.

Transaction Costs

What are these factors? As indicated, my previous work suggests that three factors, in particular, have played a crucial role in the euro's story so far: transactions costs, an anti-growth bias and issues of governance. The question is: How will enlargement affect each of the three? In each instance, my answer is unequivocal: Large numbers will simply make matters worse. Enlargement will delay even more Europe's grand dream for the euro.

Market Segmentation …

Begin first with transactions costs – the cost of doing business in euros. Transactions costs directly affect a currency's attractiveness as a vehicle for exchange transactions or international trade. At its birth, Europe's new money obviously offered a large and expanding transactional network, thus promising substantial network externalities. But even so, it was clear that the dollar would be favored by the natural advantages of incumbency unless euro transactions costs, which began high relative to the widely traded greenback, could be lowered to a more competitive level. The same scale economies that encourage use of a currency in the first place are also responsible for what specialists call "hysteresis" or "ratchet effects." Adoption of a new currency tends to be resisted unless the money can be expected to be truly cost-effective.

From the start it was understood that the cost of doing business in euros would depend directly on what could be done to improve the structural efficiency of Europe's financial markets. The point was put most cogently by Richard Portes and Hélène Rey (1998: 308): "The key determinant of the extent and speed of internationalization of the euro will be transactions costs in foreign exchange and securities markets".

On the face of it, prospects for euro transactions costs looked good. In purely quantitative terms, introduction of the new currency promised to create the largest single-currency capital market in the world. That expansion, in turn, was expected to trigger major qualitative improvements in depth and liquidity, knitting previously segmented national markets together into an integrated whole. As matters have turned out, however, Europe's reach has fallen considerably short of its grasp.

In practical terms, much has been accomplished, particularly at the wholesale level where, in the words of *The Economist* (2005: 10), "financial markets in Europe became much more integrated and more interesting". The elimination of exchange risk inside the eurozone has intensified competition among financial institutions, encouraging cost-cutting, innovation and consolidation. Progress has been particularly impressive in short-term money markets, syndicated bank lending, and the corporate bond sector.

Overall, however, momentum has been slow, in good part because of foot-dragging by member governments. In 1999, the Commission drew up a comprehensive package of reforms, the so-called Financial Services Action Plan, which was supposed to be completed by 2005. But while many ambitious new Europe-wide rules have been adopted under the Plan – such as the Conglomerates Directive of 2002 and the Markets in Financial Services Directive of 2004 – implementation by member governments has been spotty at best. National resistance to market-opening measures remains stubborn, especially at the retail level – the realm of bank accounts, mortgages, insurance policies, and the like – and in equity markets. Integration continues to be impeded by a plethora of interconnected barriers, including a diversity of settlement systems that fragment liquidity and reduce transactional convenience (Berglöf *et al.* 2005). As Romano Prodi, another former Commission head, has ruefully admitted: "The euro has spurred closer integration in the EU financial system [yet] there are still many obstacles – regulatory, legal and technical – that need to be removed" (Prodi 2004: 12).

Worse, in certain key respects, it is evident that the dollar's cost advantage will persist no matter what the EU does. Most critical is the lack of a universal financial instrument to match the US Treasury bill for liquidity and convenience – a deficiency that will be difficult, if not impossible, to rectify as long as Europe, with its separate national governments, lacks a counterpart to the federal government in Washington. Under the circumstances, the best the Europeans could do was to encourage establishment of selected benchmark securities for the public debt market. Gradually three euro benchmarks have emerged: the German Bund at ten years, the French bond at five years, and the Italian bond at two years (Rey 2005: 112). But such a piecemeal approach falls far short of creating a single market as large and liquid as that for US government securities. Full consolidation of the public debt market remains stymied by variations in legal traditions, procedures, issuance calendars and primary dealer systems.

Notably, yield differentials in the public debt market have shrunk significantly since the euro was born, suggesting a greater interchangeability among national issues. But the convergence of spreads is far from complete. Investors continue to treat the debts of EMU governments as imperfect substitutes, mostly owing to differences in perceived default risk (Codogno *et al.* 2003). And these differences of perception could now be compounded as a result of a decision by the ECB in November 2005 to limit the collateral it will accept in refinancing ("repo") operations with European commercial banks. Previously, the ECB had accepted all eurozone government bonds indiscriminately, as if the debts of EMU member states were all equally creditworthy. Now, however, the Bank will be more selective. Bonds must have a single A– rating or better from at least one of the three main rating agencies (Moody's, Standard and Poor's or Fitch). Observers expect that this decision will lead commercial banks, in turn, to be much more selective in their choice of issues, accentuating yield spreads (*Financial Times*, November 9, 2005).

On balance, therefore, market segmentation has proved remarkably resilient; and that, in turn, means that the cost of doing business in euros remains a drag on the currency's attractiveness. Though efficiency gains in financial markets have been substantial, they clearly have not gone far enough to significantly improve the euro's cost-effectiveness relative to the dollar. America's greenback continues to benefit from the advantages of incumbency.

... Prolonged

None of this will be improved by enlargement. Indeed, the reverse is more likely to be true. Larger numbers will make it even more difficult to overcome the segmentation of Europe's financial markets.

The main reason is the more primitive level of development of institutions and regulatory arrangements in the accession countries, as compared with EMU's present members. Banking systems, exceptionally, are relatively advanced due to widespread foreign ownership. In the 1990s, banks in the Baltic states and East Central Europe were largely privatized. Most ended up in foreign hands, bringing immediate benefits in terms of fresh capital and innovation. Other sectors, however, have lagged behind, especially markets for equities and derivatives. Regulatory and supervisory systems, despite efforts at modernization, are still largely deficient in such key areas as the assessment of credit risk (Schadler *et al.* 2005: 41–42). Weaknesses like these are likely to encourage foot dragging by new members even more pronounced than that of existing EMU members, for two reasons.

First is the sheer cost of the adjustments that will be required to knit the new entrants into the eurozone's nascent capital market. Since they start from a lower level of development, they will need even more extensive reforms to get up to speed. But since these are by no means rich economies, governments could prove to be even more stubborn in their resistance to further market-opening measures.

Second is the higher risk of financial crisis in the accession countries as they move into the eurozone. Most of these economies offer relatively high rates of return on capital, making them attractive targets for investment. Analysts generally expect that with the elimination of exchange risk, there will be even greater incentives for capital inflows, which eventually could generate overheating, asset price bubbles and unsustainable increases of indebtedness. The risk is concisely summarized by a recent IMF study: "Rapid credit growth looms on the horizon for each [accession country] ... A critical concern with rapid credit expansion is the risk of banking distress or even a banking crisis ... Adjustment in the aftermath of overheating or asset price bubbles may well be difficult without an exchange-rate instrument to effect needed changes of relative prices" (Schadler *et al.* 2005: 56, 65–66). Worries about such vulnerabilities could make governments even less willing to rush into the process of financial integration.

For both reasons, the path to efficiency gains in financial markets could be even more obstructed than in the present EMU of thirteen. If anything, enlargement will prolong the segmentation of financial markets. Significant reductions in the cost of doing business in euros will long remain beyond Europe's grasp.

Anti-Growth Bias

A second critical factor inhibiting the internationalization of the euro is a serious anti-growth bias that appears to be built into the institutional structure of EMU. By impacting negatively on yields on euro-denominated assets, this bias directly affects the currency's attractiveness as a long-term investment medium.

When EMU first came into existence, eliminating exchange risk within the European region, a massive shift was predicted in the allocation of global savings as compared with holdings of European assets in the past. Yet international portfolio managers have been slow to move into the euro. Liquid funds have been attracted when there was prospect of short-term appreciation. But underlying investor preferences have barely budged, in good part because of doubts about prospects for longer-term economic growth in the eurozone. In turn, one of the main causes for such doubts seems to lie in the core institutional provisions of EMU governing monetary and fiscal policy, the key determinants of macroeconomic performance. In neither policy domain is priority attached to promoting real output. Rather, in each, the main emphasis is on other considerations that tend to tilt policy in a deflationary direction, imparting a distinct anti-growth bias to the eurozone as a whole. Opportunities for future investment returns are therefore more limited than they might be otherwise.

Here too there is reason to believe that enlargement will simply make matters worse. Overall, the economies of the accession countries may be small as compared with older members. Together, they add less than 10 per cent to the GDP of the EU as a whole. Nonetheless, their entrance into the eurozone can be expected to tilt monetary and fiscal policy even more in a deflationary direction, further dampening investment returns.

Monetary Policy

On the monetary policy side, the European Central Bank, unlike many other monetary authorities, was created with just one policy mandate – to maintain price stability. Moreover, the ECB is formally endowed with absolute independence, largely insulating it from political influence. Legally, the ECB is free to focus exclusively on fighting inflation, even if over time this might be at the cost of stunting real growth. In practice, naturally, the ECB is not wholly insensitive to growth concerns. Nonetheless, the overall orientation of ECB priorities is clear. Since EMU's start, the bias of monetary policy has mainly been toward restraint, not expansion.

With enlargement, the ECB's restrictive bias may be expected to become even more pronounced owing to an inherent tendency toward higher inflation in the EU's new member economies. All of the accession countries are relatively poor compared with the older partners. All will be seeking to catch up to the income levels of the more advanced economies by promoting productivity gains in key sectors. Generally, in such situations, productivity gains tend to be more rapid for tradable goods (exports and import-competing production) than for nontradables, since tradables face the most competition and tend to attract the largest share of technology-intensive foreign direct investment. However, as wages in the tradables sectors rise with productivity, they also bid up wages in nontradables production, which in turn forces up the prices of nontradables relative to those of tradables. The result is an increase of aggregate inflation even though tradables prices are held down by competition from abroad – a process known as the Balassa-Samuelson effect (Schadler *et al.* 2005: 5).

The pressures of the Balassa-Samuelson effect are already evident in many of the accession countries, including especially Hungary and Slovakia. Only a few, such as the Czech Republic and Lithuania, have come even close to matching the low inflation experience of the eurozone's best performing economies. True, all the new members are making a determined effort to keep prices under control. With luck, most may even be able to compress their inflation rates long enough to meet the first of the Maastricht Treaty's four convergence criteria (relative price stability). Once inside EMU, however, they almost certainly will find it difficult to suppress sustained price increases for long.

Over time, higher inflation in the accession countries could be avoided only by allowing an appreciation of their nominal exchange rate. But once they become part of the eurozone, that option is ruled out *ex hypothesi*. Hence the average inflation rate for the EMU as a whole will be subject to systematic upward pressure, inducing an even more restrictive monetary policy than has prevailed until now. The ECB can be expected to get even tougher in fighting inflation. That in turn will lower even more prospects for growth of returns on euro-denominated assets.

Fiscal Policy

The story is much the same on the fiscal policy side, where eurozone governments have formally tied their hands with their controversial Stability and Growth Pact (SGP). The SGP, first set up in 1997, was intended to implement the "excessive deficit procedure" called for by the Maastricht Treaty (Article 104c). In effect, it extrapolates from the third of the Treaty's four convergence criteria (fiscal stability) to the period after countries join the eurozone. The key provision is a strict cap on national budget deficits at 3 per cent of GDP. The tight restraint makes it difficult for elected officials to use budgetary policy for countercyclical purposes, to offset the anti-growth bias of monetary policy.

Here also, we know, practice has increasingly diverged from principle, with a number of EMU's present members – including, most notably, France and Germany – repeatedly missing the SGP's 3 per cent target. We also know that little has been accomplished to make the Pact more effective. Many specialists in Europe have called for the Pact's revision. But while some limited reforms were enacted in 2005, appeals for more radical changes have made no noticeable headway. To some, these facts mean that the SGP has no "bite." But can anyone doubt that deficits might be even larger yet in the absence of the Pact? Historically, many EMU governments routinely ran deficits in excess of three per cent; most had to struggle to qualify for membership in the first place. *De facto*, therefore, if not *de jure*, the SGP straitjacket remains a constraint on eurozone countries, perpetuating an anti-growth bias in fiscal policy, too. And here also the restrictive impact is likely to become even more pronounced as EMU grows in size.

The reason is simple. EU membership imposes a heavy burden on government budgets. Once accepted, new members must begin contributing to the central EU budget. They must also conform to all of the requirements of EU legislation, the *acquis communautaire*, which will compel them to increase spending on such vital needs as infrastructure, social services, and environmental quality. Though most will find some of the pressure alleviated by financial assistance from EU institutions, net benefits will be limited by co-financing requirements. Overall, therefore, there is no doubt that fiscal policy in the accession countries will be severely tested. Membership could raise budget deficits by amounts as large as 3 or 4 per cent of GDP unless offset by higher taxes or parallel expenditure cuts (Kenen and Meade 2003: 5–7)

Accordingly, most new members can be expected to be persistently preoccupied with deficit reduction, leaving little leeway for the use of budgetary policy to counterbalance a restrictive monetary policy. Only the Baltic states and Slovenia today seem able to live comfortably under the SGP's three per cent cap. Elsewhere, substantial deficit problems are the rule, particularly in the largest accession countries (Czech Republic, Hungary, Poland and Slovakia). Almost certainly, austerity measures will be called for that could have the effect of retarding real growth.

The net impact will be considerable. It may be an exaggeration to claim, as has the president of the Czech Republic, that the rigidities of the SGP will create weak and dependent "transfer economies" like East Germany after reunification (Klaus

2004: 176). The outlook need not be that dismal. But for many of the accession countries, budget constraints will be tight; and given the economic weight of the most fiscally troubled of the new members, it does not seem unreasonable to expect that for the entering group as a whole, budgetary policy will on balance be tilted in a deflationary direction. Overall, the extra fiscal pressures will add substantially to EMU's anti-growth bias, again lowering prospects for improvement of returns on euro-denominated assets.

Governance

Finally, there is the governance structure of EMU, which for the euro's prospects as an international currency may be the biggest obstacle of all. The basic question is: Who is in charge? The answer, regrettably, has never been clear. From the start, uncertainty has reigned concerning the delegation of monetary authority among governments and EU institutions. The Maastricht Treaty, being the product of a complex political negotiation, naturally embodies a variety of artful compromises and deliberate obfuscations. The result is a strikingly high degree of ambiguity in provisions for the management of the eurozone. Jurisdictional lines are anything but transparent; the details of accountability are equivocal and obscure. None of this is apt to cultivate an easy confidence in the euro. Indeed, market actors outside EMU may be excused for hesitating to commit themselves to what looks rather like a pig in a poke – even if transactions costs could be lowered to competitive levels and even if returns on European assets could be significantly improved.

Three key provisions may be cited. First is the governance of EMU's core institution, the European Central Bank. Second is the delegation of responsibility for ensuring financial stability across the eurozone as a whole. And third is the issue of external representation: Who speaks for the euro on the broader world stage?

The European Central Bank

Practical operational control of monetary policy lies in the hands of the ECB's executive board, made up of the president, vice-president, and four other members. Overall managerial authority, however, is formally lodged in the Governing Council, which in addition to the six-member executive board include the heads of the central banks of all participating states, each with the same voting rights. From the start, it was understood that the large size and mixed representation of the Governing Council might be inconsistent with efficient or transparent governance.

The issue was obvious. Even before enlargement, the Governing Council – with the six executive board members and twelve national governors – was already bigger than the top managerial unit in any other central bank in the world. Observers were quick to question how decisions would be made with so many bodies around the table. Discussions would undoubtedly be time consuming and complicated. In the words of one informed observer: "The mere thought of a *tour-de-table* is exhausting" (Meade 2003: 129). Organization theory teaches that the costs of preparing and making policy rises not just in proportion but exponentially with the number of people involved. Hence the conventional advice is to keep executive units small in order to maximize decision-making efficiency. The prescribed size of the Governing Council was almost certainly too great for serious and productive dialogue. The ECB had a "numbers problem".

Sooner or later, it seemed, real power would have to devolve to a smaller "inner" group formally or informally charged with resolving differences on critical issues, as so often happens in large organizations. But who would be included in this exclusive club? Would it be the executive board, which might be expected to take a broad approach to the eurozone's needs and interests? Or would it be a select coterie of central-bank governors, whose views could turn out to be more parochial? No one could be sure.

Enlargement simply makes the numbers problem worse. Upon joining the EU, all ten accession countries immediately gained observer status on the Governing Council, with voting rights to follow once they adopt the euro. That would put the number at 28, with even more governors to be added down the road as Bulgaria, Romania, and other candidate governments successfully negotiate their way into the EU (or if Britain, Denmark, or Sweden ever decide to join). A gaggle of thirty or more strong-willed individuals could hardly be considered conducive to efficient decision making. As one source commented sarcastically, enlargement would leave the governing council with "too many to decide on where to go to dinner, let alone agree on how to run monetary policy for more than 400 million people" (Baldwin 2001). Of particular concern, once EMU was up and running, was the risk that equal voting rights for all council members would give excessive weight to smaller countries in setting policy parameters (Berger *et al.* 2004; de Grauwe 2004; de Haan *et al.* 2004).

To their credit, Europe's leaders recognized the problem early on and sought to provide a remedy. In March 2003, following a proposal from the ECB, the European Council (comprising the heads of state or government of all EU members) approved a reform of the Governing Council restricting votes to a smaller total on a rotating basis (ECB 2003). Membership of the Council will continue to include the executive board and all national central-bank governors; moreover, all six members of the executive board will retain their individual votes. But voting rights of national governors are now to be limited to no more than fifteen and will rotate among governors according to a specified formula, taking explicit account of the diversity among member states. The rotation will start once fifteen countries have adopted the euro and will be implemented in two stages, as follows:

1 With participation of between fifteen and twenty-two member states, eurozone countries will be divided into two groups, using size as a criterion. Size will be measured by a weighted average of an economy's share in total EU GDP and total assets of monetary financial institutions. A first group of governors originating from the five largest states will receive four votes. The second group of up to seventeen governors will receive up to eleven votes.

2 Once participation on the Governing Council moves beyond twenty-two member states, a third group of up to five governors from the smallest countries will be formed with up to three votes. Correspondingly, the number of voting rights of the middle group will be reduced from eleven to eight. The four votes of the five biggest countries will remain unchanged.

The remedy, however, may be worse than the disease, creating more problems than it solves. On the one hand, the reform leaves intact the large number of bodies at the table. Every national governor, as well as the six executive board members, will continue to participate in all policy discussions, with full speaking rights. The approach has been defended on the grounds that it should facilitate consensus building, contribute to a better flow of information, and strengthen the norm of collective responsibility (Cukierman 2004: 70). But it can also be criticized for perpetuating all the gross inefficiencies of the ECB's numbers problem. As one astute observer puts it, the Governing Council will remain "more like a mini-parliament than a decision-making body" (Gros 2003: 124).

On the other hand, the reform introduces several new ambiguities that add even more to uncertainties surrounding decision making at the ECB. How, for instance, will votes rotate within each of the two (eventually three) groups? Will the rules for rotation be the same in all groups? How often will the membership of groups be adjusted as economies change in size? And could the formula for measuring size itself be changed at any time? Transparency is hardly served by such a complex arrangement.

Worse, the reform may well deepen rifts within the Governing Council, since the rotation model is so unabashedly state-based. Votes are allocated strictly along lines of national identity. In principle, governors are supposed to be fully independent professionals making monetary policy objectively for the eurozone as a whole. In practice, they may now be forgiven for thinking first of their own countries rather than in terms of collective interests. In the words of a prominent German economist: "The reform proposal does not meet the rationale of an integrative monetary policy ... It re-nationalizes European monetary policy" (Belke 2003: 122). The current president of the ECB, Jean-Claude Trichet, has already more than once been forced to reprimand individual governors for publicly opposing established policies that seemed inconsistent with the needs of their home economies (*New York Times*, February 3, 2006: C6).

The danger would not be so serious if all EMU economies were largely convergent in real terms. The reality, however, is just the reverse. Econometric analysis shows little correlation of output shocks between the accession countries, on the one hand, and the older members of the eurozone, on the other (Berger *et al.* 2004; Hall and Hondroyiannis 2006). Except for Slovenia and, to a lesser extent, Cyprus, synchronization of business-cycle activity between the two groups appears to be quite weak. National policy preferences, therefore, are likely to diverge sharply as well.

The shame is that an alternative model was at hand that might have avoided many of these problems. Reacting to the ECB's initial proposal, the European Parliament recommended a radically different approach based on a redistribution of authority between the Executive Board and Governing Council. A broader range of practical powers over interest rates and intermediate policy objectives would be delegated to the Executive Board, converting it into a full-fledged monetary committee. Responsibilities of the Governing Council, by contrast, would be limited to questions of general strategy and guidelines for the monetary regime. The Governing Council, which presently meets twice a month, would instead convene no more than once or twice a year.

With this alternative, no changes would have been required in either the size or the voting rules of the Governing Council. Lines of accountability, however, would have been far clearer. In its operations, the Executive Board would have been directly answerable to the Governing Council, much as the board of executive directors at the International Monetary Fund is ultimately responsible to the Fund's board of governors. EMU's Governing Council, in turn, would have stood as the institutional embodiment of European monetary sovereignty. But member governments, clearly, were reluctant to give up their direct representation in the decision making process. Hence the European Council never even seriously considered the Parliament's alternative model. Instead, the unwieldy proposal of the ECB was swiftly approved and ratified, storing up the risk of serious problems in the future.

Financial Stability

Serious problems could also arise from EMU's provisions for maintenance of financial stability. No monetary regime is invulnerable to the risk of occasional crisis. At any time, asset prices could become excessively volatile, adversely affecting real economic conditions; or there might be a spreading contagion of illiquidity or insolvency among monetary institutions. Financial systems are inherently fragile. Unfortunately, the prevailing rules of the eurozone are not at all clear about who, ultimately, is responsible either for crisis prevention or for the management of crises should they occur. Transparency is not served in these circumstances, either.

According to the Maastricht Treaty, the European Central Bank is expected to "contribute to the smooth conduct of policies pursued by the competent authorities relating to the prudential supervision of credit institutions and the stability of the financial system" (Article 105.5). But no specific tasks are assigned to the ECB to help forestall crisis, and none may be assumed by the ECB unless expressly delegated by the Council of Ministers (Article 105.6). Though linkages may have grown among national financial markets since the euro's birth, the ruling principle remains decentralization, otherwise known as subsidiarity – the notion that the lowest level of government that can efficiently carry out a function should do so. Formal authority for prudential supervision and regulation continues to reside at the national level, as it did before EMU. Each central bank is charged with responsibility for the financial institutions based within its own national borders.

Nor does the ECB have specific powers to deal with any crises that might occur. General language in the Maastricht Treaty does appear to empower the

Bank to backstop TARGET, the large intra-European clearing system, in the event of a payments gridlock or other difficulties. One of the basic tasks of the ECB, declares the Treaty, shall be "to promote the smooth operation of payment systems" (Article 105.2). But for any other contingency, such as a sudden wave of illiquidity in the banking sector, the Treaty is as uncommunicative as the Oracle of Delphi. Nothing is said about any authority for the ECB to act as a lender of last resort. Economist Garry Schinasi says that this silence makes the ECB the "ultimate 'narrow' central bank" (Schinasi 2003: 3). The ECB has a mandate for price stability but not for financial stability.

The Treaty's silence has been a source of much debate. Some specialists interpret it as a form of "constructive ambiguity" – an indication that, in practice, the ECB's crisis-management powers could be enhanced if and when needed. As one legal commentator puts it: "The wording of the subsidiarity principle leaves the door open for a possible Community competence" (Lastra 2003: 57). But others disagree, arguing that because the responsibility has not been specifically transferred, it must remain at the national level. The Treaty's language is seen as restrictive rather than permissive.

In practice decentralization rules here, too. As in pre-EMU Europe, the lender-of-last-resort function is left to the individual central banks. And again, each central bank remains responsible only for financial institutions within its own national borders. Beyond that, all is opaque. No one, it appears, is directly accountable for the stability of the eurozone as a whole.

Can such a decentralized arrangement be counted on to assure smooth operation of the overall system? There is certainly room for doubt. What would happen, for instance, if in a given country a large financial institution with extensive cross-border business were to find itself in trouble? Would the national authorities be evenhanded in their response, fully recognizing the interests of claimants elsewhere in the eurozone? Or would they act protectively, even at the risk of conflict with the regulatory authorities of partner countries? We have no way of knowing. The scheme "may work well", observes Schinasi, "but this still remains to be seen ... It is [not] obvious that national supervision in Europe would tend, as a first priority, to focus on European priorities ... It is difficult to imagine the national supervisor pursuing European interests first and national interests second" (Schinasi 2005: 119–120). The possibility that central banks might work at cross-purposes, provoking or aggravating a crisis, is certainly not outside the realm of possibility. There is no Invisible Hand for public agencies. Decentralized decision making among governments without some form of coordination is potentially a recipe for disaster.

Here too, enlargement just makes the situation worse, for two reasons. First, once again, is the numbers problem. If uncoordinated decision making is risky with a dozen central banks in the game, how much more vulnerable is an EMU of double or perhaps even triple that number? Recall organization theory's suggestion that with expansion, decision-making problems increase not just proportionally but exponentially. This does not mean that as the eurozone grows, financial instability becomes unavoidable. There is no certainty about such matters. But it does mean that with each new member, the probability of some kind of crisis keeps on rising.

Second, compounding the numbers problem, is the relative poverty of the accession countries as compared with the present membership of EMU. On the one hand, this means that their supervisory institutions, on average, are apt to be more rudimentary – less practiced at the essential tasks of monitoring markets and assessing risk. On the other hand, it means that in their eagerness to catch up with the EU's more advanced economies, they are apt to do all they can to promote lending for productive investment. The combination is deadly. The result, as previously noted, could be an excessively rapid expansion of credit, testing the limits of financial prudence and risking overheating and asset price bubbles. The ice under the feet of the eurozone will grow increasingly thin.

External Representation

Finally, there is the issue of external representation. Who is to speak for the eurozone on broader macroeconomic issues such as policy coordination, crisis management, or reform of the international financial architecture? Here there is no answer at all, leaving a vacuum at the heart of EMU.

No single body is designated to represent EMU at the IMF or in other global forums. Instead, the Maastricht Treaty simply laid down a procedure for resolving the issue at a later date, presumably on a case-by-case basis (Article 109). Some sources excuse this on the grounds that it achieved a balance between the need to convey a common position and the prerogatives of member states. But that seems far too kind. In fact, it was a cop-out, a diplomatic formula to mask failure to reach agreement.

At a minimum, the text compounds confusion about who is in charge. At worst, it condemns the eurozone to lasting second-class status, since it limits the group's ability to project power on monetary matters. As booster Fred Bergsten laments: "Europe still speaks with a multiplicity, even a cacophony, of voices ... Organizational reforms that enable the countries making up Euroland to act together and speak with a single voice will probably be an essential prerequisite of full European equivalence with the United States" (Bergsten 2005: 33). The point has been best put by political scientists Kathleen McNamara and Sophie Meunier: "As long as no 'single voice' has the political authority to speak on behalf of the euro area, as the US Secretary of the Treasury does for the American currency, the pre-eminence of the United States in international monetary matters, as in other realms, is likely to remain unchallenged" (McNamara and Meunier 2002: 850). Washington has no single phone number to call when negotiations are required.

Clearly, the phone number cannot be in Frankfurt, where the European Central Bank is headquartered. In international monetary forums, countries are normally represented not by central banks but by finance ministers or equivalent – public officials with the political clout to speak for their respective governments. The ECB obviously cannot claim that kind of authority. Indeed, it is difficult to imagine the elected governments of Europe ever delegating such a fundamental power to an institution that has been deliberately designed to be as free from political influence as possible.

Alternatively, some have suggested the appointment of a single individual with sufficient credentials and legitimacy to act as interlocutor for the eurozone (Henning 1997; McNamara and Meunier 2002; Zimmerman 2004) – a Mr. (or Ms) Euro, as it were. Precedent exists, of course, in the realm of foreign and security affairs, where EU members already agreed a decade ago to name a single high representative to stand for them all – a Mr. Europe (presently Javier Solana of Spain). But experience has shown that Mr. Europe's ability to speak authoritatively for the entire EU is persistently hamstrung by policy differences among individual governments. A single appointed official cannot ignore or overrule the preferences of diverse sovereign states.

The most practical solution would be a collective one, centered on the informal committee of EMU finance ministers that has emerged since the birth of the euro – what has come to be known as the Eurogroup. Like comparable EU institutions, such as the Council of Ministers or European Council, the Eurogroup could be represented at any given time by its chair; the chairmanship itself, as with those other institutions, rotates periodically among members. In 2005 the Eurogroup chair began attending meetings of the Group of Seven, but with no specified responsibilities. A more effective approach might be to explicitly delegate authority to the chair to speak on behalf of the eurozone.

Some criticize the idea, fearing that it could lead to a politicization of monetary policy in the eurozone and might even compromise the independence of the ECB. But such apprehensions seem overblown. Participation in international forums by America's Treasury Secretary, for instance, has by no means compromised the independence of the Federal Reserve. In fact, this kind of division of labor between central bank and finance ministries is the rule around the world, not the exception. For EMU, the advantage of the Eurogroup is that it does embody the necessary degree of political authority. At last, there would be not only a single number to call but also someone empowered to pick up the phone.

So what is stopping EMU? Romano Prodi says that it is "a lack of will" (Prodi 2004: 14). But that is surely an oversimplification. The question is: Why is there a lack of will? The answer, plainly, has to do with the lingering influence of national sovereignty. Though EMU members may share a joint money, their interests are hardly identical. Divergent circumstances and preferences make them reluctant to give up the right to speak for themselves. Even after more than half a decade of living with the euro, national identity trumps collective interest.

Once again, enlargement just makes the situation worse. Adding the accession countries will not only amplify the numbers problem, complicating decision making. Entrance of such a diverse group of relatively poor economies will also multiply and deepen internal cleavages, making it increasingly difficult to hammer out common positions on external issues. The fundamental rationale for developing a single voice for EMU, McNamara and Meunier remind us, "lies in the potential … to project the image of a unified, strong Europe to key international political and financial actors" (McNamara and Meunier 2002: 851). Enlargement will leave the Europeans further from that goal than ever.

Conclusion

The bottom line, therefore, seems clear. Bigger will not be better, despite the increased potential for network externalities that comes with enlargement. On the contrary, bringing the accession countries into EMU will only exacerbate the impact of factors impeding the euro's emergence as an international currency. By prolonging the segmentation of Europe's financial markets, larger numbers will delay any significant reduction of the cost of doing business in euros. By adding to inflationary and budgetary pressures, enlargement will reinforce the anti-growth bias built into the institutional structure of EMU. And by further complicating an already complex governance structure, the new entrants will cloud even more the fundamental question of who is in charge. None of this is calculated to make the euro more attractive to outside users.

Could the risks be even worse? Could EMU founder under the weight of enlargement? Though unlikely, the possibility cannot be lightly dismissed. The eurozone's problems, writes the respected economist Anna Schwartz, "will only worsen with the inclusion of new members. Is this a recipe for political disintegration? Would the euro survive political disintegration?" (Schwartz 2004: 25). Others warn of "EMU's coming stress test" (Gros *et al.* 2005), which could lead to unilateral secessions. Italy's welfare minister, concerned about his country's weakening export performance, has publicly called for a reintroduction of the lire and even tried to collect enough signatures for a referendum on the matter. He is unlikely to be the last politician to use the euro as a scapegoat for disappointing economic performance.

Given Europe's historical commitment to the integration process, however, breakdown seems improbable. EMU will not be allowed to fail. As *The Economist* writes: "A break-up of the euro area is still in the realm of small probability rather than likelihood" (*Economist*, 11 June 2005: 69). The real question is whether EMU can succeed. Can the euro ever rise above its defects to become a genuine rival to the dollar? Will the "old dream of enthusiasts", at long last, be realized?

The answer, regrettably, is also in the realm of small probability rather than likelihood. Nothing is impossible, of course – particularly if the United States continues to mismanage its own currency as badly as it has in recent years. America's payments deficit widened to over $800 billion in 2005 (more than 7 per cent of GDP) and could soon top a trillion dollars. The more the external deficit grows, threatening a crisis for the greenback, the more attractive the euro could begin to appear, whatever its defects. But that is hardly a case of leading from strength.

The fundamental problem for EMU is the mismatch between the domain of its currency and the jurisdictions of its member governments. The euro is a currency without a country – the product of an international agreement, not the expression of a single sovereign power. Its success, therefore, is critically dependent on the continued cooperation of EMU's member states, which can hardly be guaranteed for all time. Should it be any wonder, then, that outsiders might hesitate to commit themselves to the currency's future? Never before has the world adopted an international money that was not backed by a centralized political authority.

Monetary unions among sovereign states have existed before, of course, without major disruption. In the contemporary era one thinks of the East Caribbean Currency Area or the CFA Franc Zone in Africa. But these have all involved relatively small developing countries with no aspiration to major currency status. EMU, by contrast, encompasses some of the largest economies on the face of the earth and has never hidden its grand global ambitions. Unfortunately, Europe's divisions have never been hidden, either. For that reason, prospects for the euro's international role were poor even before enlargement. Enlargement of the eurozone's membership will simply make them even poorer.

References

Alogoskoufis, G. and Portes, R. (1997), "The Euro, the Dollar, and the International Monetary System", in Masson, P.R., Krueger, T.H. and Turtelboom, B.G., eds, *EMU and the International Monetary System* (Washington: International Monetary System), 58–78.

Baldwin, R. (2001), "The ECB's Numbers Problem", *Financial Times*, December 4, 15.

Bank for International Settlements (March 2005), *Triennial Central Bank Survey: Foreign Exchange and Derivatives Market Activity in 2004* (Basle).

Belke, A. (May/June 2003), "The Rotation Model is Not Sustainable", *Intereconomics*, vol. 38, no. 3, 119–124.

Berger, H., de Haan, J. and Inklaar, R. (2004), "Restructuring the ECB", in Berger, H. and Moutos, T., eds, *Managing European Union Enlargement* (Cambridge, MA: MIT Press), 29–66.

Berglöf, E., Fulghieri, P., Gual, J., Mayer, C., Luis Pita Barros, P. and Vives, X. (2005), *Integration of European Banking: The Way Forward*, Monitoring European Deregulation 3 (London: Centre for Economic Policy Research).

Bergsten, F. (1997), "The Impact of the Euro on Exchange Rates and International Policy Cooperation", in Masson, P.R., Krueger, T.H. and Turtelboom, B.G., eds, *EMU and the International Monetary System* (Washington: International Monetary System), 17–48.

Bergsten, F. (2005), "The Euro and the Dollar: Toward a 'Finance G–2'?", in Posen, A.S., ed., *The Euro at Five: Ready for a Global Role?* (Washington: Institute for International Economics), 27–39.

Codogno, L., Favero, C. and Missale, A. (October 2003), "Yield Spreads on EMU Government Bonds", *Economic Policy* 37, 503–527.

Cohen, B. (September 2003), "Global Currency Rivalry: Can the Euro Ever Challenge the Dollar?", *Journal of Common Market Studies*, vol. 41, no. 4, 575–595.

Cukierman, A. (2004), "Restructuring the ECB: Comments", in Berger, H. and Moutos, T., eds, *Managing European Union Enlargement* (Cambridge, MA: MIT Press), 67–72.

De Grauwe, P. (2004), "Challenges for Monetary Policy in Euroland", in Torres, F., Verdun, A., Zilioli, C. and Zimmermann, H., eds, *Governing EMU: Economic, Political, Legal and Historical Perspectives* (Badia Fiesolana, Italy: European University Institute), 363–388.

De Haan, J., Berger, H. and Inklaar, R. (2004), "Is the ECB Too Decentralized?", in Sinn, H.-W., Widgrén, M. and Köthenbürger, M., eds, *European Monetary Integration* (Cambridge, MA: MIT Press), 71–97.

De Larosière, J. (2002), "The Euro: An Opportunity for Europe and for the International Monetary System", in *The Euro in the International Arena: The Euro 50 Group Roundtable* (New York: Euro 50 Group), 9–19.

Economist (2005), "Open Wider: A Survey of International Banking", supplement, 21 May.

Eichengreen, B. (1997), "Comment on Bergsten", in Masson, P.R., Krueger, T.H. and Turtelboom, B.G., eds, *EMU and the International Monetary System* (Washington: International Monetary System), 49–57.

European Central Bank (May 2003), "The Adjustment of Voting Modalities in the Governing Council", *Monthly Bulletin*, 73–83.

European Commission (November 2005), *Second Report on the State of Practical Preparations for the Future Enlargement of the Euro Area* (Brussels).

European Central Bank (December 2005), *Review of the International Role of the Euro* (Frankfurt).

Gros, D. (May/June 2003), "An Opportunity Missed!", *Intereconomics*, vol. 38, no. 3, 124–129.

Gros, D., Mayer, T. and Ubide, A. (2005), *EMU At Risk*, 7th Annual Report of the CEPS Macroeconomic Policy Group (Brussels: Centre for European Policy Studies).

Gros, D. and Thygesen, N. (1998), *European Monetary Integration: From the European Monetary System to European Monetary Union*, 2nd ed. (New York: Addison Wesley Longman).

Hall, S. and Hondroyiannis, G. (2006), "Measuring the Correlation of Shocks Between the EU–15 and the New Member Countries", Working Paper No. 31 (Athens: Bank of Greece).

Henning, R. (1997), *Cooperating with Europe's Monetary Union*, Policy Analyses in International Economics 49 (Washington: Institute for International Economics).

Kenen, P. and Meade, E. (October 2003), "EU Accession and the Euro: Close Together or Far Apart?", International Economic Policy Brief PBO3–9 (Washington: Institute for International Economics).

Klaus, V. (2004), "The Future of the Euro: An Outsider's View", *Cato Journal*, vol. 24, nos 1–2 (Spring/Summer), 171–177.

Lastra, R. (2003), "The Governance Structure for Financial Regulation and Supervision in Europe", *Columbia Journal of European Law*, vol. 10, no. 1 (Fall), 49–68.

McNamara, K. and Meunier, S. (October 2002), "Between National Sovereignty and International Power: What External Voice for the Euro?", *International Affairs*, vol. 78, no. 4, 849–868.

Meade, E. (May/June 2003), "A (Critical) Appraisal of the ECB's Voting Reform", *Intereconomics*, vol. 38, no. 3, 129–131.

Mundell, R. (2000), "The Euro and the Stability of the International Monetary System", in Mundell, R.A. and Cleese, A., eds, *The Euro as a Stabilizer in the International Economic System* (Boston: Kluwer Academic), 57–84.

Portes, R. and Rey, H. (1998), "The Emergence of the Euro as an International Currency", in Begg, D., von Hagen, J., Wyplosz, C. and Zimmermann, K.F., eds, *EMU: Prospects and Challenges for the Euro* (Oxford: Blackwell), 305–332.

Prodi, R. (2004), "The Euro and Enlargement", in Deardorff, A.V., ed., *The Past, Present and Future of the European Union* (New York: Palgrave Macmillan), 6–20.

Rey, H. (2005), "The Impact of a Five-Year-Old Euro on Financial Markets", in Posen, A.S., ed., *The Euro at Five: Ready for a Global Role?* (Washington: Institute for International Economics), 111–116.

Schadler, S., Drummond, P., Kuijs, L., Murgasova, Z. and van Elkan, R. (2005), *Adopting the Euro in Central Europe: Challenges of the Next Step in European Integration*, Occasional Paper No. 234 (Washington: International Monetary Fund).

Schinasi, G. (2003), "Responsibility of Central Banks for Stability in Financial Markets", Working Paper WP/03/121 (Washington: International Monetary Fund).

Schinasi, G. (2005), "Financial Architecture of the Eurozone at Five", in Posen, A.S., ed., *The Euro at Five: Ready for a Global Role?* (Washington: Institute for International Economics), 117–122.

Schwartz, A. (2004), "Global Order and the Future of the Euro", *Cato Journal*, vol. 24, nos 1–2 (Spring/Summer), 19–26.

Wyplosz, C. (1999), "An International Role for the Euro?", in Dermine, J. and Hillion, P., eds, *European Capital Markets with a Single Currency* (New York: Oxford University Press), 76–104.

Zimmermann, H. (2004), "Ever Challenging the Buck? The Euro and the Question of Power in International Monetary Governance", in Torres, F., Verdun, A., Zilioli, C. and Zimmermann, H., eds, *Governing EMU: Economic, Political, Legal and Historical Perspectives* (Badia Fiesolana, Italy: European University Institute), 233–247.

PART IV
The Euro and the European Economic Governance

Chapter 9

Running an Enlarged Eurozone. Reforming the ECB Governing Council: Efficiency, Representation and National Economic Interest

David Howarth

Introduction

On December 19, 2002, in preparation for the coming into force of the Treaty of Nice, the European Central Bank (ECB) Governing Council (GC) adopted a recommendation on new GC voting procedures following the enlargement of the eurozone (formally approved on February 3, 2003).[1] Prior to this agreement, there was a growing literature on the manner in which enlargement should or might affect ECB decision making institutionally, including Buiter (1999), Fatum (2000), Baldwin *et al.* (2001a, b), Bjorksten (2000), Eichengreen and Ghironi (2001) and de Grauwe (2000). This chapter contributes to the literature focusing on the efficiency of monetary policy making and the coherence of monetary policy making for economically diverse states – including de Grauwe (2000), Gros and Hefeker (2000), European Parliament (2001) and Deutsche Bundesbank (2001) – and the literature on the legitimacy of the existing decision making structures of the European Central Bank, including ECB (2002), Leino (2001), de Haan and Eijffinger (2000), Buiter (1999) and Issing (1999). Recently, Heisenberg (2003) has attempted to bridge discussions about efficiency, transparency, enlargement and democratic legitimacy.

1 This ECB recommendation, under Article 10.6 of the Statute of the European System of Central Banks and of the European Central Bank, for a Council Decision on an amendment to Article 10.2 of the Statute of the European System of Central Banks and of the European Central Bank (ECB/2003/1; 2003/C29/07) was submitted by the European Central Bank to the Council on February 3, 2003. The decision of the Council, meeting in the composition of the Heads of State or Government, was taken on March 21, 2003, after taking into consideration the opinions of the European Commission and the European Parliament. The agreed amendment was then recommended to the member states for ratification in accordance with their respective constitutional requirements.

This chapter is more limited in scope, analyzing the recent agreement on GC reform in terms of national economy size reflected in the bargaining power of the ECB GC members and macroeconomic preference. The December 2002 and February 2003 agreements on reform were subject to consensual decision making in the GC and subject to the unanimous approval of national finance ministers in Ecofin. While acting in an *ad personam* (that is, independent and personal) capacity, the NCB governors and Executive Board (EB) members agreed upon a reform which – conforming *barely* to treaty-based principles of equality and representativeness and addressing *inadequately* concerns about GC decision-making inefficiency – reflected national macroeconomic policy preferences and particularly the preferences of the member states (MS) with the largest economies. In order to prevent enlargement from contributing significantly to decision-making inefficiency, pre-existing principles of eurozone representativeness were distorted in a manner which reflected the macroeconomic preferences of most current eurozone MS and in particular the largest MS.

The Difficulties Posed by Enlargement: Size Matters …

The 2000 Intergovernmental Conference, which preceded the Nice Summit, agreed upon the reform of several EU institutions to cope with a considerable increase in member state numbers, yet largely ignored the impact of enlargement upon the operation of the ECB. Article 10.6 was introduced in the Statute of the ESCB and of the ECB calling upon the ECB Governing Council to present a recommendation "as soon as possible" following the entry into force of the Treaty of Nice on the necessary institutional reforms in the bank to cope with enlargement. While the new EU member states were expected to respect most of the convergence criteria and, following accession, could potentially include their currencies in the Exchange Rate Mechanism (ERM) II, they could only participate in the eurozone at a later stage. At the time of writing (early 2007), six of the new member states are ERM II members: Cyprus, Estonia, Latvia, Lithuania, Malta and Slovakia. On January 1, 2007, Slovenia became the thirteenth eurozone member and the Governing Council expanded to nineteen members.

The impact of eurozone enlargement looms large for the ECB principally because it highlights existing problems with the operation of the Governing Council – problems that reflect the uneasy balance between equality, representativeness and decision-making efficiency and effectiveness. The ECB Governing Council is already the largest monetary policy committee of any central bank (the voting contingent of the Federal Open Market Committee (FOMC) of the US Federal Reserve has only twelve members). There is a growing body of work on optimal monetary policy committee (MPC) size to best ensure decision -making efficiency and effectiveness (see Blinder 2004; Sibert 2003 and 2006). Sibert (2006) examines the economics literature on monetary policy making by committee and the literature on groups in the other social sciences – especially social psychology – focusing on the effect of size on group performance and decision outcomes. She concludes that the optimal number of

MPC members is at least five and not much beyond this. On the basis of such studies, personal experience and observation, many other observers argue that the ECB Governing Council is too large. At eighteen (now nineteen) members it is conducive neither to maximum efficiency nor to effectiveness in monetary policy making – in particular on technical as opposed to political aspects (notably, the specification of the ECB's operational goals) (see for example, de Haan *et al.* 2005; Eijffinger 2006; Sibert 2006). Future enlargements exacerbate such concerns. Amongst others, Willem Buiter, a former member of the Monetary Policy Committee of the Bank of England, complains of the Governing Council's size prior to Greek accession:

> A group of 17 is already too large for the serious and productive exchange of views, discussion and group decision making. … A squad of 21 will be quite unwieldy. Thirty would be a mob. … Based on my own limited experience, a policy making body with seven members would probably be optimal (Buiter 1999: 200).

The GC was empowered to change (by unanimity) its own practices if it found problems or potential problems in its decision making (Statute on the ESCB and the ECB Article 12.3). There is much scope for its procedures to evolve – such as the creation of more working groups – and the work of the GC can involve more activity at the ECB level or through the NCBs. However, the size problem still matters.

Some monetary economists have argued that the problem could be resolved by emulating the US Federal Reserve Board, by increasing the power of the Executive Board (EB) in relation to the NCB governors and rotating GC places among the member states (Favero *et al.* 2000). Others see the creation of a Monetary Board detached from the MS NCBs as the only effective way to resolve the efficiency problem (Baldwin *et al.* 2001a, b). However, such recommendations ignore the unique character of both the Eurosystem as a "federal" banking system and the EU as a political entity. First, the centre (the ECB) is considerably less dominant in the Eurosystem than in the American system. The NCBs retain considerably more power than the US Federal Reserve District Banks and the governors have final say – thanks to their majority in the GC – over the allocation of functions. Any reform to strengthen the EB at the expense of the GC would be challenged on grounds of legitimacy: despite their *ad personam* status (and *not* national representatives), the strong presence of the NCB governors on the GC was considered vital to selling the EMU project to skeptical national publics. The arrangements of the US Federal Reserve Board were developed just over 60 years ago, around 160 years after the creation of the United States as a country and long after the conclusion of the Civil War successfully asserted federal government authority. There is obviously no parallel situation in the EU.

Buiter (1999) also recommends – even without eurozone enlargement – restricting the size of the GC to nine members and the EB to four. However, it could be argued that the EU lacks the legitimacy as a political system to deny MS a permanent seat on the ECB GC. No other EU-level institution currently denies member states representation.[2] It was unlikely that the existing NCB governors or MS governments would be willing to lose the right to a permanent seat. Officially, each NCB governor is there in a personal capacity as an experienced expert on central banking not as a national representative per se. In theory, therefore, a rotation of governors (either all or only the less populated MS) would be an adequate resolution of the size problem: a particular group of them should be as representative of informed opinion as all of them. However, the governors are *de facto* national representatives because they each come from one of the MS and are most familiar with their own national economies and banking systems. De Grauwe *et al.* (1999) also note that there is nothing in the treaties to prevent NCB governors from prioritizing the economic interests of their own MS. It would be difficult for the governors to present the perspective of other member states as effectively as their own and thus highly problematic to exclude certain member states from voting on a permanent basis.

Alternative Reform Proposals

In addition to variants of the rotation system (discussed below), five alternative reform proposals were considered and rejected by GC members: a constituency model, a system of weighted voting, a double majority system, the creation of a Monetary Board and an election system. A constituency model, based on regional groupings as in the World Bank and the IMF, was rejected. Officially (ECB 2003; Mersch 2003) it was argued that this would violate the principle of independence of the individual NCB governors in that they would become *de jure* representatives of a specific constituency rather than operate on an *ad personam* basis (in a personal capacity). The extension of the system of weighted voting was deemed contrary to the "one member, one vote" principle established in Article 10.2 of the Protocol to the TEC on the statute of the ESCB and ECB. This statute allows weighted voting (excluding EB members) only on matters pertaining to shareholdership, that is, NCB capital. GC members also rejected the kind of double majority system (number, population and/or GDP to be considered) adopted in the Nice Treaty for the Council which, concerning an intergovernmental body, was not seen to be a relevant precedent for GC reform. The NCB governors from the smaller MS were concerned that the need for a double majority would result in a kind of *directoire* dominated by the largest MS. One variant of this model required a majority vote including at least three of the six EB members, with any GC member possessing the right to verify that a pre-

2 It should be noted that the ECB enjoys something of a special status and is not a Community institution in the legal sense. The Nice Treaty (Article 4(2)) requires the Council to adopt a rotation of European Commission places totalling below the number of MS once this number reaches twenty-seven. The Draft Treaty Establishing a Constitution for Europe (Article I-26(6)) specifies this further, allowing – after one full Commission term under existing rules – for the number of Commissioners to equal two-thirds the number of MS (subject to possible modification by the European Council acting unanimously).

set GDP level was represented, thus (currently) giving the French and German NCB governors the possibility of blockage if that level was set at 62 per cent.[3] The creation of a Monetary Board consisting of EB members and a few NCB governors – along lines recommended by Baldwin *et al.* (2001a) – was rejected for contradicting the core principles of decentralization and representation, especially given the overwhelming significance of national (as opposed to EU level) macroeconomic policy making. The model of the American Federal Reserve was thus explicitly rejected. Finally, an election system was rejected on several grounds: an unrestricted election might infringe the representativeness criteria, result in the creation of a "market" for votes and undermine cooperation among GC members.

Rotation System

The rotation system for voting in the GC is impressively complex for the uninitiated, and the lack of transparency in the preparation of the proposed reforms – itself suggestive that considerations beyond the core principles and efficiency goals were influential in determining the system agreed upon – has been criticized by several ECB watchers, notably the well-known German monetary economist Daniel Gros (2003). According to the agreement, the number of NCB governors exercising a voting right would be capped at fifteen, while all governors would continue to attend meetings. When the number of NCB governors in the GC exceeded fifteen, voting rights would be exercised on the basis of a rotation system, designed to ensure that the NCB governors with the right to vote would be from member states which, taken together, were representative of the eurozone's economy as a whole. Consequently, the NCB governors would exercise a voting right with different frequencies depending on an indicator of the relative size of the economies of their member states within the eurozone. Based on this indicator, NCB governors would be allocated to different groups.

Initially, there would be two groups. The governors from the five member states with the largest economies (currently Germany, France, Italy, Spain, Netherlands) would form one rotating group possessing four votes (thus only four of these five governors would have the right to vote at any one time with a voting frequency of 80 per cent). The governors from the other member states (numbering eleven to seventeen) would form the second rotating group, sharing eleven votes. Once the total number of member states in the eurozone increased beyond twenty-two (up to twenty-seven, that is, the current EU member states and the twelve accession countries listed in the Protocol on enlargement annexed to the Treaty of Nice), three groups would be established. The first would remain the same. The second group would consist of the NCB governors from the countries with the next largest economies, sharing eight votes on a rotational basis. The size of this group would

3 The EP's Monetary and Finance Committee, with a German *rapporteur*, also made a proposal for a double majority, consisting of, first, the population and, second, the total size of the economy and the financial sector.

equal the total number of governors divided by two (then rounded up to a full number if necessary). The third group would consist of the governors from the countries with the smallest economies sharing three votes on a rotational basis. The members of the EB would preserve their permanent voting rights.

The division of MS into the two/three groups would reflect their share in the eurozone according to a composite indicator of "representativeness" consisting of principally the member states' GDP at market prices (five-sixths weight in the indicator) and its total assets of the aggregated balance sheet of monetary financial institutions (TABS-MFI) (one-sixth weight). The data on GDP would be provided by the European Commission, while the rules for the calculation of the key for subscription of the ECB's capital would apply (Article 29.2 Statute of the ESCB). The data on TABS-MFI would be defined on the basis of an existing Council Regulation (No. 2533/98 of November 23, 1998) concerning the collection of statistical information by the ECB. This data would be updated every five years. The GC proposed that a two-thirds majority of *all* its members would be required to decide on the initial adaptation of the voting rights in the two-group system as the number of eurozone member states increased. The same procedure of a two-thirds majority of *all* members would apply to the definition of the precise implementing provisions for the rotation of voting rights within each group (for example, the time interval between the rotation of voting rights).

The Official Justification

The agreement on the rotation system reflects the concern of many GC members (especially EB members and NCB governors from the larger participating MS) with regard to the potential inefficiencies of an excessively large GC raised by Buiter (1999), Baldwin *et al.* (2001a, b) and others. A principal concern was that one form of representativeness (one member, one vote) would override representation of the actual eurozone economy as simple majority voting could. Such a possibility currently exists in the system of representation and voting in the GC. However, the possibility would increase considerably if all the accession NCB governors obtained voting rights. The ECB argued that a system of rotation with varying voting rights on the basis of reasonable economic criteria ensured the true equal treatment of the NCB governors and "sufficient" levels of representativeness. The design of the rotation system was, according to the ECB, guided by the following principles:[4]

- The "*equality*" of NCB governors ("one member, one vote" principle) is maintained by allowing all to attend all GC meetings. Even though all the governors do not vote all the time, the votes all carry the same weight regardless of the size of national economies. No NCB governor retains a permanent vote thus preserving an element of "equality".

4 The fifth principle was transparency (of the wording of the text outlining the rotation system). ECB Press Statement, December 20, 2002.

- The principle of "*ad personam participation*" (allowing all GC members to attend all meetings in a personal and independent capacity rather than representatives of a specific MS *per se*) is preserved.
- *Representativeness* is preserved in the sense that voting NCB governors will be representative of the entire eurozone (even though some NCB governors are not voting) yet there is no "renationalization" in the sense of governors being required to represent specific regions.
- *Consistency* is to be maintained during the transition from two to three phases by avoiding that governors of certain NCBs move randomly up and down between certain groups.

The rotation system was defended also in terms of not discriminating against the NCB governors of countries acceding to the eurozone in the future. Four of the new MS were expected to enter the second rotating group, while the strong possibility existed that many of the remaining countries would move eventually from the third to the second group with economic growth.

Debates on the Number and Composition of Rotating Groups, Voting Rights, Composite Indicator and Representativeness

Two or Three Rotating Group Models

This was debated at length in the GC. Alternative proposals of two group models of different sizes were debated. These were rejected because of concerns by several of the NCB governors of being placed in a rotating group with governors from MS with much smaller economies. The NCB governors from the largest MS also sought to create a small group with relatively high voting frequency. Thus the three-group model – with NCB governors from large, medium and small MS respectively – was the preferred option from the start of discussions with the intermediary phase of a two-group model.

Eighteen versus Twenty-One Votes

The concern for decision-making efficiency encouraged the governors from the largest MS to favor maintaining the existing eighteen votes, while several governors from the smaller MS defended a higher number of voting members to ensure greater voting frequency in the second and third groups. The compromise reached was twenty-one votes: six permanent votes for the EB members and up to fifteen rotating votes for the governors.

Representativeness Indicator

The NCB governors from several of the medium-sized MS (the Netherlands and so on) preferred to avoid the use of population criteria given that this would allow several of the CEEC NCB governors to replace existing MS governors in the second group and allow Poland to replace the Netherlands in the first group. The official logic for excluding the population criterion (ECB 2003; Mersch 2003) is curious: this was seen as inappropriate as the ECB is "an economic and not a political body", even though the population criterion is already used in addition to GDP for determining MS capital contributions to the ECB and voting on these contributions. Most MS preferred just using the GDP criterion. However, the NCB governors from some of the current eurozone MS (notably Luxembourg) also sought to include recognition of the financial sector. This was defended in reference to the experience of the American Federal Reserve System which grants the president of the New York Reserve Bank permanent voting rights in the Federal Open Market Committee (FOMC).[5] TABS-MFI was adopted as the broadest measure of the financial sector, with an existing definition in EU law and an established and consistent statistical framework.

Compromising Representativeness and Efficiency

The reform proposed by the ECB Governing Council has been widely criticized by academics, journalists, non-eurozone central bank officials and politicians. Gros (2003: 1) has been particularly outspoken in his criticism, arguing that "the solution proposed by the ECB is worse than the status quo. It is inefficient, opaque, internally inconsistent and arbitrary"[6] (see also Bofinger 2003). After several debates and expressions of expert opinion, the reform proposals were rejected by the European Parliament's Committee on Economics and Monetary Affairs on the grounds of their "complexity" – although this rejection was not binding upon the Council. The parliamentary committee voted to retain the "status quo", that is, the preservation of votes for all NCB governors, with an enlarged Executive Board of nine members, thus challenging the validity of claims of a size–efficiency trade-off. However, if rotation were to be adopted, the parliamentary committee accepted the use of a composite indicator, based on the criteria of economy and financial market size *but also* population, thus challenging the legitimacy of the ECB's more restricted criteria (European Parliament 2004).

On efficiency grounds, the proposed reform does not address the concerns that the ECB Governing Council is already too big: the Governing Council is set to

5 The other eleven Federal Reserve District Banks presidents rotate into four voting positions on the FOMC. The US Federal Reserve Act makes no reference to the relative weight of US states, while section 2 of the Act establishes the criteria of convenience and "customary course of business" to determine voting weights.

6 In addition to the points made in the text, Gros challenges the lack of clarity and the arbitrariness surrounding the rotation of NCB governors with voting rights. He provides an alternative for the reform of the ECB developed by the CEPS Macroeconomic Policy Group – which involves the Governing Council meeting less often and setting the guidelines for monetary policy, while the Executive Board assumes more control over the execution of monetary policy – and urges the European Commission to propose an alternative reform for adoption by the Council.

grow to twenty-one members from the present eighteen. Preventing some NCB governors from voting is not the same as preventing them from speaking and they will continue to attend all Governing Council meetings. Thus the potential for cacophony that concerns Buiter (1999) and others remains. The nod in favor of efficiency was managed only in the context of a great distortion of the principle "one member, one vote" with the new rotation system reflecting national economic size. The reform – in order to ensure representativeness – moves in the opposite direction to the preference of those observers who advocate a more center-heavy US Federal Reserve model (de Haan *et al.* 2005; Eijffinger 2006; Favero *et al.* 2000) or the Monetary Board proposed by Baldwin *et al.* (2001). The reform places increased emphasis on representation of the eurozone economy rather than member states, but all NCB governors can continue to attend Governing Council meetings and there is an increased number of voting members.

The new form of representativeness reflected in the rotation system and the failure to meet efficiency objectives reflects the macroeconomic preferences of the five eurozone member states with the biggest economies more than the other current and future member states. The establishment of two/three groups for rotation, with the NCB governors from the five member states with the biggest economies assured more frequent voting rights than the other governors, seems to contradict the *ad personam* status of the NCB governors. The reform officially recognizes that the status of the NCB governors should vary, and this in turn suggests that the governors are not to be treated as truly independent people operating in a personal capacity; that their home member state is of relevance and determines their status, at least by guaranteeing governors from member states with larger economies a more frequent vote than those from member states with smaller economies.

Of course, one might see the proposed reform as "politically reasonable" and legitimate in that they recognize that economy and financial market size do in fact matter: if there must be rotation, why should the governors of the banks of Malta and Slovenia be treated the same as the Bundesbank president? Clearly, the member states with the biggest economies have already lost out in terms of a "representativeness" that reflects economic size. Officially, their central bank governors possess the same vote as the others on all decisions except those having to do with the capital of the ECB. The adoption of the new rotational scheme is a way of potentially strengthening this kind of "representativeness", if only to a limited degree. Put another way, the "representativeness" of one governor–one vote has been qualified by a "politically reasonable" "representativeness" that accepts the relevance of economy size. This qualification reflects the reality that most eurozone citizens are preoccupied, first and foremost, with conditions in their national economy rather than the eurozone economy as a whole. While this qualification no doubt reflects the power concerns of NCB governors from the largest member states, it might also reflect a concern with regard to public perception in these member states of the legitimacy of eurozone monetary policy making.

Crucially, the two/three rotating group system and the agreed cap of twenty-one for Governing Council voting members reflects the macroeconomic preferences of the largest member states (especially Germany and France). The voice of the five largest member states is hardly diminished by the proposed reform, dropping from five out of eighteen to four out of twenty-one (in a eurozone of twenty-two member states or more). It might also be argued that *de facto* over-representation of the large member states in the Governing Council is set to continue. Howarth and Loedel (2005) show that the underlying objective of equal national representation was undermined with the first appointment of the Executive Board in 1998 and the (almost) constant representation of the four largest member states on the Executive Board.[7] These Executive Board members are expected to maintain a focus on the entire eurozone, as required by the Statute of the ESCB and of the ECB. Nonetheless, the overrepresentation of large member states does challenge the principles of equality and representativeness. At the very least, it can be argued that having served most, if not all, of their career in their member states of origin, the Executive Board members are more familiar with their home economy than other national economies. As explained below, this familiarity can have an impact on monetary policy-making preferences. If Executive Board members are to be considered potential national representatives in disguise, the twenty-one maximum membership of the Governing Council established in 2003 only slightly diminishes the weight of the largest five member states from currently nine out of eighteen to eight out of twenty-one. It is very likely (interviews, ECB 2004) that the French and German NCB governors (and perhaps even the Italian and Spanish ones) preferred a double majority system of GDP size and voting members – or a voting system weighted according to GDP – which would have given two or three of these governors an effective veto on all monetary policy making. Clearly, such a system would have been unacceptable to the large majority of NCB governors. It would also have posed considerable risks for the public's perception of the legitimacy of eurozone monetary policy making – especially, in the event of a future move to greater transparency in the Governing Council.[8]

---

7 Three replacements since June 2004 demonstrate the continuity of large member state representation: the Spanish Executive Board member Eugenio Domingo Solans was replaced by another Spaniard, Jose Manuel Gonzalez-Paramo; the Italian Tommaso Padoa-Schioppa by Lorenzo Bini Smaghi; and the German Ottmar Issing by Jürgen Stark. France was not represented on the Executive Board for only a brief period following the replacement of Christian Noyer as ECB vice-president and the accession of Jean-Claude Trichet as president. However, this was an inevitable interruption given that Noyer's departure was part of the controversial compromise allowing Trichet to take office. The extent to which the French President went in 1998 to ensure the appointment of the Bank of France Governor, Trichet, as the ECB president, further suggests the importance attached to securing Executive Board places by the largest member states.

8 There is disagreement among legal scholars whether primary Community law prohibits the publication of minutes of the meetings of the Governing Council. It has been argued by some that Article 10.4 of Statute of the ESCB and of the ECB limits transparency in this regard (Amtenbrink 1999). Article 10.4 states: "The proceedings of the meetings shall be confidential. The Governing Council may decide to make the outcome of its deliberations public." Although no provision in the TEC (and specifically Article VII or the Protocol on the Statute of the ESCB and of the ECB) necessarily blocks transparency, the ECB Governing Council members justified their 1998 decision to prevent disclosure of Governing Council minutes as a necessary evil to prevent the exertion of domestic

The Economic Danger of "Equality"

In the context of enlargement, one principal consideration linked to the different economies and economic needs of the future eurozone member states likely contributed to the reform preferences of the largest member state NCB governors (interviews, ECB 2004). Given the more rapid expansion of their economies over the medium to long term, the future member states would have much higher inflation on average than existing member states and considerably higher inflation than France and Germany (and even Italy and Spain). Completely equal member state NCB governor representation on the Governing Council in an enlarged eurozone would result in the over-representation of inflation-prone member states and the possible establishment of an entrenched bias in favor of higher interest rates. This over-representation arguably already exists in the current Governing Council, where inflation differentials between the member states have spilled over to private and public differences between ECB Governing Council members on interest rate changes, and vociferous criticism by certain Executive Board members of certain member states with higher inflation (Howarth and Loedel 2005).

The fear of over-representation is linked to two related concerns. The first is the extent to which national policy preferences shape the governors' (and even the Executive Board members') positions. The second is the structural differences of the national economies. Regarding the first concern – as already noted – no explicit provision in the TEC and the Statute of the ESCB and of the ECB prevents a NCB governor from presenting policy positions based on domestic data and national needs (de Grauwe *et al.* 1999; Meade and Sheets 2002). There have been a small number of studies which attempt to differentiate between policy making on the basis of national preferences and policy making on the basis eurozone-wide preferences and the low inflation target of the ECB (for example, de Grauwe *et al.* 1999; Heinemann and Huefner 2004; Sanchez-Santos and Varela 2003). The jury is out on whether or not national preferences have had a "distorting" effect on ECB monetary policy making and this article does not attempt to enter into this debate. However, it is important to emphasize that the presence of a much larger number of NCB governors from small- and medium-sized national economies with relatively high inflation creates additional pressure for a monetary policy which focuses less on the interests of the biggest member state economies (Heinemann and Huefner 2004).[9]

---

political pressures on national central bankers (ECB 1999). In effect, non-transparency might also the decrease the appearance of NCB governors advocating monetary policy changes that conform to national preferences (Howarth and Loedel 2005).

9 Heinemann and Huefner (2004) apply different economic approaches to determine if national preferences rather than a eurozone focus determine ECB interest rate decisions. Using the ordered probit approach, these authors conclude that national preferences (based on controlling national inflation rates rather than the eurozone inflation rate) do affect monetary policy – although they accept clear limitations to their study. Given the increased divergence in the economies, and inflation rates, among member states in a future enlarged eurozone. These authors argue that: "If for EMU-12 there is some evidence that

The likelihood of a considerable inflation differential in the future enlarged eurozone is due to the Balassa-Samuelson effect: inflation rates in the poorer ten CEECs will be systematically higher than in wealthier current member states and will likely remain so for some time (Baldwin 2001b; Bjorksten 2000; Égert *et al.* 2003; Égert 2005; Eichengreen and Ghironi 2001). In 2004, for example, there was an inflation rate of 3.7 per cent for the ten future member states and 4.4 per cent for the twelve (the ten plus Romania and Bulgaria) versus an average of 2 per cent for the current eurozone (ECB 2005). If we are to assume that all NCB governors view inflation risks similarly – despite the ECB's overall inflation target of or close to 2 per cent over the medium term – those governors from the future member states would tend to prefer tighter monetary policy while those from many of old member states would prefer a looser policy. Baldwin *et al.* (2001b) thus complain of a strong potential for a disjuncture between the requirements of the economy of the entire eurozone (more than 70 per cent of which is made up of the five largest member states) and the preferences of the smallest fourteen (sixteen) member states that will form a majority of members in the Governing Council of an enlarged eurozone of twenty-two (twenty-four) member states. The economic situation of the ten (twelve) accession countries thus creates difficulties for the entire eurozone and problems for monetary policy making. Without the 2003 reform to Governing Council voting procedures, member states with only 6 per cent of the eurozone GDP (2000 figures) (but 35 per cent of the population) would have controlled ten voting positions on the Governing Council. In the future enlarged eurozone of twenty-four member states, Germany, France and Italy would comprise 67 per cent of the GDP yet – according to the old voting system – would have held only three of the NCB governors' twenty-four votes or 12.5 per cent (assuming Sweden, Denmark and Britain stay out but all the new accession countries, Romania and Bulgaria come in). In a monetary union of twenty-seven member states, the smallest seventeen would represent only 10 per cent of the eurozone's economy yet would form a majority of votes in the Governing Council (Berger 2002). Without reform, all newcomers to the eurozone – with the exception of the United Kingdom – will have greater political than economic weight.

In addition to the concern about inflation differentials between the larger and future poorer member states, the largest member states also had other economic reasons to seek to preserve their relative voting power in the Governing Council. The differences in monetary transmission mechanisms due to national economic structural differences and different national banking systems – see Angeloni *et al.* (2003), Bank of England (1999), Corsetti and Pesenti (1999), de Grauwe (2000) and EP (2001) – can result in different monetary policy preferences. Interest rate changes have significantly different effects on the national economies of the eurozone (although understanding the precise impact is an inexact science given

---

divergence is not irrelevant in the Governing Council this should be even more pronounced for EMU-27. In this sense our first results back the case for adjusting the representation and/or voting weights in the Governing Council in favour of the countries with large GDP shares as recommended by the ECB" (556).

the complexity of variables in the national economies). Therefore, while NCB governors might agree on the need for an interest rate change, a consideration of the impact of the change on national economies might encourage them to push for varying levels of change. Several variables can be mentioned. There are different levels of consumer and public debt: thus interest rate changes will have a considerably different impact on consumer and public spending in different member states. The maturities of debt also vary considerably: for example, because firms in Italy and France have shorter-term loans than the firms in other eurozone member states, they are more affected by ECB interest rate changes. Furthermore, the degree to which interest rate changes are buffered by national banks varies (Angeloni *et al.* 2003). The economic structures of the future new member states of the eurozone will likely vary as much as the current member states. Thus, the concern of the current large member state NCB governors regarding new member state voting is not only related to their economic differences as a group but rather the further dilution of large member state concerns regarding the impact of interest changes.

Conclusion

Disenfranchising a significant number of the smaller member states was thus considered vital to the preservation of the macroeconomic preferences of the largest member states but also the perception of the legitimacy of eurozone monetary policy making for the citizens of these member states. However, the only way that the NCB governors from the existing smaller member states would agree to this reduction of total votes was if rotation was to apply to all the member states and if the established principles of equality ("one member, one vote") and representativeness were respected officially. These treaty-based principles were distorted to become, in effect: "one member, one vote only some of the time with varying frequency determined by economy and financial market size".[10] For the full eurozone of twenty-seven members including all current EU member states, Romania and Bulgaria, the total number of votes and frequency of voting will vary considerably: four out of five and 80 per cent frequency for the first group; eight out of fourteen or 57 per cent for the second; and three out of eight or 37 per cent for the third. Even with fewer eurozone members, the preferences of the smallest (and crucially the future poorer) member states are much less likely to prevail and those of the larger member states more likely to be asserted. The insistence that economy and financial market size matter over population size (however reasonable from the perspective of monetary policy making) was also reflected in the preferences of the smallest of the current large member states (notably the Netherlands) and other current small member states, few of which would end up in the third rotating group. With the possibility (however remote) of future Turkish entry into the eurozone, even German, French and Italian NCB

10 Author's own words.

governors had a clear interest in establishing group selection by economy and financial market size as opposed to GDP and population size.

Given the lack of transparency surrounding the intra-ECB discussions and negotiations on Governing Council reform, the precise policy positions of the different NCB governors and the precise nature of internal debates are impossible to determine for the time being. However, the reform agreed upon suggests that the NCB governors of the largest member states defended policy positions conforming to national macroeconomic interests, even though compromise that took on board the concerns of other current eurozone NCB governors and respected – albeit only in a highly distorted manner – treaty-based principles was necessary. The distortion reflects possible efforts to weaken the representation of the NCB governors from the future CEEC member states in order to diminish a structurally determined bias in favor of higher interest rates. The distortion also reflects the interests of the NCB governors of the largest member states to maintain their disproportionate representation in the Governing Council in order to ensure their relatively strong influence on interest rate changes affecting their economies in a particular way due to specific national economic structures. The reform of Governing Council voting procedures transforms the underlying concept of "representativeness" in the eurozone. It undermines the principle of member state representation that has been (and remains) vital to the legitimacy of ECB policy making (and EMU more generally), while strengthening the relevance of national economic size and the representation of the entire economy of the eurozone (rather than its member states and their populations). The official ambition to avoid enlargement contributing *significantly* to decision-making inefficiency can arguably be said to have been met. However, inefficiency was, nonetheless, potentially worsened and the core concerns about size raised by many monetary economists were not addressed.

Some monetary economists have granted qualified praise to the agreed reform of the ECB Governing Council and the creation of the three rotating groups. They do so on the grounds that this reform moves in the right direction towards a truly desirable voting system that aligns "political power and economic weight" of national central bank governors as closely as possible (de Haan *et al.* 2005; Eijffinger 2006; see also Berger *et al.* 2004). Such a system is, according to these authors, "the best way" – short of the centralization of operational policy making in the Executive Board – "to ensure that national interests will not unduly influence ECB policy-making" (Eijffinger 2006: 97). Their argument doubts the *ad personam* participation of NCB governors and the possibility that they can make monetary policy decisions without specific reference to their own national economies. If NCB governors can in effect represent national economic concerns over those of the eurozone as a whole, the alignment of voting power in the Governing Council with economic weight negates the possibility of reflecting this bias in ECB monetary policy. These observers are concerned with the policy-making inefficiencies created by emphasizing NCB governor equality and member state representativeness. They also believe that treating NCB governors equally in terms of voting rights in the Governing Council results in the over-representation of the smaller national economies of the eurozone, which in turn damages effective ECB monetary policy. The problem will worsen with enlargement.

The analysis adopted in this paper accepts that these considerations might well have influenced the reform agreed by the Governing Council members. However, it is argued here that the move in the direction of aligning political (voting) weight and economic weight runs contrary to the "equality" and "representativeness" principles in a manner which undermines ECB and EMU legitimacy. The argument that political weight should reflect economic weight responds to the legitimacy and power concerns of the governments of the largest eurozone national economies. However, the way in which this argument denies the equality and *ad personam* participation of NCB governors – by emphasizing that they represent member state economies – undermines the legitimacy of the ECB and in turn the EMU project. Rooted in a contested EU political system, ECB and EMU legitimacy relies to an unclear extent on equal member state representation, however indirect and qualified by the principle of *ad personam* participation. The agreed Governing Council reform of December 2002 and February 2003 fudges the principles of equality, representativeness and *ad personam* participation of the Governing Council members. Yet the reform does not entirely discard these principles. The reform is potentially damaging to ECB and EMU legitimacy but it is considerably less so than the reform proposals driven solely by either efficiency concerns or the recognition of member state economic weight or both. The monetary economists who advocate such proposals would do well to consider "input" as well as "output" legitimacy.

References

Amtenbrink, F. (1999), *The Democratic Accountability of Central Banks: A Comparative Study of the European Central Bank* (Oxford: Hart Publishing).

Angeloni, I., Kashyap, A., Mojon, B. and Terlizzese, D. (2003), "Monetary Transmission in the Euro Area: Where Do We Stand?", in Angelino, I., Kashyap, A. and Mojon, B., eds., *Monetary Policy in the Euro Area* (Cambridge: Cambridge University Press).

Baldwin, R., Berglof, E., Giavazzi, F. and Widgren, M. (2001a), *Nice Try: Should the Treaty of Nice Be Ratified?* (Washington, DC: Brookings).

Baldwin, R., Berglof, E., Giavazzi, F. and Widgren, M. (2001b), "Preparing the ECB for Enlargement", CEPR Discussion Paper No. 6.

Bank of England (1999), "The Transmission Mechanism of Monetary Policy", *Bank of England Quarterly Bulletin*, vol. 39, no. 2.

Berger, H. (2002), "The ECB and Euro-Area Enlargement", IMF Working Paper No. 02/175.

Bjorksten, N. (2000), "Economic Catching Up in the Enlarged Euro Area: Implications for the Common Monetary Policy", EUI Working Papers, RSC, no. 2000/52. See http://www.ieu.it/RSC/WP-Texts/00_52.pdf.

Bofinger, P. (2003), "Consequences of the Modification of the Governing Council Rules", Briefing Paper, European Parliament Committee for Monetary and Economic Affairs, 17 February.

Buiter, W. (1999), "Alice in Euroland", in *Journal of Common Market Studies*, vol. 37, no. 2, 181–209.

Corsetti, G. and Pesenti, P. (1999), "Stability, Asymmetry and Discontinuity: The Outset of Euroepan Monetary Union", *Brookings Papers on Economic Activity* (Washington: Brookings).

Deutsche Bundesbank (October 2001), "Monetary Aspect of the Enlargement of the EU", Monthly Report (Frankfurt: Deutsche Bundesbank). See http://www.bundesbank.de/en/monatsbericht/textteil/bericht10/01/mb1001ges_e.pdf.

Égert, B. (2005), "Balassa-Samuelson Meets South Eastern Europe, the CIS and Turkey: A Close Encounter of the Third Kind?", *European Journal of Comparative Economics*, vol. 2, no. 2, 221–243.

Égert, B., Drine, I., Lommatzsch, K. and Rault, C. (2003), "The Balassa-Samuelson Effect in Central and Eastern Europe: Myth or Reality?", *Journal of Comparative Economics*, vol. 31, no. 3, 552–572.

Eichengreen, B. and Ghironi, F. (2001), "EMU and Enlargement", unpublished manuscript. See http://fmwww.bc.edu/ec–p/WP481.pdf.

Eijffinger, S.C.W. (2006), "Change at the ECB Executive Board", *Intereconomics*, vol. 41, no. 2, March/April, 93–99.

European Central Bank (ECB) (November 2002), Monthly Bulletin. See http://www.ecb.int/pub/pdf/ mb200211en.pdf.

European Central Bank (ECB) (2003) *Annual Report 2002* (Frankfurt: ECB).

European Central Bank (ECB) (2004) *Annual Report 2003* (Frankfurt: ECB).

European Parliament (EP) (2001), "Monetary Policy Transmission in the Euro Area" (Luxembourg: Directorate-General for Research). See http://www.europarl.eu.int/workingpapers/econ/pdf/110rev_en.pdf.

Fatum, R. (2000), "Economical and Political Implications of Bargaining Versus Voting in a Monetary Union", Santa Cruz Center for International Economics, Working Paper No. 00–16. See http://sccie.ucsc.edu/papers/workingpapers/ 2000/sccie–00–16.pdf.

Favero, C., Freixias, X., Persson, T. and Wyplosz, C. (2000), *One Money, Many Countries: Monitoring the European Central Bank 2* (London: CEPR).

de Grauwe, P. (2000), "Monetary Policies in the Presence of Asymmetries", *Journal of Common Market Studies*, vol. 38, no. 4, 593–612.

de Grauwe, P., Dewachter, H. and Aksoy, Y. (1999), "The ECB Decision Rules and Macroeconomic Performance", CEPR Discussion Paper No. 2067.

Gros, D. and Hefeker, C. (July 2000), "One Size Fits All: National Divergences in a Monetary Union", CEPS Working Paper No. 149.

Gros, D. (February 2003), "Reforming the Composition of the ECB Governing Council in View of Enlargement. How Not to Do It!", briefing paper for the Monetary Committee of the European Parliament (Brussels: CEPS). See http://www.europarl.eu.int/comparl/econ/pdf/emu/ speeches/20030217/gross.pdf.

de Haan, J. and Eijffinger, S.C.W. (2000), "The Democratic Accountability of the European Central Bank: A Comment on Two Fairy-Tales", *Journal of Common Market Studies*, vol. 38, no. 3, 393–407.

de Haan, J. , Eijffinger, Sylvester C.W. and Waller, Sandra (2005), *The European Central Bank: Credibility, Transparency, and Centralization*, Boston: MIT Press.

Heinemann, F. and Huefner, F. (2004), "Is the View from the Eurotower Purely European? – National Divergence and ECB Interest Rate Policy", *Scottish Journal of Political Economy*, vol. 51, no. 4, 544–558.

Heisenberg, D. (2003), "Cutting the Bank Down to Size: Efficient and Legitimate Decision-Making in the European Central Bank After Enlargement", in *Journal of Common Market Studies*, vol. 41, no. 3, 397–420.

Howarth, D. and Loedel, P. (2003), *The European Central Bank: The New European Leviathan?* (Basingstoke: Palgrave).

Issing, O. (1999), "The Eurosystem: Transparent and Accountable of 'Willem in Euroland'", *Journal of Common Market Studies*, vol. 37, no. 3, 503–519.

Leino, P. (2001), "The European Central Bank and Legitimacy: Is the ECB a Modification of or an Exception to the Principle of Democracy?", Harvard Jean Monnet Working Paper, 1/01. See http://www.jeanmonnetprogram.org/papers/00/001101.html.

Meade, E. and Sheets, N. (1999), "Regional Influences on US Monetary Policy: Some Implications for Europe", London: Centre for Economic Performance Working Paper. See http://cep.lse.ac.uk/pubs/download/dp0523.pdf.

Mersch, Y. (2003), "The Reform of the Governing Council of the ECB", Panel Statement, Central Bankers' Panel, European Banking and Financial Forum, Prague, March 25. Reproduced in BIS Review, 16/2003.

Sanchez-Santos, J. and Varela, D. (2003), "Representative or Independent? A Rational Choice Model of Interest Rate Decision-Making by the European Central Bank", paper presented at the UACES Annual Research Conference, September 2–4, 2003, Newcastle, UK. See http://www.udc.es/rrii/ajm/papers/ECBpaper08.pdf.

Sibert, A.C. (2003), "Monetary Policy Committees: Individual and Collective Reputations", *Review of Economic Studies*, vol. 70, no. 3, 649–665.

Sibert, A.C. (2006), "Central Banking by Committee", *International Finance*, Summer, vol. 9, no. 2, 145–168.

Chapter 10

The Political Economy of Eurozone Enlargement: The Motives, Prospects and Implications for the EU and its Member States

Ramunas Vilpisauskas

Introduction

The State of Affairs: Nominal Convergence

> Contrary to often-heard concerns, the main question regarding the future of the European single currency is not who is going to leave, but who is going to join.
> (Alhearne and Pisani-Ferry 2006: 1).

New EU member states from Central and Eastern Europe that joined the EU in May 2004 have committed themselves to become members of the Economic and Monetary Union ("EMU" – the eurozone). The accession into the eurozone could therefore be seen as the "left over" from the accession negotiations that will be undertaken when the necessary conditions are met. Unlike Great Britain and Denmark, these countries have no "opt outs". After entering the EU, they immediately entered the third stage of the EMU to become the member states with a status of temporary derogation.[1]

Even though within some new members, such as Poland, there have been calls for the referendum on joining the eurozone, meeting the convergence criteria is the most important factor that will to a large extent determine the timing of accession of new EU members. By now most new EU members have indicated their plans to apply for the evaluation of their status with regard to the convergence criteria and to introduce the euro in the next one to three years (see Table 10.1). Only Polish authorities have not clearly expressed their preferences regarding the target date of introducing the euro, although some analysts predict that Poland will join the eurozone around 2012–2013 (*Financial Times*, February 17, 2006).

The divergence of the target dates to a large extent reflects the diversity of fiscal indicators and exchange rate policies in the new member states. As a rule, countries with a history of fixed exchange rates as well as comparatively better

1 For an overview of the issues surrounding the enlargement of the eurozone see, for example, Tiusanen and Kinnunen (2005).

Table 10.1 The Existing Exchange Rate Regime in NMS, Date of Entering the ERMII and the Plans to Introduce Euro

Member State	Exchange Rate Regime	Date of Entering the ERM II	Plans to Introduce Euro
Slovenia	Managed float	June 2004	Joined on January 1, 2007
Lithuania	Currency board	June 2004	From 2010
Estonia	Currency board	June 2004	From 2010
Poland	Float	—	January 1, 2011
Latvia	Managed float exchange rate pegged with euro	May 2005	From 2011
Slovakia	Managed float	November 2005	January 1, 2009
Hungary	Target zone (EUR)	—	After 2012
Czech Republic	Managed float	—	By 2010

Sources: Deutsche Bank Research, April 2006; National Central Banks.

fiscal policy indicators have more ambitious aspirations to introduce euro. It should be noted that current new EU members from Central and Eastern Europe apply different exchange rate regimes that date back to the start of transition reforms in the first half of 1990s. Some, like Poland and Czech Republic, have floating exchange rates, which will have to be tightened and the fluctuations limited to the degree set by the Exchange Rate Mechanism II. Others, like Estonia and Lithuania, have currency boards which have been in place for more than a decade and imply monetary policy which is more restricted than being part of the monetary union.

The monetary regime existing in particular country also determines the degree of policy adjustment required during the accession into the eurozone. For example, unlike the experience of most current eurozone members, which restricted the freedom of their monetary institutions during the creation of the monetary union, the countries with currency boards are going through somewhat the opposite process of bringing more discretion into their monetary policy making. Actually, application of the currency board with a peg to the anchor currency euro practically means participation in the eurozone, though with a theoretical possibility of altering the exchange rate of national currency. There have been debates about the different transition regimes from the currency board arrangement to the monetary union and the need to devalue national currency before the introduction of euro (Gulde, Kahkonen and Keller 2000; Katsimi 2004). However, it could be argued that the history of currency boards in the Baltic states provides a strong basis for the participation in the Exchange Rate Mechanism II and the introduction of euro under the existing exchange rate rules, provided that conditions for flexibility are maintained, while the attempts to revalue before irrevocably fixing the exchange rate could create more uncertainty and destabilize expectations. The possibility of maintaining the currency board arrangement during the participation in the ERM II has been foreseen by the European Central Bank and used by both Lithuania and Estonia, which joined the ERM II in 2004. Although recently the calls for the new member state governments to preserve the option to revalue (devalue) the national currency against euro before introducing the latter have intensified, the history of the currency board and related benefits minimize the need for such an option for these countries (Atkins January 2006: 2; Munchau January 30, 2006: 15). Since the viable currency board arrangement implies the existence of strict policy discipline, the relatively healthy fiscal policy indicators of Lithuania and Estonia could also be partly explained by the monetary regime in place.

The comparative analysis of fiscal indicators against both the convergence criteria and the indicators of the current EMU member states illustrates several trends (see Figures 10.1(a) and 10.1(b)). All new EU member states are within the limits of the public debt criteria of 60 per cent of GDP (with the exception of Malta and Cyprus, which are not discussed in this chapter), with some, such Estonia, coming close to only 5 per cent of public debt. In this respect, the contrast with the state of the current eurozone members with an average of public debt reaching 70 per cent of GDP is the most visible. This could most probably be explained by the different history of the Central and Eastern European countries.

(a)

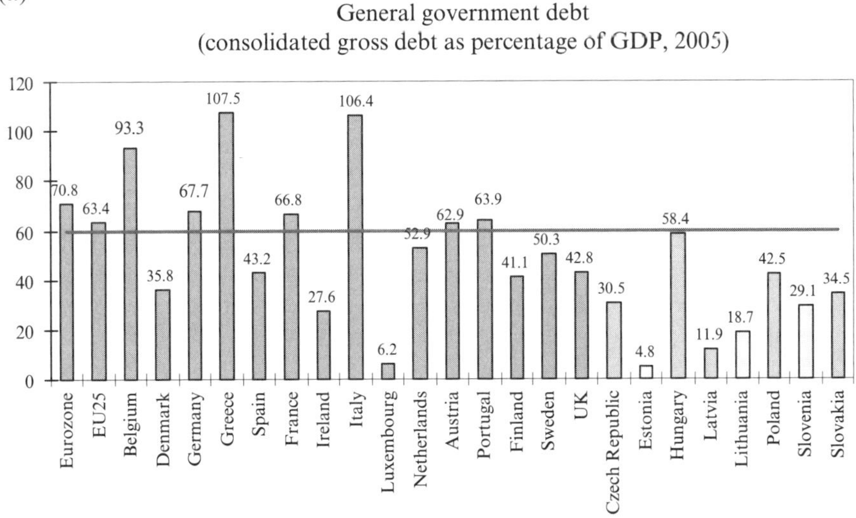

(b)

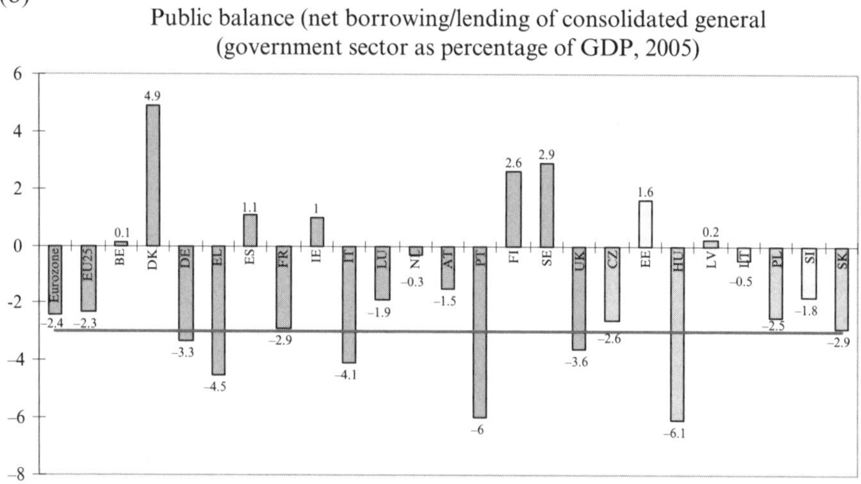

Figure 10.1 The Budgetary Deficits and Public Debt Indicators of New Member States and Eurozone Countries

Source: Eurostat.

The budgetary deficit criteria is met by some of the new member states, in particular the Baltic states (Estonia running budgetary surplus) and Slovenia. Partly, the reduction of the budgetary deficits is a result of the dynamic economic growth of these countries during the last five to six years, which has been reflected in the growth of budgetary income. Taking into account the forecasts which predict similar medium-term growth rates, the prospects for balancing national budgets are quite good.

The long-term interest rates have also been down in recent years, mostly as a result of economic policy reforms, competition in the banking sector and growing credibility of public policies in these countries, in particular with the accession into the EU becoming a reality (see Figure 10.2).

It should be noted that prospective accession into the EU (and the EMU) structured the expectations of international investors and contributed to the reduction of interest rates in new members. Although this did not lead to such a significant surge of foreign direct investment (FDI) into the new members as previously expected (Baldwin, Francois and Portes 1997: 127–170), the opportunities for cheap borrowing led to the rapid growth of credits and real estate market prices, which in turn have been fuelled by the expectations of price increases after the introduction of euro in these countries.

The state of new members meeting the inflation criteria is rather mixed (see Figure 10.3). Although some countries such as Slovenia only recently experienced the decrease of inflation to meet the convergence criteria, to other new EU members, which have been among the first to join the ERMII, inflation recently became the main risk factor threatening their prospects of joining the EMU in

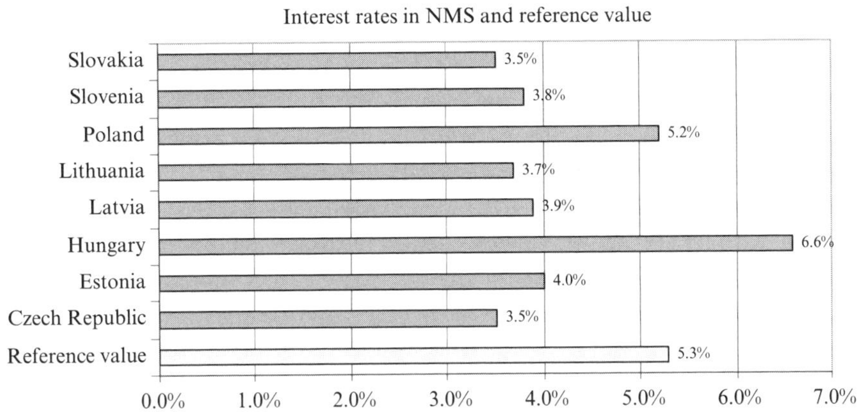

Figure 10.2 Interest Rates in New Member States and Eurozone Countries

Source: Deutsche Bank Research, April 2006.

2007. By the time of writing, it is already quite certain that not only Estonia was going to miss the target of joining the eurozone only because of its high inflation rate, but that the most likely entry date has been postponed till 2010 or even later.

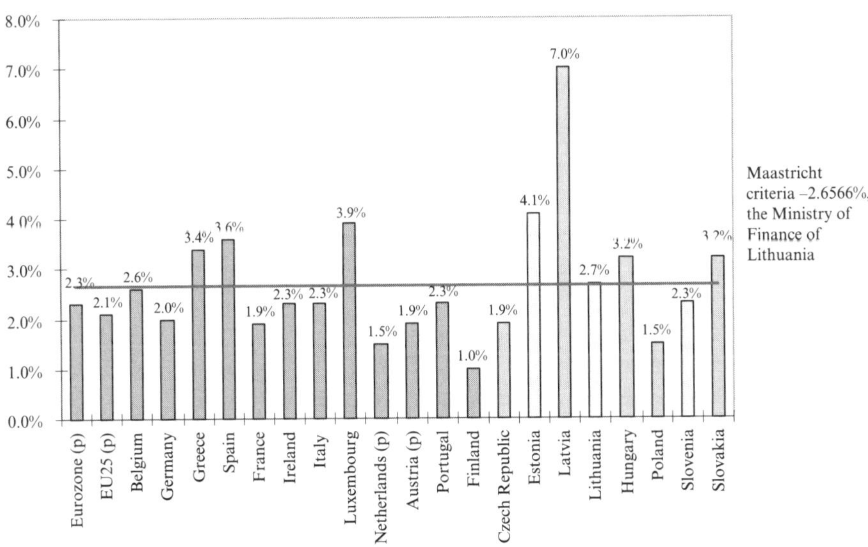

Figure 10.3 Inflation Rates in New Member States and Eurozone Countries

Sources: Eurostat, April 2006; the Ministry of Finance of Lithuania.

Interestingly, Lithuania had been balancing for several months on the limit of exceeding the inflation criteria which, for example, in February 2006 was exceeded by 0.1 percentage point. The European Commission announced that the prospects of Lithuania (as well as Slovenia) to introduce the euro from the start of 2007 would be evaluated and presented in May 16, 2006. Eventually, the decisions regarding the accession of these first two new member countries under evaluation have been made in the Council. Although just at the time of Council decisions Lithuania's annual inflation equaled the Maastricht criteria, on the basis of recommendations from the Commission which judged that meeting inflation criteria in Lithuania was unsustainable, the Council decided that Lithuania's accession into the eurozone had to be postponed. At the same time, Slovenia was judged to be ready to join the EMU in 2007.

The position of Lithuania, the third country in the group of new member states which joined ERM II in 2004, is likely to cause most debates which could have broader implications for the interpretation of the convergence criteria and their application. Despite the fact that for several years the country experienced zero inflation or deflation amidst its impressive economic growth and relatively healthy fiscal stance, recent increase of inflation due to the growth of oil prices, domestic administrative price increases and convergence process became a risk for the accession into the EMU in 2007 (and most likely up till 2010).

To be sure, the European Commission assesses the readiness of any new member to introduce euro on the basis of meeting convergence criteria, the process which is described as a purely technical exercise (Parket and Condon 2006: 2). However, the political symbolism attached to the accession into the eurozone together with the very close divergence from the calculated inflation criteria (in the case of Lithuania diverging only by less than 0.1 percentage point) is likely to invoke (or revive) the debates about the meaning of nominal convergence criteria, the concept of sustainability and the fair application of convergence criteria to all the member states of the EU whatever their size and economic weight.[2]

These debates could have important implications for the future discourse about the planned accessions into the eurozone and therefore are briefly presented below. First, the methodology of calculating the inflation by selecting the three member states with the lowest inflation indicators from the group of EU–25 rather than from the eurozone members of twelve (thirteen from 2007) could be questioned (the rule of best performers of price stability). This rule implies that countries that do not belong to the eurozone can affect the perspectives of the prospective members to introduce single currency. Another questions have to do with the notion of "best performance" and what could it mean – the lowest inflation rate (and related concept of outlier), the target rate set by the ECB or some other reference, and how many (one, two or three) of those countries used as a reference should be selected. Another important issue which is likely to be among the most debated in the context of eurozone enlargement is the effect of convergence and whether the methodology of adding 1.5 per cent to the best performers in terms

2 For some arguments about the arbitrary process of selecting the members ready to join the euro area see Munchau, January 2006: 15.

of price stability when calculating the Maastricht inflation criteria to assess the candidate economies is relevant in the current economic situation of enlarged EU with strongly divergent economic growth rates in the eurozone and new EU member states.[3] Besides, a very strict interpretation of convergence criteria applied to the new member states in the context of a number of current eurozone members breaching the criteria and the recent relaxation of Stability and Growth Pact might (and already did) provoke claims about the application of double standards and avoiding the fundamental principle of equal treatment.

It should be noted, that divergent inflation rates in the eurozone members and candidate countries have been partly a result of the factors such as growing oil prices which affect new members more significantly due to the larger share of the energy products in the basket of goods used to calculate the consumer price index (other factors including the excise duties harmonized upwards to reach minimum EU levels, increase of the administered prices of utilities partly due to the revaluation of infrastructure company assets and increase of the price of energy resources set by external suppliers from Russia). Therefore significant increase of the world oil prices recorded in recent years has had relatively more important impact on the inflation in new members.

Even though this might be interpreted as a sign of the lack of real convergence, such divergent responses to global trends as well as inflation differentials resulting from the catching-up of new members should not make them more vulnerable to the asymmetric shocks provided that other conditions facilitating real convergence are in place. Among these conditions the flexibility of the economy, i.e. price and wage flexibility are particularly important. As many analysts maintain, the flexibility is the key factor in allowing to absorb the asymmetric shocks under the conditions of monetary union (Mody and Rosenberg February 2006: 14). The next section addresses the perspectives for the real convergence and the issue of flexibility.

The State of Affairs: Real Convergence

The increase in economic and social diversity is one of the most important effects of the recent EU enlargement. Although the diversity of preferences is often associated with the transaction costs in making collective decisions in the EU institutions, economic diversity is also an important factor in assessing the perspectives and implications of being part of the single currency area.

New EU member states have been growing relatively faster than the eurozone members and catching up with the former (see Figure 10.4).

3 The so-called Balassa-Samuelson effect resulting from divergent increase of productivity have been estimated by different sources to add between 1.0 and 3.0 percentage points to the inflation rate (de Grauwe and Schnabl (2004). Though more recent estimates, for example, the Bank of Lithuania, set this indicator at a lower rangte of 0.3–0.9 percentage points.

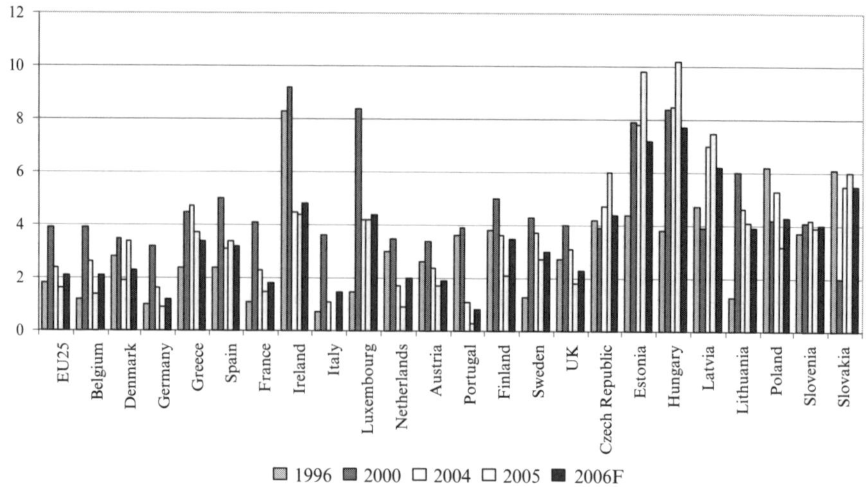

Figure 10.4 GDP Growth Rates of the EU Members

Source: Eurostat.

The catching-up process is a natural outcome of economic integration of richer and poorer economies. Although the speed of catching up depends on the mix of domestic policies, the inflow of capital into the new member states and the outflow of labor into the richer member states is a process which reflects the economic arguments about the differences in the rates of return on different factors of production. However, the relative differences of per capita income among the EU member states are still significant (see Figure 10.5).

Future catching up in the monetary union (or under the arrangement of national currency pegged to euro) will be absorbed by the domestic structures. The degree of asymmetries is a factor of similarities between the economic structures and the degree of economic integration of new member states with the eurozone members.

Although the new member states have reached similar share of services in their GDP compared to the EU average, they still differ in terms of the significance of agricultural activities and industrial structures, which are comparable to southern Europe and increasingly competing with rapidly growing Asian economies. In terms of economic integration, new EU member states are already relatively integrated into the eurozone through trade and investment links (see, for example, Rostowski 2003; Walter *et al.* 2006).

These differences in the level of economic development, which reflects productivity differentials as well as economic structures, strengthen the importance of flexibility of new member state economies. Flexibility is going to be the key factor in coping with economic shocks and developing towards sustainable convergence with the rest of eurozone.

Although it has been admitted that new member states are relatively more flexible than the eurozone members (Alhearne and Pisani-Ferry 2006: 7), relatively

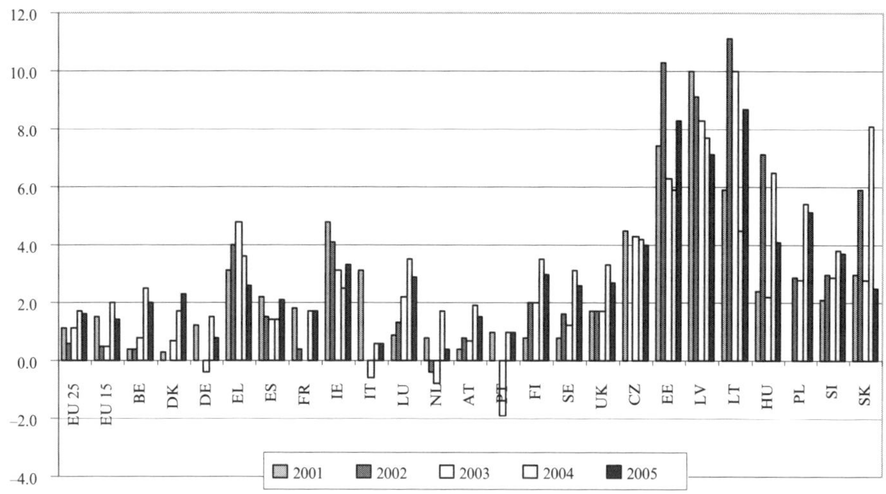

Figure 10.5 Growth Rates of Real GDP per capita in the EU Members

Source: Eurostat

little attention has been given to the indicators of flexibility. Internal flexibility could be evaluated on the basis of international surveys assessing the flexibility of labor markets, wages and other variables.

To sum up, the new member states that aspire to join the monetary union compare relatively well in terms of internal flexibility of factors of production with the current eurozone members, although the latter show significant differences. As it will be argued in the next section, the issue of domestic economic flexibility will reinforce the debates about the implementation of the Lisbon agenda, the advantages of different economic and social models which exist in Europe and their prospects in the global economy. Such a discourse could have important political implications for the domestic policies of the current eurozone members, the prospective enlargement of the eurozone and further deepening of integration in the EU.

The Political Economy of Enlarging the Eurozone

The creation of the eurozone from the very start has been surrounded by debates about the political motives and institutional implications of pooling sovereignty in the field of monetary policy. Interestingly, most economic writings on the creation of the monetary union eventually admit that only political economy factors can explain the timing and the choice of the design of monetary union.

Similarly, the enlargement of the eurozone is going to become an important political project which could, on the one hand, be seen as an important sign of the attractiveness and vitality of the eurozone and the EU. If the current (probably

Table 10.2 GDP per capita in PPS (EU–25=100)

	1996	2002	2004	2005F	2006F
Eurozone	110.7	107.7	106.7	106.2	105.7
EU15	109.5	109.4	108.6	108.2	107.9
Belgium	118.0	117.5	118.4	117.5	117.5
Germany	118.0	108.6	108.6	108.1	107.4
Greece	69.8	77.2	82.0	83.6	84.7
Spain	86.9	95.2	97.6	98.3	98.2
France	112.8	112.2	109.3	108.9	108.2
Ireland	102.2	132.9	137.0	138.4	139.8
Italy	115.5	110.1	105.8	103.6	103.1
Luxembourg	196.5	220.3	238.6	243.3	247.7
Netherlands	119.1	125.3	124.4	123.7	123.6
Austria	126.4	119.9	122.6	122.5	121.9
Portugal	74.8	79.5	72.4	71.2	70.0
Finland	103.9	114.7	113.9	113.6	115.2
Sweden	115.6	113.7	117.4	118.4	119.2
UK	109.0	116.0	116.2	115.9	115.8
Czech Republic	70.0*	66.3	70.3	73.3	75.0
Estonia	34.7*	45.0	51.2	55.8	58.2
Latvia	30.2*	38.7	42.8	46.8	49.5
Lithuania	34.7*	41.9	47.8	51.0	53.3
Hungary	48.4*	58.1	60.1	61.9	63.2
Poland	42.1*	46.3	48.8	49.8	51.0
Slovenia	68.9*	74.5	79.1	80.9	82.5
Slovakia	45.5*	51.0	53.0	55.4	57.3

* Estimate.

Source: Eurostat.

too optimistic) plans for the enlargement of the euro area materialize with nine countries joining it between 2007 and 2010, its population will increase from 309 million to 345 million, and if all current EU members with a derogation are accepted, it would increase by additional 47 million (Commission of the European Communities 2005: 4). On the other hand, the growth of economic weight of the eurozone will be significantly smaller than its population growth: under the first scenario its aggregate GDP will increase by only 3.7 per cent, while under the second its GDP would grow by further 6.2 per cent. It might be

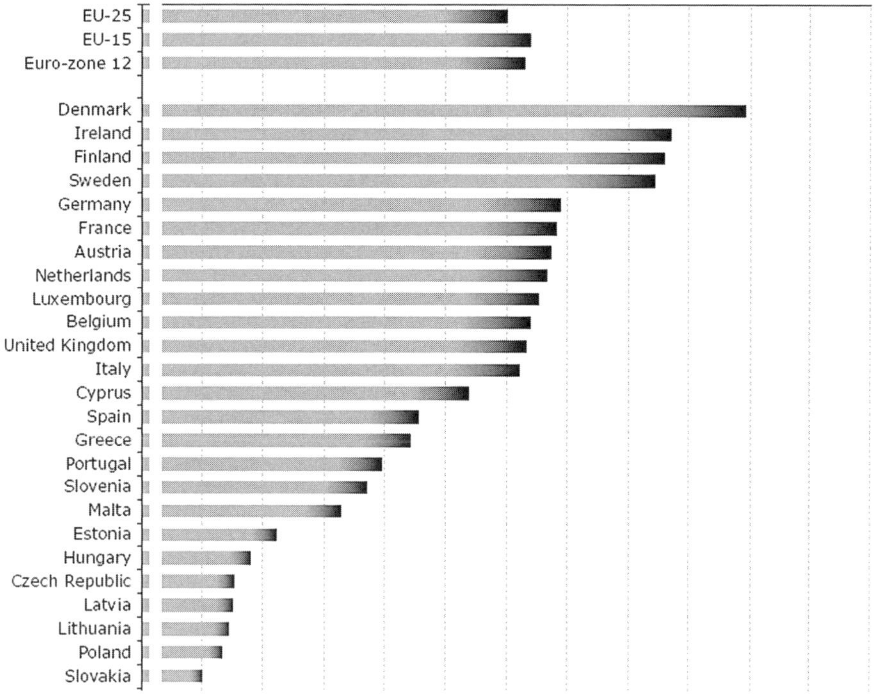

Figure 10.6 Comparative Price Levels in 2003

(Comparative price levels of final consumption by private households, including indirect taxes EU–25=100)

Source: Eurostat.

interpreted as leading to more difficulties in making decisions affecting directly wider market with a relatively insignificant increase in its economic weight,that is, less coherence with relatively insignificant gains in economic weight. Moreover, the accession of new members into the euro area might be surrounded by similar political interpretations as the enlargement of the EU about its consequences for the further deepening of integration in the EU. In general, as some analysts note, "today's European political mood is at odds with idealism of the euro's creators" (Atkins 2006: 3).

It should be noted that accession of the new EU members into the eurozone has been discussed in academic writings by raising a number of points. In the economic writings, as prior to the creation of the euro area, the optimum currency area model has been used to assess the implications of enlarging the monetary union, attention has been given to the optimum strategies for new members of coping with divergent growth rates and possible asymmetric and the resulting need to chose the best regime of exchange rate mechanism during the accession into the ERMII and later into the eurozone (see, for example, de Grauwe and Schnabl 2004), the meaning of convergence criteria (Folsz 2003), the revision of the Stability and Growth Pact on the basis of forecasted effects of eurozone

Table 10.3 Economic Freedom Index, WEF and Investment Climate Survey Indicators of New Member and Old Member States

Country	Economic Freedom Index	Growth Competitiveness Index (by WEF)		Doing Business (World Bank)
EU–25	2005	2005	2004	2006
Belgium	22	21	25	18
Czech Republic	21	38	40	41
Denmark	8	4	4	8
Germany	19	15	13	19
Estonia	7	20	20	16
Greece	57	46	37	80
Spain	33	29	23	30
France	44	30	27	44
Ireland	3	26	30	11
Italy	42	47	47	70
Latvia	39	44	44	26
Lithuania	23	43	36	15
Luxembourg	4	25	26	—
Hungary	40	39	39	52
Netherlands	16	11	12	24
Austria	18	21	17	32
Poland	41	51	60	54
Portugal	30	22	24	42
Slovenia	38	32	33	63
Slovakia	34	41	43	37
Finland	12	1	1	13
Sweden	19	3	3	14
UK	5	13	11	9

Source: Eurostat.*Sources*: Deutsche Bank Research, April 2006; National Central Banks.

enlargement (Schelkle 2004: 890–908), and the timing of accession (Rostowski 2003). Other authors focused on the institutional issues of enlarging the euro area, in particular, the impact of accession on the functioning of the European Central Bank, the transparency, legitimacy and efficiency of its monetary policy (Heisenberg 2003: 397–420).

However, what has received relatively little attention is the potential political effect of enlarging the monetary union to the domestic discourses about structural reforms in the founders of the EU and the eurozone linked to the broader debates about competitiveness. Although it has been argued that the enlargement of the euro area might reinforce pressures on the labor markets of Germany and other founders of the monetary union and thereby make them reluctant to show their support for this project (Rostowski 2003), the issue of economic flexibility in the context of ongoing structural reforms merits more attention. The recent focus on protective measures and "national champions" in some eurozone members as well as controversy surrounding the adoption of the services directive are good indications of political sensitivities that surround the issue of structural reforms and increasing competition. The enlargement of the EU has already been associated with the growing labor competition from the new members and the enlargement of the eurozone might only reinforce this perception.

Furthermore, if the public statements of the French and other political leaders can be an indication of the political significance that French and some other founding members attach to the monetary union and single currency, the eurozone is projected as a basis for the future possible projects of enhanced cooperation among the core of EU member states (Parker and Atkins 2006: 4). This is not a new vision and rather reflects the old debates about the need accompany the monetary union by closer political union as an instrument of democratic legitimization (Gros 2006: 1). The most frequently mentioned examples of enhanced cooperation include harmonization of direct taxes and alignment of social policies. Both possibilities are regarded with caution by most new member states of the EU, and therefore their participation could be seen as a potential break for the initiation of deeper integration.

To conclude, the first round of new members' accessions into the eurozone could have important implications for the discourse about the monetary policy in the EU, its relationship to domestic structural reforms and the new projects of (deeper) integration. This is reviving the debates not only similar to the ones which have been present during the creation of the monetary union, but also to the arguments about the benefits and potential side effects of EU enlargement. Although the Maastricht criteria are more precisely defined than EU membership criteria, it is still going to be politically charged process with political reasoning and implications behind the technical decisions.

References

Alhearne, A. and Pisani-Ferry, J. (2006), "The Euro: Only for the Agile", Bruegel Policy Brief No. 1: 1, 7.

Atkins, R. (January 2006), "Bundesbank Warns on Eurozone Rush", *Financial Times*, January 23, 2006, 2.

Atkins, R. (February 2006), "Heading Up or Tailing Off? Why Eurozone Economic Recovery Hangs in the Balance", *Financial Times*, February 16, 2006, 3. See http://www.ft.com.

Baldwin, R., Francois, J.F. and Portes, R. (April 1997), "The Costs and Benefits of Eastern Enlargement: The Impact on the EU and Central Europe", *Economic Policy* 24, 127–170.

Commission of the European Communities, Communication from the Commission to the Council, the European Parliament, the European Economic and Social Committee, the Committee of the Regions and the European Central Bank. (2005), "Second Report on the Practical Preparations for the Future Enlargement of the Euro Area", November 4, 2005, COM, 545 final, Brussels.

Financial Times (2006), "Poland Could Be the Last New Member State to Adopt the Euro", February 17, 2006. See http://www.ft.com.

Folsz, A. (2003), "The Monetary Framework after Accession – A Political Economy Analysis of the ERMII", European Integration Online Papers, No. 2.

Grauwe, P. and Schnabl, G. (2004), "Nominal versus Real Convergence with Respect to EMU Accession. How to Cope with Balassa-Samuelson Dilemma", EUI RSC Working Paper No. 2004/20.

Gros, D. (January 2006), "Will EMU Survive 2010?", Center for European Policy Studies, 1.

Gulde, A.-M., Kahkonen, J. and Keller, P. (January 2000), *Pros and Cons of Currency Board Arrangements in the Lead-up to EU Accession and Participation in the Eurozone*, IMF Discussion Paper PDP/00/1.

Heisenberg, D. (2003), "Cutting the Bank Down to Size: Efficient and Legitimate Decision-Making in the European Central Bank after Enlargement", *Journal of Common Market Studies*, vol. 41, no. 3, 397–420.

Katsimi, M. (2004), *Exchange Rate Strategies towards EMU for Accession Countries with Currency Boards*, EUI RSC Working Paper No. 2004/18.

Mody, A. and Rosenberg, C. (February 2006), Letters to Editor: Why Lithuania and Estonia Could Fare Well in Eurozone, *Financial Times*, February 8, 2006, 14.

Munchau, W. (January 2006), "Monetary Union Is Not for the Poor", *Financial Times*, January 30, 2006, 15.

Parker, G. and Atkins, R. (2006), "Eurozone Rules under Fire as Lithuania Fails to Join", *Financial Times*, May 16, 2006, 2.

Parket, G. and Condon, C. (2006), "Slovenia Gets Euro Go-Ahead but Lithuania's Inflation Too High", *Financial Times*, May 16, 2006, 2.

Rostowski, J. (October 2003), "When Should the Central Europeans Join the EMU?" (Warsaw: Center for Social and Economic Research).

Schelkle, W. (October 2004), "EMU's Second Chance: Enlargement and the Reform of Fiscal Policy Coordination", *Journal of European Public Policy*, vol. 11, no. 5, 890–908.

Tiusanen, T. and Kinnunen, J. (2005), "EU's Eastern Enlargement and the Future Expansion of the Eurozone", Laappeenranta University of Technology, Northern Dimension Research Center, Publication 23.

Walter, N. *et al.* (2006), "Estonia, Lithuania, Slovenia: Poised to Adopt Euro. Views on Medium and Long-Term Convergence", Deutsche Bank Research, April 3, 2006.

Chapter 11

The Euro and Economic Reforms: The Case of Spain

Sebastián Royo

Introduction

In 2006 Spain commemorated twenty years of European Union membership. EU integration was a catalyst for the final conversion of the Spanish economy into a modern Western-type economy. Indeed, one of the key consequences of its entry into Europe has been that membership has facilitated the modernization of its economy (see Tovias 2002). This is not to say, however, that membership was the only reason for this development. The economic liberalization, trade integration, and modernization of the Spanish economy started in the 1950s and 1960s and Spain became increasingly prosperous over the two decades prior to EU accession.

Yet the actual accession of Spain after 1986 forced the political and economic actors to adopt economic policies and business strategies consistent with membership and the *acquis communautaire* (which included the custom union, the Value Added Tax (VAT), the Common Agriculture and Fisheries Polices and the external trade agreements; and later the Single Market, the Exchange Rate Mechanism (ERM) and the European Monetary Union).

EU membership also facilitated the micro and macro economic reforms that successive Spanish governments undertook throughout the 1980s and 1990s. In a context of strong support among Spanish citizens for integration, membership became a facilitating mechanism that allowed the government to prioritize economic rather than social modernization and hence, to pursue difficult economic and social policies (that is, to reform their labor and financial markets), with short-term painful effects. Moreover, the decision to comply with the EMU Maastricht Treaty criteria led to the implementation of macro and microeconomic policies that resulted in fiscal consolidation, central bank independence, and wage moderation.

The overall economic results have been very beneficial. Spain has closed the wealth gap with the richest European countries (*El País*, January 2, 2006). In 20 years per capita income has grown 20 points, 1 point per year, to reach close to 90 per cent of the EU–15 average. With the EU–25, Spain has already reached the average. It has grown on average 1.4 percentage points more than the EU since 1996, as shown in Figure 11.1.

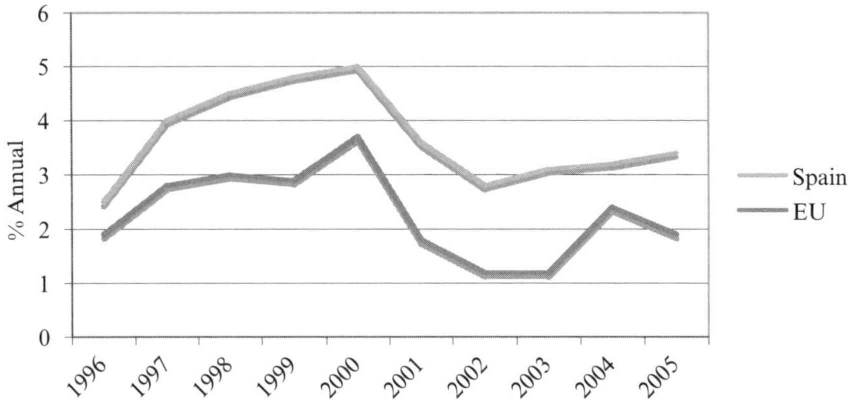

Figure 11.1 GDP Growth

Furthermore, the Spanish economy has led an extraordinary process of convergence and has integrated into the international economy. The integration with Europe has deepened: 90 per cent of the foreign direct investment (FDI), 87 per cent of the tourists, 74 per cent of the exports and 66 per cent of the imports come form the EU. EU integration has also allowed Spanish companies and people to access international markets, expand internationally and access capital abroad. One of the outcomes of this process has been the growing importance of Spanish multinational firms (like Telefonica, Banco de Santader and ACS), which have become leaders in their markets.

Spain has also benefited extensively from European funds: approximately 150,000 million euros were received from agricultural, regional development, training and cohesion programs. These funds have represented 24 per cent of the annual agrarian income (80,000 million euros in twenty years). They have also contributed to the dramatic improvement of infrastructures (40,000 euros in twenty years): in 1986 Spain had 773 km of highways, in 2006 6,267 km, and 4 km in every 10 have been funded with European funds; in 1986 it did not have any high-speed trains. Today it has three lines and, for every 100 euros invested in trains, 38 have come from Europe. Currently there are nine major ongoing infrastructure projects that will be partially funded with EU funds. Spain has also received 12,000 million euros from the cohesion funds that have helped fund projects such as the high-speed train from Madrid to Barcelona (3,518 million in EU funds). While these funds represent "only" 1 per cent of the FDI they have played a central role because they have generated opportunities that have led to initiatives and reforms that have been key for the modernization of the Spanish economy.

The integration process also faced difficulties. The process of industrial restructuring was very painful and destroyed thousands of jobs (unemployment reached 23 per cent in the early 1990s). The elimination of the corporate tax and the introduction of the VAT in the 1980s were also traumatic. EU integration also brought more controls and accountability to public financial accounts. Moreover, the 1992 crisis of the European Monetary System was devastating for the Spanish economy: it led to three devaluations and the destruction of most of the jobs that had been created in the second half of the 1980s. Finally, the decision to join the European Monetary Union was also painful: it imposed fiscal consolidation.

The overall effects of EMU have also been positive: it has contributed to macroeconomic stability, it has imposed fiscal discipline and central bank independence, and it has lowered dramatically the cost of capital. As we will see, without the euro the huge trade deficit would have already forced a devaluation and the implementation of more restrictive fiscal policies. Despite all these achievements the Spanish economy still faces serious competitive challenges. This chapter will illustrate that EU and EMU membership have not led to the implementation of the structural reforms necessary to address these challenges. On the contrary, EMU has contributed to the economic boom fueled by record-low interest rates, thus facilitating the postponement of necessary economic reforms. Spain faces a competitiveness challenge that requires significant structural reforms. This challenge, however, is not a problem of European institutions, but of national policies. I will conclude that the process of economic reforms has to be a domestic process led by domestic actors willing to carry them out.

The chapter is divided into five sections. The first one examines the main economic consequences of European membership for the Spanish economy. The second analyzes the economic convergence process and its challenges. The third section discusses the deterioration in the competitiveness of the Spanish economy and its symptoms. The fourth one explores the main shortcomings of the Spanish economy. The chapter closes with some recommendations to address the competitive challenges.

Spain in the European Union

Since 1986 the Spanish economy has undergone profound economic changes. EU membership has led to policy and institutional reforms in the following economic areas: monetary and exchange rate policies (first independent coordination, followed by accession to the ERM, and finally EMU membership); reform of the tax system (that is, the introduction of the VAT and reduction of import duties); and a fiscal consolidation process. These changes have led to deep processes of structural reforms aimed at macroeconomic stability and the strengthening of competitiveness of the productive sector. On the supply side, these reforms sought the development of well-functioning capital markets, the promotion of efficiency in public services, and the enhancement of flexibility in the labor market. As a result markets and prices for a number of goods and services have been deregulated and liberalized; the labor market has been the subject of limited deregulatory reforms; a privatization program was started in the early 1980s to roll back the presence of the government in the economy and to increase the overall efficiency of the system; and competition policy was adapted to EU regulations. In sum, from an economic standpoint the combined impetuses of European integration and economic modernization have resulted in the outcomes shown in Figure 11.2.

• The end of economic isolation	• Increasing competition
• Institutional reforms	• Industrial restructuring
• Tax harmonization	• Capital flow liberalization
• Openness of the Iberian economies	• Deregulation
• Nominal convergence	• Lower inflation
• Capital infrastructure effort	• Fiscal consolidation
• Financial liberalization	• Cohesion policies
• Central Bank independence	• Lower nominal interest rates
• Privatization	• Internationalization
• FDI in Iberia	• Higher efficiency
• Labor market reform	• Deregulation
• Reduction in government subsidies	• Economic growth

Figure 11.2 The Spanish Economic Transformation

At the time of accession, it was considered that a critical factor in determining the final outcome of integration would depend upon the pattern of investment, which would bring about important *dynamic effects*. Spain had a number of attractions as a production base, including good infrastructure, an educated and cheap labor force and access to a market with a growing potential. In addition, EC entry would add the incentive of further access to the EC countries for non-EC Iberian investors – for example, Japan or the United States. As expected, one of the key outcomes of integration has been a dramatic increase in foreign direct investment, from less than 2 per cent to more than 6 per cent of GDP over the last decade. This development has been the result of the following processes: economic integration, larger potential growth, lower exchange rate risk, lower economic uncertainty and institutional reforms. EU membership has also resulted in more tourism (which has become one of the main sources of income for Spain).

Another significant dynamic effect has been the strengthening of Spanish firms' competitive position. As a result of enlargement Spanish producers gained access to the European market, which provided additional incentives for investment and allowed for the development of economies of scale, resulting in increasing competitiveness. By the 1980s, Spain was already facing increasing competition for its main exports – clothing, textiles, leather – from countries in the Far East and Latin America, which produced all these goods at a cheaper costs by exploiting their low wages. As a result of this development, the latter countries were attracting foreign investment in sectors where traditionally Spain had been favored. This situation convinced the Spanish leaders that they had to shift toward more capital-intensive industries requiring greater skills in the labor force but relying on standard technology –for example, chemicals, vehicles, steel and metal manufacturing. In this regard, Spain's entry to the EC facilitated this shift. Indeed, the country gained access to the EC market, thus attracting investment that would help build these new industries. Finally, Spain also benefited from the EU financial assistance programs – the European Regional Development Fund, the Social Fund, the Agriculture Guidance and Guarantee Fund, the newly created Integrated Mediterranean Program for agriculture and later on from the Structural and Cohesion Funds.

EU integration has also allowed the Spanish economy to become integrated internationally and to modernize, thus securing convergence in nominal terms with Europe. As a result of these reforms, the process of financial liberalization, and the significant decline in real interest rates, Spain was successful meeting the Maastricht convergence criteria (see Table 11.1). Indeed, on January 1, 1999, Spain became a founding member of the European Monetary Union. In the end, the country, which as late as 1997 was considered an outside candidate for joining the eurozone, fulfilled the inflation, interest rates, debt, exchange rate and public deficit requirements established by the Maastricht Treaty. This development confirmed the nominal convergence of the country with the rest of the EU.

Table 11.1 Compliance of the EMU Convergence Criteria for Spain 1993–2004

Year	Inflation (per cent growth)	Long-term interest rate	Public sector deficit (as per cent of GDP)	Government debt (as per cent of GDP)
1993	4.6	10.2	6.9	60.0
1994	4.7	10.0	6.3	62.6
1995	4.7	11.3	7.3	65.5
1996	3.6	8.7	4.6	70.1
1997	1.9	6.4	2.6	68.8
2004	3.3	3.64	0.3	62.6

Source: Commission and EMU Reports.

The EU contributed significantly to this development. Indeed, structural and cohesion funds have been the instruments designed by the EU to develop social and cohesion policy within the European Union, in order to compensate for the efforts countries with the lowest per capita income relative to the EU (Ireland, Greece, Portugal and Spain) would need to make to comply with the nominal convergence criteria. These funds, which amount to just over one-third of the

EU budget, have contributed significantly to reducing regional disparities and foster convergence within the EU. As a result major infrastructure shortcomings have been addressed and road and telecommunication networks have improved dramatically both in quantity and quality. In addition, increasing spending on education and training have contributed to the upgrading of the labor force. In sum, these funds have played a prominent role in developing the factors that improve the competitiveness and determine the potential growth of the least developed regions of the country (Sebastián 2001: 25–26).

During the 1994–1999 period, EU aid accounted for 1.5 per cent of GDP in Spain and, for instance, in 2001 Spain was allocated nearly 63 per cent of the EU's structural funds budget (US$ 27.8 billion). Overall in absolute terms Spain is the country that has benefited the most from the structural and cohesion funds. Between 1989 and 2006 it received (excluding the funds from the Common Agricultural Policy CAP) more than 100,000 million euros (at 1999 prices). In 2005 Spain received 7.878 billion euros from the structural and cohesion funds (24 per cent of the total or 50 per cent of the cohesion ones: 1.386 billion). EU funding has allowed rates of public investment to remain relatively stable since the mid-1980s. Indeed, the percentage of public investment financed by EU funds has been rising since 1985, to reach average values of 15 per cent for Spain. Moreover, the European Commission has estimated that the impact of EU structural funds on GDP growth and employment has been significant: GDP rose in 1999 by 3.1 per cent in Spain. Overall, these funds, given their impact on the demand side (public work and so on) and on the supply side (they have increased the productive capacity of the Spanish economy), have contributed to economic growth. It is estimated that on average these funds have added 0.4 percentage points to yearly economic growth during the 1989–2006 period, or the equivalent of 600 euros per habitant and per year (Herce 2006: 4, Negocios). The 2007–2013 EU budget agreement guarantees that Spain will be a net recipient until that date, but the bulk of the funds will be channeled to the new member states (representing between 3–4 per cent of their GDP, which will allow them to create 2.5 million jobs).

In sum, the combined impetuses of lowering trade barriers, the introduction of the VAT, the suppression of import tariffs, the adoption of economic policy rules (such as quality standards or the harmonization of indirect taxes), and the increasing mobility of goods and factors of production that come with greater economic integration, have boosted trade and enhanced the openness of the Spanish economy. After 1999, this development has been fostered by the lower cost of transactions and greater exchange rate stability associated with the single currency. For instance, imports of goods and services in real terms as a proportion of GDP rose sharply in Spain (to 13.6 per cent in 1987 from 9.6 per cent in 1984), while the share of exports shrank slightly (to 15.8 per cent of GDP from 16.6 per cent in 1984, and from 17.1 per cent of real GDP in 1992 to 27 per cent in 1997). As a result, the degree of openness of the Spanish economy has increased sharply over the last twenty years. Henceforth, changes to the production structure and in the structure of exports, indicators of the degree of competitiveness of the Spanish economy (that is, in terms of human capital skills, stock of capital, technological capital) show important improvements, although significant differences remain in comparison to the leading developed economies (which confirms the need to press ahead with structural reforms). These achievements verify that in terms of economic stability Spain is part of Europe's "rich club".

This economic success however, has fostered a sense of complacency, which has allowed for a delay in the adoption of necessary structural reforms. Despite all the significant progress accomplished during the past two decades, Spain still has considerable ground to cover to catch up with the richer EU countries and to improve the competitiveness of its economy. Given the existing income and productivity differentials with the richer EU countries, Spain has to continue and intensify the reform process.

Convergence with the EU

The above section highlights the benefits of EU and euro membership for the Spanish economy. Yet the process of nominal convergence has advanced at a faster pace than real convergence. The country's income levels remain behind the EU average, as shown in Table 11.2.

Table 11.2 Divergence of GDP Per Capita 1980–2004

	1980	1985	1990	2000	2004
EU totals	100.0%	100.0%	100.0%t	100.0%	100.0%
Spain	74.2%	72.5%	77.8%	81.0%	97.2%

Source: European Union.

Indeed, twenty years have not been enough. While there is significant controversy over the definition of real convergence, most scholars agree that a per capita GDP is a valid reference to measure the living standards of a country. This variable, however, has experienced a cyclical evolution in Spain with significant increases during periods of economic expansion and sharp decreases during economic recessions. Spain's European integration has revealed both convergence and divergence, nominal and real. As we will see below, since 1997 inflation in Spain has exceeded the EU average every year.

Since the new EU member states that joined in 2004 are significantly poorer, enlargement has reduced the EU's average gross domestic product per capita by between 10–20 per cent. This is the so-called "statistical effect". Before enlargement (and the statistical effect) per capita income had increased "only" 16 percentage point in Spain since 1986. In Portugal the figure was 14.2 per cent, and in Ireland, by contrast, it increased 38 per cent. Only Greece, with an increase of 6.8 per cent, has had lower real convergence than Spain and Portugal. A possible explanation for this development has been the fact that while Spain grew between 1990 and 1998 an average of 2.1 per cent, Portugal grew 2.5 per cent, and Ireland

7.3 per cent over the same period. This growth differential explains the divergences in real convergence. Other explanations include the higher level of unemployment (on average 15 per cent in Spain during the last decade); the low rate of labor participation (active population over total population, which currently stands at 61 per cent; expanding the Spanish labor participation rate to the EU average would increase per capita income to 98.2 per cent of the EU average); the inadequate education of the labor force (only 28 per cent of the Spanish potential labor force has at least a high school diploma, in contrast with the EU average of 56 per cent); low investment in research and development (R&D) and information technology (the lowest in the EU, with Spain ranking 61st – spending even less proportionally than many developing countries including Vietnam – in the World Economic Forum's *Global Report of Information Technologies 2002–2003*) and relative poor infrastructure (road mile per 1,000 inhabitants in Spain is 47 per cent of the EU average and railroads stand at 73 per cent). The inadequate structure of the labor market, with high dismissal costs, a relatively centralized collective bargaining system and a system of unemployment benefits that guarantees income instead of fostering job search, have also hindered the convergence process (*El País*, February 14, 2000).

An important factor in the convergence surge after 2000 was the substantive revision of the Spanish GDP data as a result of changes in the National Accounts from 1995–2000. These changes represented an increase in GPD per capita of 4 per cent in real terms (the equivalent of Slovakia's GDP). This dramatic change was the result of the significant growth of the Spanish population since 1998 as a result of the surge in immigration (in 2003 population grew 2.1 per cent). The inclusion of the new population data in the 2001 census resulted in the revision of all the macroeconomic data. Spain's per capita income has moved closer to the EU average, growing from 73.7 per cent in 1986 (the year of accession), to 79.1 per cent in 1992 (SEA) and 83.4 per cent in 1999 (EMU). If we take into account the twenty-five member states, the growth differential has also been positively increased from 88.2 per cent in 1996 to 97.2 per cent in 2004 (or 89.7 per cent in terms of the EU–15). Between 2000 and 2004 the Spanish economy experienced a rapid process of convergence increasing four points and reaching 97.2 per cent. This development was the consequence of three factors: (1) demographic changes (the percentage of the working age population over total population), (2) the participation rate (the percentage of people employed over the working age population) and (3) labor productivity (GDP/ number of people employed), as shown in Table 11.3.

The key factor in this acceleration of convergence, given the negative behavior of productivity (if productivity had grown at the EU average, Spain would have surpassed the EU per capita average by three points), has been the important increase in the participation rate, which was the result of the reduction in unemployment, and the increase in the activity rate (proportion of people of working age that has a job or is actively seeking for one) that followed the incorporation of female workers into the labor market and immigration growth. Indeed between 2000 and 2004 the immigration population has multiplied by three and has grown from 0.9 million to 2.8 million (Oficina Económica del Presidente October 2005).

Table 11.3 The Determinants of Real Convergence in Spain 2000–2004 (EU–25=100)

	Per capita rent	Labor productivity	Participation rate	Demographic factor
2000	92.7	99.0	91.8	102.4
2004	97.2	96.8	98.5	102.8
Difference	+4.5	–2.2	+6.7	+0.4

Source: OEP 2005, 18.

The Loss of Competitiveness

During the last decade Spain has accumulated intense disequilibria. While the economy continues with robust growth (3.1 per cent in 2004 and 3.4 per cent in 2005; more than double the rate in the eurozone area as a whole), economic success is on shaky ground because it is being driven by the construction industry and private consumption. Indeed, robust economic growth cannot mask worrying imbalances in the existing economic model in which growth is largely driven by domestic demand: strengths in consumption (domestic demand has increased at rates of 10 per cent in 2005) and residential investment, combined with high indebtedness levels (110 per cent of the available income), and the negative contribution of the external sector to growth (for example, in 2005 it rested two points to growth). This pattern is not sustainable.

One of the consequences of EMU membership for Spain has been the convergence of interest rates, which declined more than twelve percentage points since 1996. This has led to record-low interest rates in the country (negative in real terms) and an explosion in credit and mortgages. Over the last decade and a half, financial deregulation, rising incomes (linked to the lower unemployment rates), immigration growth and strong demand from foreigners (increasing by a multiple of six compared to the first half of the 1990s), who have been purchasing real state in Spain, have all led to an upsurge of real state demand. Consequently prices have increased 130 per cent since 1997 (on average nominal prices went up 17 per cent annually over the last few years), and the ratio of average house prices to average incomes in comparatively much higher than in other countries. According to some estimates, construction makes up to almost 17 per cent of GDP (between 1985–1995 it represented an average of 13.5 per cent) and residential construction reached 8.3 per cent of GDP in 2004 (between 1985–1995 it represented an average of 13.5 per cent) (Gros 2005). The US market has grown moderately in comparison. This situation has led some observers to talk about a "real estate bubble". While the empirical evidence is not conclusive, there is no question that this situation is risky. Since most mortgages have variable rates, the savings rate is very low, and the rate of indebtedness of Spanish families has increased (before 1990 it represented 60 per cent of disposable income and since then it has grown to 110 per cent), mortgage holders are very vulnerable to interest rate increases from the ECB.

The real estate bubble has overshadowed the lack of competitiveness of the Spanish economy. The degree of competitiveness is a critical variable to establish the potential for growth and development of economies in the short and medium terms because it helps determine the share of domestic demand that is satisfied with products from abroad and the share of external demand that is satisfied with internal production. In this regard, the loss of competitiveness of the Spanish economy is a very worrisome development. The current account deficit is a key symptom of Spain's loss of competitiveness.

The Trade Deficit

Spain has a very open economy: exports represented 25.7 per cent of GDP in 2004 and imports 29.3 per cent. Yet Spain's trade deficit has widened sharply and has caused a blowout in the current account shortfall, which has reached 7 per cent of GDP, the highest in the industrialized world. Indeed, Spain has developed a "dual economy" in which the manufacturing/industrial sector on the one hand and the service/construction one on the other, have diverged in terms of performance. While the construction sector is booming (over 700,000 houses were built in Spain in 2004, more than the total in France, Germany, Belgium, Holland and Luxembourg combined), manufacturing production regressed 0.4 per cent in 2005 (the automobile sector declined almost 9 per cent in 2005) and exports are not experiencing almost any growth.

The pressure on the manufacturing sector has intensified in the last two decades. By the 1980s Spanish firms were already facing increasing competition for their main exports – clothing, textiles, leather – from countries in the Far East and Latin America, which produced all these goods at a cheaper costs exploiting their low wages. As a result of this development, the latter countries were attracting foreign investment in sectors where traditionally Spain had been favored. These concerns intensified further due to increasing fears about new competition from the central and eastern European countries after the enlargement of the European Union (Sebastián 2001: 22). The major source of concern was due to the fact that these countries specialize in labor-intensive and low-to-medium technology products (such as machinery, electrical equipment, textile goods and automobiles), sectors that make up a large proportion of Spanish trade (7.4 per cent, 7.3 per cent, 4.5 per cent and 20 per cent, respectively, of total Spanish exports to the EU–15), and in which competitiveness via prices is of particular importance. At the same time, in the central and eastern European countries labor costs are between 20 per cent and 60 per cent lower than those of the EU.

Furthermore, the increasing threat of outsourcing (for example, companies like Samsung, Philips, Panasonic and Levi's have closed their plants in Catalonia in the last few years) and the worrisome pattern of decreasing foreign direct investment (FDI) coming into Spain (it has fallen in half during the 2000–2003 period, from 40,728 million euros in 2000 to 22,705 million in 2003), have intensified the pressure on manufacturing firms. In 2005 FDI started to recover with an increase of 71 per cent or 17.3 billion euros.

The lack of competitiveness is reflected in the record trade deficit. Spain's current account deficit for the first eleven months of 2005 reached 7.35 per cent of GDP (61 billion euros or $75 billion), increasing almost 60 per cent between January and November 2005 (with exports up 4.45 and imports up 11.4 per cent). To place this figure in perspective, in the US the deficit is 5.8 per cent. This imbalance has been affected by the soaring cost of energy imports, which have risen 40 per cent since 2004. The European Commission has estimated that the current account deficit in 2006 will reach 8.3 per cent in 2005 and 9.1 per cent in 2007. These levels are not sustainable.

Several reasons explain the evolution of the trade deficit:

1. The decoupling between production and domestic demand: increasing internal demand has led to a growth in imports that has been hindered by the appreciation of the euro, the crisis in the larger European economies, and the growing competition from other countries.
2. The savings rate is insufficient to cover investment projects. The current account deficit shows the disequilibria between savings and private investment. While the public sector is no longer in deficit, the private one shows a large deficit (particularly the one from non-financial societies).
3. Spanish exports are concentrated in a few markets. 70 per cent of Spanish exports go to the EU–15. Yet, the average growth of Spanish markets in the last five years has been 4.5 per cent, while global markets grew 7 per cent. The slow growth of European economies has had a deleterious effect on Spanish exports,
4. The limited degree of technological sophistication of Spanish products. High technology exports only represent 8 per cent of the total (less than half of the EU–15 average). Most Spanish exports are labor intensive, which make them very vulnerable (Oficina Económica del Presidente October 2005: 27–28).

Challenges

One of the main lessons from EMU is that countries should join only when their economies are sufficiently flexible. Indeed in order to prosper in a monetary union, countries need a sufficient degree of wage and price flexibility. Unfortunately the Spanish successive governments have failed to implement the necessary reforms to increase the flexibility of the economy and consequently, as we have seen, Spain has gradually lost competitiveness against the rest of the EMU countries. At the root of this problem lie the following shortcomings.

Inflation

Inflation remains one of the main economic challenges for the Spanish economy. The Spanish inflation rate has exceeded the eurozone's by an average of more than 1 percentage point each year and in 2004 the gap widened to 1.5 points. In 2005, once again, it finished the year with disappointing results. The consumer price index (CPI) jumped to an annual 4.2 per cent, almost doubling the government estimates for the year, and 1.8 points higher than in the eurozone as a whole. This is the worst result since 2002, when it reached 4 per cent. While this increase has been largely attributed to the oil and food (particularly olive oil) price increases, it further damaged the already deteriorating competitiveness of the Spanish economy. The price differential between Spain and the eurozone stood at the end of 2005 at 1.8 points (2.4 per cent in the eurozone), the highest among all the eurozone members and the third largest of all the EU members (only ahead of Slovakia and Lithuania). This is the highest differential since 2003 and unfortunately there are no signs that it will be abating, as shown in Table 11.4.

Table 11.4 CPI Evolution in January

	1997	1998	1999	2000	2001	2002	2003	2004	2005	2006
Variation	2.8	1.9	1.5	2.9	2.9	3.1	3.8	2.3	3.1	4.2

Source: INE.

Most observers attribute the growing differential in Spain's inflation rate with the eurozone to the fact that there continue to be barriers to entry in the service sector, particularly in the gas and electricity sectors (*El País*, February 18, 2006). Persistent high inflation also undermines Spain's economic growth and undercuts the ability of Spanish exporters to compete with other European countries. A continuation of this pattern for a few more years would wipe out Spanish exports.

The Labor Market

Employment figures have been very positive: employment grew in 2005 over 3 per cent (0.4 more than in 2004) and the participation rate has grown from 56.3 per cent in 2000 to 61.1 per cent in 2004 closing the gap with the EU average 65 per cent. In 2005 the Spanish economy created 894,000 jobs (4.9 per cent more in 2004), the total number of employed people reached 19,314,300, and unemployment declined to 8.7 per cent the lowest figure in decades. These impressive results, however, cannot mask the weakness of this development: the temporary rate has grown from 30.8 per cent in 2004 to 33.7 per cent in 2005, the highest by far in Europe; productivity rates have been negative (declined 1.3 per cent in 2005); and there are wide disparities in the quality of work between men and women. Indeed, according to the OECD, women's wages are almost 20 per cent lower than men's (in Europe the average is 16 per cent); female unemployment is at 11.6 per cent – twice as high as male unemployment; the "glass ceiling" is hard to break (more than two-thirds of Spain's top 35 listed companies have no female board directors, and only 6 per cent of directorships are held by women) and female workers are more likely to be stuck in low-paid short-term work (*Financial Times*, March 4–5, 2006: 2).[1]

The lack of competitiveness has been further hastened by the spectacular growth of temporary employment, which has helped to more than halve Spain's official unemployment rate since the 1993 recession to 8.7 per cent, and has contributed to a 60 per cent increase in the number of people in work during the last decade. From 1984 through 1997 the number of temporary contracts increased from 7.5 per cent to 39 per cent of the total. Henceforth the level of temporary work among new workers in Spain rose from 61 per cent in 1987 to 81.5 per cent in 1990, doubling the proportion of the active population on temporary contracts during that period from 15 per cent to 30 per cent (and accounting for 90 per cent of all employment contracts). In addition, almost 50 per cent of the staff is temporary in small firms (see Bentolila, Segura and Toharia 1991, 237–238 and Richards and Polavieja 1997, 13–23).[2] The temporary rate stands (in 2006) at 33.7 per cent of the labor force, a level twice as high as the EU one (13.6 per cent). With only 10 per cent of the active working population, Spain accumulates 31 per cent of the temporary workers in the eurozone, and there are more temporary workers in Spain that in Italy, UK, Belgium and Sweden combined. This problem is not abating; on the contrary, the current level of temporality is the highest one ever with the exception of the 1994–1995 period.[3] Of the 900,000 new jobs created in Spain in January to June of 2005, two-thirds carried contracts of six months or less.

In addition, the industrial relations framework does not provide the necessary flexibility (either internal or external) for firms to deploy and organize their labor force (Nuñez 2005). A central challenge for Spanish firms and employers is to find a balance between the reduction of temporary levels and the rigidity of some contracts. In a context of relatively high dismissal costs (general entitlement to 45 days' pay for every year worked) and high employers' share of social security contributions as a percentage of wages (which is among the highest in Europe) employers have been using these contracts as instruments to introduce flexibility in their labor force in order to be able to adapt it to market conditions, technological change and demand. They are often accused of abusing temporary contracts – hiring people until the end of July, the start of the holiday season in Spain, and then renewing them in September to avoid paying for holidays.

1 In response to this challenge the Socialist government has proposed a new law that will oblige companies with more than 250 workers to introduce "equality plans" to eliminate discrimination against women in pay, benefits and promotion.

2 Despite the efforts from the trade unions, fixed-term employment has remained persistently high, and it is increasing in the public sector where it represented over 20 per cent of all employment in 2003. One of the reasons is the high rate of turnover experienced by temporary workers (in abuse of the law): in 1994 each temporary worker had signed an average of two contracts per year, but in recent years the figure was three. Half of the temporary contracts have a duration of less than a month. See EIRO, *2003 Annual Review for Spain*.

3 This development is also partly a consequence of the productive structure of the country, very dependent on seasonal activities like tourism, agriculture, and construction. See *El País* (August 10, 2005).

Temporary work, however, limits the incentives of employers to invest in their workers, the commitment of employees to their firms, and hinders the development and implementation of training programs, with negative consequences on productivity. These contracts pay as little as €4 an hour and offer little, if any training. Furthermore, the trend towards temporary working is stifling innovation and worker mobility, and job insecurity leads to a lack of enterprise among young people with university degrees (*Financial Times*, October 21, 2005: 3). Employers are starting to recognize the perverse consequences of these developments (Jiménez Aguilar 1997: 12–13) and demand a reduction in the costs of dismissals and social security contributions.[4] The generalization of this practice has led to the establishment and institutionalization of a model based on low costs that is no longer competitive.[5]

Rigidities in the labor market further hinder economic adjustment in cases of shocks and make it more difficult to adopt new technologies. Yet, according to the OECD (1999) Spain remains among the least flexible economies, as shown in Figure 11.3.

This problem has been compounded by the fact that Spain entered the euro at undervalued exchange rate and subsequently it lost competitiveness against the eurozone because of above-average wage increases and inflation. Unit labor costs have continued to rise, not so much because of higher nominal wages (which have grown moderately), but because of a fall in productivity (see Table 11.5).[6]

Figure 11.4 shows that since 2000 unitary labor costs have increased over the EU–15's causing an important loss of competitiveness.

Productivity

The unfavorable evolution of unitary labor costs is closely associated to the insufficient growth of productivity (see Figure 11.5).

According to the *Conference Board*, Spanish labor productivity suffered the biggest fall in 2005 of all the countries in the OECD, with a drop of 1.3 per cent (in the EU it was up 1.1 per cent), and OECD data shows that during the

4 Although employers' associations frequently express their antagonism toward trade unions, criticize an environment that they consider hostile to them, and demand greater labor market flexibility, in private, during the course of the interviews that I conducted with their leaders they recognized the need for greater cooperation and stressed the benefits of concentration. One of the leaders of the CEOE, Jiménez Aguilar, has recognized that the increasing segmentation of the labor market between permanent and temporary workers "hinders workers' professional training, their motivation, and in sum the competitiveness of the firm and the quality of its products".

5 In Valencia, for example, many companies that used to produce textiles or shoes have seen their low-cost competitive advantage eroded as a result of competition from Asia and have been forced to close their plants and import products from China. They are now focusing on design and distribution, activities that require little labor.

6 The surge of immigration, which resulted in a sharp increase in the participation rate, has led to a decrease in average remuneration per worker (about 3.7 per cent between 2002–2004).

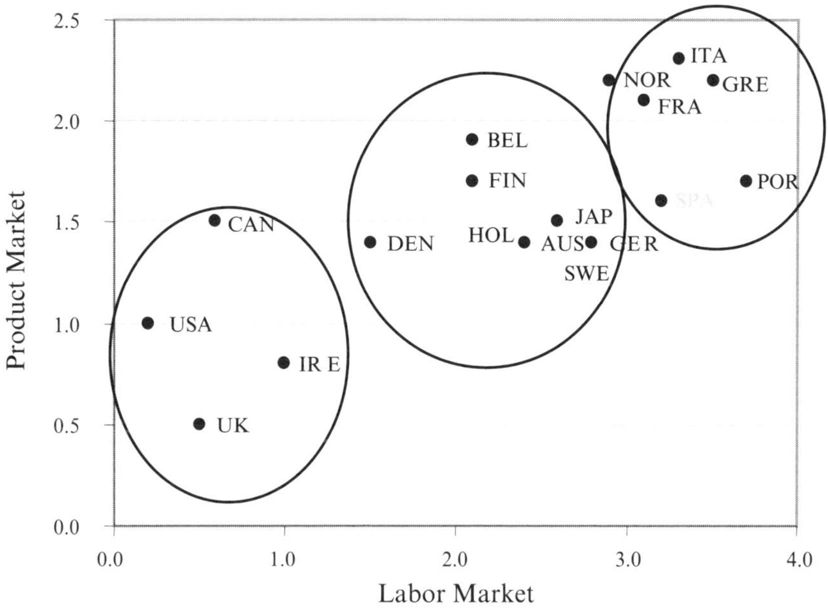

Figure 11.3 Index of Product and Labor Market Regulation (1998)

Table 11.5 Wage Increases Negotiated in Collective Agreements in Spain, 2000–2004

Year	Wage increase	CPI real year average	Purchasing capacity
2000	3.6	3.4	0.2
2001	3.7	3.6	0.1
2002	3.8	3.5	0.3
2003	3.5	3.5	0.7
2004	4.0	4.4	0.4

Sources: MTAS; Estadísticas de Convenios Colectivos.

1994–2003 period Spain was placed next to last among 30 developed countries. While we know little about what determines productivity growth in advanced economies, some of the reasons for the lackluster productivity performance in the Spanish economy may include heavy regulation, public spending (that is, public sector productivity shows a decline), low rate of investment, low skill levels in human capital, poor infrastructure (for example, congestion in roads, or problems in retail and wholesale distribution), mediocre performance in innovation and expenditure on R&D, poor intellectual property protection, poor science base (that is, the reduced number of scientific publications) and weak presence in high-

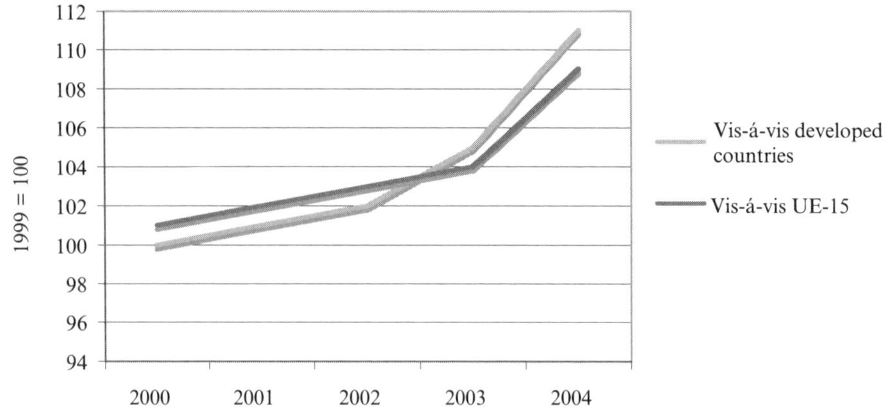

Figure 11.4 Competitiveness of Unit Labor Costs

Source: OEP 2005: 30.

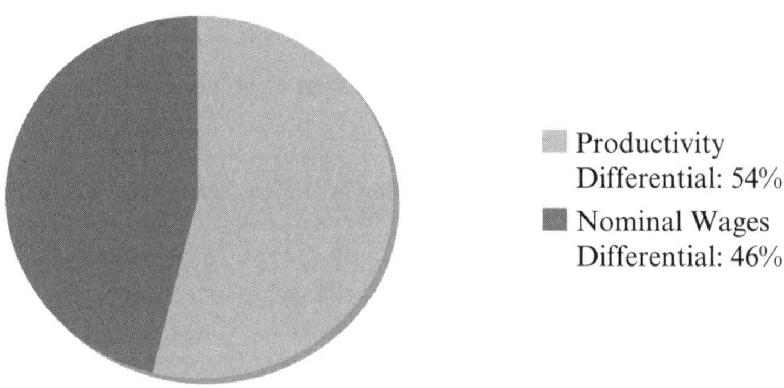

Figure 11.5 Determinants of Loss of Competitiveness in the Spanish Economy

Source: OEP 2005: 31.

technology industries. Finally, this drop can also be explained by a massive wave of immigration with lower levels of education, which also increased the working population and reduced average workers' contribution to GDP (*El País*, February 18, 2006; see Wolf 2005).

The Economic Structure

An economic structure based on small and medium enterprises (SMEs) with companies that have the capacity to adapt to changing environments has produced benefits such as flexibility, openness to innovation, fluid communication channels and employment creation. However, the small dimension of these firms generates deficiencies that hinder their competitiveness. For instance, they have difficulties exporting and competing in international markets, they generally fail to use new technologies and managerial tools, they have problems raising capital and accessing public funds for research and development, they have little purchasing power and a tendency to under utilize their productive capacity and they lack resources to train their workforce. More importantly, their size limits the possibility of economies of scale necessary to compete and improve productivity.

Moreover the small dimension of Spanish companies makes it also difficult for them to generate the collective goods that these firms need to compete successfully. Most firms employ production strategies that rely on a relatively skilled labor force. Yet they do not have strong incentives to invest in their workers because they are vulnerable to "hold up" by their employees or the "poaching" of skilled workers by other firms. Employees, for their part, do not have strong incentives to share with management the information that they gain at work, because they would be open to exploitation. Finally, the dimension of Spanish firms hinders their options to raise capital to innovate and their ability to invest in new technologies. These shortcomings should lead the economic actors to support institutional mechanisms to help coordinate their activities and provide the necessary collective goods to succeed in the global economy.

Other Indicators

Spain lags well behind in other critical areas: since most employment is in sectors based on intensive and low qualified labor, only 36 per cent of Spanish employees work with new technologies; the percentage of the population that participates in professional training programs is merely 5.8 per cent, well below the 9 per cent EU average; Spain is listed 20th in the *Global Competitiveness Index* (GCI) on the innovation capacity and technological development of Spanish firms; and while investment in R&D has increased over the last five years (1998–2003) at an average of 7.6 per cent, the percentage of investment in R&D (at 1.1 per cent of the GDP) is still lagging behind the 1.93 per cent EU average.

Productivity is also affected by capital stock deficiencies. Despite the spectacular improvement in infrastructures, Spain still lags behind the EU and public investment, which had experienced rates over 9 per cent in the 1990s, decelerated markedly between 2000 and 2003. This development is particularly worrisome in the context of the spectacular population growth of the last five years. This deficit in capital stock requires that the government continue investing in infrastructures to close the gap (see Table 11.6).

The quality of human capital is also deficient. While the quality of labor has improved, according to the International Program for Student Evaluations, Spanish students are below OECD averages in reading and comprehension, math and sciences (see Table 11.7).

In addition, while changes to the production structure and in the structure of exports, indicators of the degree of competitiveness of the Spanish economy (that is, in terms of human capital skills, stock of capital, technological capital) have shown some improvements, significant differences remain in comparison to the leading developed economies. The European Commission is reporting that the EU

Table 11.6 The Stock of Infrastructure of the Spanish Economy

	2000	2001	2002	2003	2004
Public investment growth	–8.9	9.2	9.0	1.2	6.7
Infrastructure growth	3.3	3.6	3.4	3.6	3.6
Infrastructure growth per capita	2.5	2.0	1.7	1.4	2.5
Infrastructures per capita (UE–15=100)	84.2	84.1	82.3	79.4	80.0

Source: OEP 2005: 36.

Table 11.7 The Education of the Spanish Labor Force, Per Cent of Population

	2000	2001	2002	2003	2004
Illiterate	0.5	0.5	0.4	0.4	0.4
Primary education	25.2	23.5	22.2	20.4	18.9
Secondary education	46.5	47.4	48.1	49.5	49.9
University education	27.8	28.7	29.3	29.7	30.8

Sources: OEP 2005: 37.

is "losing the battle on competitiveness", and in a list of 44 indicators, including economic performance, reform, employment and research, Spain (together with Portugal and Greece) is among the worst performing countries in the majority of the areas.[7] According to the Global Competitiveness Index (GCI) Spain is placed 23rd in the world, and in some of the categories computed in the ranking (for example, the quality of public institutions) Spain is performing even poorer than in previous years.

The country's poor record on innovation is also deteriorating even further. Although Spanish scientists account for 4 per cent of the world's published

7 See *Financial Times* (January 13, 2003): 3. Spain has lost three positions (is listed at number twenty) in the Globalization Index published by *Foreign Policy* (January/February 2003, no. 134, 60). In addition the *World Economic Forum* has placed Spain and Portugal among the least competitive countries in the European Union (only Greece is behind) in its *Report on Global Competitiveness*. This report examines economic conditions in 80 countries focusing on two main indexes: MICI (Microeconomic Competitiveness Index), which measures the quality of business development, and the GCI (Growth Competitiveness Index), which examines growth perspectives in five to eight years based on macroeconomic stability.

research, the country lags behind other European countries in innovation league tables based on patent filing (*Financial Times*, October 21, 2005: 3). Data from the European Office of Patents indicates the level of patents in Spain is only 19 per cent of the European average and 11 per cent of the United States'. Furthermore, according to the latest European Commission's *Innovation Scoreboard* Spain is "losing ground" and is placed 16 among EU countries. One of the central problems, according to the report is the "very weak performance of entrepreneurial spirit". The rate of enterprise creation in Spain is merely 10 per cent (versus 11.2 per cent in Europe) and of the new companies created 70 per cent do not have paid employees. This can be partly explained because of the precariousness of the job market, which leads youngsters to look for security above everything else and many look for jobs as civil servants. Other problems include the very low level of cooperation on innovation among small and medium enterprises, which is only 38 per cent of the European average; backward steps on key indicators that measure the resources devoted to information technologies and telecommunications, which have decreased from 85 per cent to 83 per cent of the EU average; and finally, while there has been significant progress on R&D expenditures in the public and private sectors, Spain is still lagging far behind the EU average (the expenditures in the public sector have increased from 64 per cent to 70 per cent of the EU average and from 45 per cent to 49 per cent in the private sector). Spain invests 1.05 per cent of GDP in R&D, less than half the EU average. At the current pace it would take twenty years to reach the EU average. Finally, Spain also shows a significant deficit in relation to the information society and the use of electronic trade (the percentage of Spanish companies that buy and sell on the internet is the lowest in Europe). High technology exports are only 33 per cent of the European average and have only increased two points (from 31 per cent) since 2001 (*El País*, January 13, 2006).

Conclusions

The idea of European integration became a driving force that moved reforms forward and was a fundamental factor for bringing together political stabilization, economic recovery and democratic consolidation. Indeed, the European integration process has facilitated the reincorporation of Spain into the international arena, contributed to the legitimacy of the new democratic regime, acted as a buffer in controversial issues (such as decentralization or the implementation of economic reforms) and has facilitated and accelerated the process of convergence and modernization of financial, commercial and manufacturing structures. Overall the impact of membership has been very beneficial. While there have been painful changes (for example, the process of industrial restructuring or fiscal reforms) with traumatic effects (unemployment levels reached over 20 per cent in the early 1990s), these changes would have been necessary anyway. European integration accelerated the reforms but at the same time it allowed for an orderly implementation that benefited from the experiences and support of other European countries (and funds). The impressive rates of economic growth experienced by the country during the last twenty years are closely connected with EU membership. The sharp decline in interest rates that resulted from EMU integration, the transfer of European funds to Spain, the implementation of more orthodox fiscal policies, and the opening of the Spanish economy are all examples of outcomes associated with European membership. Finally, without the euro, the huge trade deficit would have already forced a devaluation and the implementation of more restrictive fiscal policies.

Yet despite all the significant progress accomplished during the past two decades, the Spanish economy confronts difficult challenges in the new millennium. In comparison with other European countries, the Spanish economy is experiencing faster rates of growth. Yet it has not reached the development levels, particularly in technology, of the richest European countries. Furthermore, the competitive position of the Spanish economy has deteriorated lately and this is a very worrisome development that must be addressed. Failure to do so may have dire consequences. Some observers have argued that Spain is about to experience a German-style economic stagnation or worse (Gros 2005), while others are raising the possibility that Spain may have to leave the euro (Munchau February 20, 2006 and *Financial Times*, January 30, 2006).

From an economic convergence standpoint, given the existing income and productivity differentials with the richer countries, Spain will have to continue raising its living standards to bring them closer to the current EU average. For this to happen, it is necessary for the Spanish economy to grow faster than the other rich European countries. This will require further liberalization of its labor structures (both internal and external), as well as increasing competition within its service markets and improving the utilization of their productive resources. Convergence will also demand institutional reforms in R&D policies, in education, improvement of civil infrastructures, as well as further innovation, an increase in business capabilities, more investment in information technology and better and more efficient training systems. Moreover, Spain needs to find the right balance of labor flexibility and worker incentives to promote productivity. A successful convergence policy will also require a debate about the role of public investment and welfare programs. In Spain, increases in public expenditure to develop its welfare state have caused imbalances in the national accounts. Yet it still spends significantly less in this area than its European neighbors (Spain spends 6.3 points less on welfare policies than the EMU average). Effective real convergence would demand not only effective strategies and policies, but also a strong commitment on the part of Spanish citizens to achieve this objective.

Moreover, the Spanish economy still has considerable ground to cover to improve its competitiveness. Since the country is part of EMU and any adjustment through a devaluation of its currency is no longer feasible, the only way for Spain to regain lost competitiveness is through a long period of wage moderation and increasing productivity. This will demand improvements in the working of markets and the elimination of distortions, as well as further liberalization of the economy particularly in the gas and electricity sectors and enhanced energy efficiency to diminish the country's continuing dependence on import energy, which contributes to inflation. Furthermore it will require the use of new technologies and increasing spending on research and development.

A competitiveness agenda will have to focus on productivity growth, which is even more important in Spain than nominal wage growth. To address this shortcoming will demand actions to improve policy across a wide front: higher investment in infrastructure, improvements in land-use planning, efforts to increase the quality of education, rigorous promotion of competition in all areas of the economy, tax simplification and rationalization of existing regulations (see Wolf 2005). Furthermore such agenda will demand a shift from a low-cost, low-skill manufacturing base that relies on technical design and marketing skills from elsewhere, toward more capital-intensive industries that require greater skills in the labor force and rely on standard technology – for example, chemicals, vehicles, steel and metal manufacturers, as well as a change in the existing growth model (based on relatively low production costs) in order to build a new framework based on innovation, quality, value-added and productivity.[8] Small companies have to carve out market niches in the global market and develop the technical capacity for short production runs to be able to respond to shifting demand. They have to develop their own brands and distribution networks, and create their own customer bases. This will require the development of a technological know-how and marketing techniques.

The goal must be to increase productivity by increasing the capital intensity of production. Innovation and higher productivity will require four main conditions:

- investment in capital technology (information systems and telecommunications);
- a new culture of entrepreneurship, innovation and risk;
- human capital with strong skills and the flexibility to adapt to new technologies and processes, based on a model of continuous training;
- a flexible and adaptable industrial relations framework.

Do the Spanish people want to continue building houses or do they want to increase salaries and develop a model based on value-added? There are other European countries that have developed knowledge-based economies with very strong results, and can serve as references (for example, the Scandinavian countries). Yet these challenges do not longer depend as much on Europe as they

---

8 There are some positive indicators: General Motors has recently decided to manufacture its new vehicle Meriva in the plant that it has in Fegueruela (Zaragoza), which was in competition with Gliwice (Poland). This decision has taken place in a context of outsourcing and delocalization in the Spanish automobile sector burdened by relative high labor cost and pensions. The reason for this decision was based on the higher productivity of Fegueruela's workers, facilitated by concessions from the GM workers council, which will allow for the assembly of cars in 16 hours (it takes now twenty-one hours). As a result, production costs would be similar to the ones offered by Poland (Polish workers' salaries are one-third of Feguerela's).

do on Spain itself. The wide scope of these reforms reflects the daunting challenge faced by the Spanish government. It will face growing resistance from the people likely to be hit hardest by these reforms. However, the lack of political willingness to implement these reforms will hinder the convergence process and erode further the competitiveness of the Spanish economy. It will not be easy. Globalization is forcing economies to open up markets and embrace reforms, but the current stalemate in Europe after the rejection of Europe's constitutional treaty by Dutch and French voters, growing protectionism (manifested by the opposition of national governments to cross-border mergers and acquisitions in sectors such as energy), and increasing backlash against "Anglo-Saxon" free-market capitalism will make the reform process even more difficult.

The main economic lesson from the Spanish integration to Europe is that EU and EMU have limited direct powers to enforce outcomes. The experience of Spain shows that the influence of indirect EU recommendations on policy and demonstration effects has been greater than direct action. It demonstrates the limits of peer pressure and the ability of the *acquis communautaire* to force change. The challenges facing Spain are not a problem of European institutions, but of national policies. While EU membership will facilitate (and in many cases ameliorate) adjustment costs and will provide impetus for reforms, the experience of Spain shows that this is no substitute for the domestic implementation of reforms, which should proceed further in areas such as labor, product and capital markets. Successful convergence and increasing competitiveness will hinge to a considerable degree on the ability of Spanish leaders to implement reforms in the face of domestic resistance. Lack of progress will bring economic stagnation or worse.

References

Alvarez-Miranda, B. (1996), *El Sur de Europa y la Adhesion a la Comunidad, Los Debates Politicos*, (Madrid: CIS).

Bentolila, S., Segura, J. and Toharia, L. (1991), "La Contratación Temporal en España", in *Moneda y Crédito*, no. 193, 225–265.

Cameron, D.R. (September 2002), "The Challenges of EU Accession", paper presented at the annual meeting of the *American Political Science Association* (Boston, MA).

Costa Pinto, A. and Severiano Teixeira, N. (eds) (2002), *Southern Europe and the Making of the European Union* (New York: Columbia University Press).

Costa Pinto, A. and Severiano Teixeira, N. (2002), "From Africa to Europe: Portugal and European Integration", in Costa Pinto, A. and Severiano Teixeira, N., eds, *Southern Europe and the Making of the European Union* (New York: Columbia University Press).

El País (February 14, 2000), "La Convergencia Real a Paso Lento".

El País (August 10, 2005), "España tiene más eventuales que Italia, Reino Unido, Bélgica y Suecia juntos".

El País (January 2, 2006), "Dos décadas de impulso a la economía".

El País (January 13, 2006), "España pierde terreno en innovación y baja al puesto 16 de la Unión Europea", 45.

El País (February 18, 2006), "Almunia Says Inflation Dampens Spain's Potential Growth Level", *English Edition with International Herald Tribune*. (Brussels: European Industrial Relations Observatory), *2003 Annual Review for Spain*.

Fernández Guerrero, I., González, A. and Suárez Burguet, C. (1989), "Spanish External Trade and EEC Preferences", in Yannopoulos, G.N., *European Integration and the Iberian Economies* (New York: St. Martin's Press).

Financial Times (January 13, 2003), "The EU 'Is Losing Battle on Competitiveness'", 3.

Financial Times (October 21, 2005), "'Garbage Jobs' Stifle Spanish Innovation", 3.

Financial Times (January 30, 2006), "Monetary Union Is Not for the Poor". See http://www.ft.com.

Financial Times (March 4–5 2006), "Spain Plans to Ban Sex Discrimination at Work", 2.

Fishman, R. (2001), "Shaping, Not Making, Democracy: The European Union and Spain's Post-Franco Political Transformation", paper presented at the conference *From Isolation to Integration: 15 Years of Portuguese and Spanish Membership in Europe*, Minda de Gunzburg Center for European Studies at Harvard University, November 2–3, 2001.

Gros, D. (2005), "Will EMU Survive 2010?", Centre for European Policy Studies, January 2005. See http://www.ceps.be.

Herce, J.A. (2006), "La Política de Cohesión", *El País*, November 15th, 2006, 4, Negocios.

Hine, R.C. (September 1989), "Customs Union Enlargement and Adjustment: Spain's Accession to the European Community", in *Journal of Common Market Studies*, vol. XXVIII, no. 1.

Jiménez Aguilar, J. (1997), "El Nuevo Dialogo Social Desde la Perspectiva de las Organizaciones Empresariales", paper presented during the *Jornadas sobre el Dialogo Social*. Cursos de Verano de la Universidad Complutense, El Escorial, July 9, 1997.

Magone, J. (2002), "Attitudes of Southern European Citizens Towards European Integration", in Costa Pinto, A. and Severiano Teixeira, N., eds, *Southern Europe and the Making of the European Union* (New York: Columbia University Press).

Morlino, L. (2002), "The Europeanisation of Southern Europe", in Costa Pinto, A. and Severiano Teixeira, N., eds, *Southern Europe and the Making of the European Union* (New York: Columbia University Press).

Munchau, W. (February 20, 2006), "Spain has more Reason to Quit the Euro than Italy", *Financial Times*. See http://www.ft.com.

Nuñez, J.B. (2005), "Innovación, Productividad y Empleo", *El País*, July 10, 2005.

Oficina Económica del Presidente (October 2005), *Convergencia y Empleo: Programa Nacional de Reformas de España* (Madrid: OEP).

Pérez-Díaz, V. (2002), "From Civil War to Civil Society: Social Capital in Spain from the 1930s to the 1990s", in Putnam, R.D., ed., *Democracies in Flux: the Evolution of Social Capital in Contemporary Society* (New York: Oxford University Press).

Pridham, G. (1991), "The Politics of the European Community: Transnational Networks and Democratic Transitions in Southern Europe", in Pridham, G., *Encouraging Democracy: The Institutional Context of Regime Transition in Southern Europe* (Leicester: Leicester University Press).

Pridham, G. (2001), "European Integration and Democratic Consolidation in Southern Europe", in Costa Pinto, A. and Severiano Teixeira, N., eds, *Southern Europe and the Making of the European Union* (New York: Columbia University Press).

Richards, A. and García Polavieja, J. (1997), "Trade Unions, Unemployment and Working Class Fragmentation in Spain", Working Paper No. 112 (Madrid: Centro de Estudios Avanzados en Ciencias Sociales).

Royo, S. (2005), *Portugal, Espanha e a Integração Europeia: Um Balanço* (Lisbon: Instituto de Ciencias Sociais da Universidade de Lisboa).

Royo, S. (2006), *Spain and Portugal in the European Union: Misión Accomplished?*", in Zeff, E. and Pirro, E.B., eds, *The European Union and the Member States: Cooperation, Coordination, and Compromise* (New York: Lynne Rienner Publishers).

Royo, S. (2006), "The Challenges of EU Integration: Iberian Lessons for Eastern Europe", in Roy, J. and Domínguez, R., eds, *Towards the Completion of Europe: Analysis and Perspectives of the New European Union Enlargement* (Miami: Jean Monnet EU Chair, University of Miami).

Royo, S. and Manuel, P.C. (eds) (2003), *Spain and Portugal in the European Union: The First Fifteen Years* (London: Frank Cass).

Sebastián, M. (2001), "Spain in the EU: Fifteen Years May Not Be Enough", paper presented at the conference *From Isolation to Europe: 15 Years of Spanish and Portuguese Membership in the European Union*, Minda de Gunzburg Center for European Studies, Harvard University, November 2–3, 2001.

Tovias, A. (2002), "The Southern European Economies and European Integration", in Costa Pinto, A. and Severiano Teixeira, N., eds, *Southern Europe and the Making of the European Union* (New York: Columbia University Press).

Wolf, M. (2005), "Britain Must Get to Grips with Lackluster Productivity Growth", *Financial Times*, November 8, 2005. See http://www.ft.com.

PART V
The Euro in the Global Economy

Chapter 12

Global Imbalances and the Need for Policy Adjustment

José Manuel González-Páramo[1]

Introduction

This chapter focuses on what seems to be the most popular topic among economic commentators and policy makers with an international interest: global imbalances. The interest in and attention given to global imbalances is not only proportional to the record size of the US current account deficit and the global implications of its unwinding, but also to the longevity of this debate, since the resilience of the US current account deficit has so far confounded the expectations of many economists. This chapter gives a view from the other side of the Atlantic on global imbalances. In particular, it touches upon three aspects: (1) the causes of global imbalances; (2) how worried we should be about global imbalances and (3) the need for policy adjustment.

The Causes of Global Imbalances

The chapter begins with well known facts. In 2005 the current account deficit of the United States was estimated to have reached 6.4 per cent of gross domestic product (GDP). From a global perspective, this was indeed very large for an economy the size of the United States and corresponded to around 80 per cent of the total current account surpluses in the rest of the world. In 2005 the US current account deficit reached a level that was roughly matched by the combined current account surpluses of Japan, China, other Asian economies and the oil-producing nations (see Figure 12.1).

Declining Savings in the United States

There is an ongoing debate on what has caused these imbalances and somewhat of an agreement on the role of a wide array of macroeconomic and microeconomic forces throughout the world economy that affect public and private savings and investment. Among all factors, the decline in US savings may be considered as a

1 This chapter stems from my speech in April 2006, and therefore is largely based on data ending in 2005. I would like to thank Maurizio Habib for his input to this chapter.

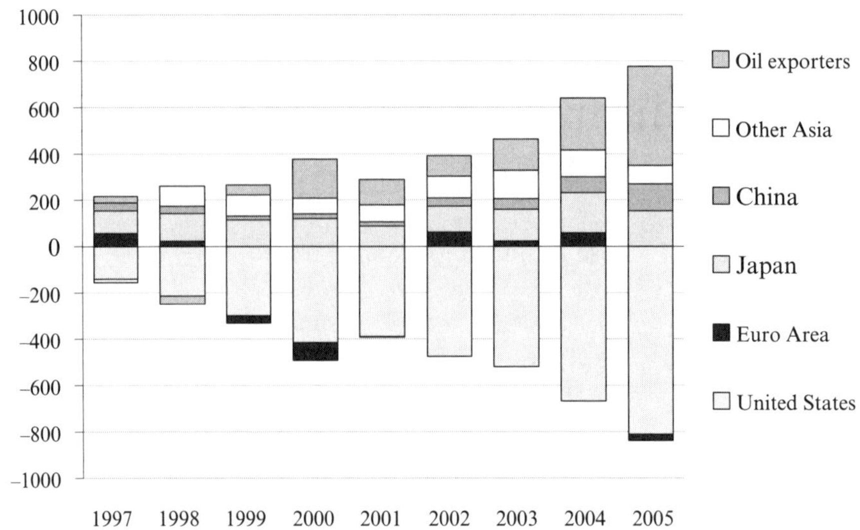

Figure 12.1 Current Account Positions, 1997–2005 (USD Billions)

Sources: IMF World Economic Outlook and ECB staff calculations.

major cause. Since 1999 the growing current account deficit in the United States has been associated with a sharp decline in savings. As a result, the US national net saving rate is currently at around 1 per cent of GDP, the lowest level since World War II. Both private and public savings have contributed to this decrease. With regards to private savings, the decline has been mainly due to a drop in net household savings that in the course of 2005 – for the first time since the 1930s – fell into negative territory (see Figure 12.2). In turn, declining household savings could be the result of substantial positive wealth effects – triggered by the asset price bubble in the second half of the 1990s and soaring real estate prices since 2000[2] – also as a consequence of the anticipation of a higher permanent income arising from a positive productivity shock, and population ageing. Low real interest rates and distortionary tax incentives (see OECD 2005 and IMF 2005a) could have also played a role in discouraging household saving.

In addition, over the past four years, the shift from budget surpluses to sizeable public deficits has contributed to lowering the national saving rate of the United States. There is an intense debate, stretching from academia to policy-making circles, on the extent to which a fiscal deficit translates into the current account. The consensus view is that there is a significant albeit partial statistical relationship between fiscal balances and current account positions, confirming partial Ricardian behavior by the private sector. This fits in with the fact that the worsening of the US current account is a long-term trend that started some fifteen years ago and that has taken place in both periods of fiscal consolidation and loosening. The

2 See, for example, Kraay and Ventura (2005) on the link between asset bubbles and the current account.

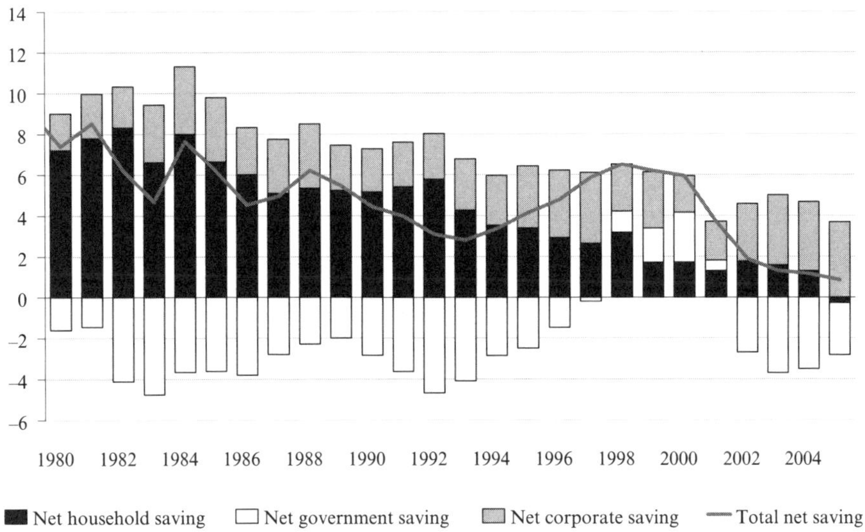

Figure 12.2 Breakdown of US Net Saving by Sector, 1980–2005 (Per Cent of GDP)

Sources: US Bureau of Economic Analysis and ECB staff calculations.

aforementioned view implies that the US fiscal position matters significantly as far as the current account deficit are concerned. The US general government fiscal balance swung from a surplus of more than 1 per cent of GDP in 2000 to a deficit of around 4 per cent of GDP in 2005, which is equivalent to a fiscal expansion by more than 5 per cent of GDP. Over the same period, the US current account deficit increased from 4.2 per cent of GDP to 6.4 per cent of GDP, widening by more than 2 per cent of GDP owing, *inter alia*, to high oil prices and a deteriorating oil trade balance[3] (see Figure 12.3). These figures imply an elasticity between fiscal balances and current account positions of around 0.25, if one excludes the increase in the oil bill. This is fully consistent with some of the empirical estimates for the link between the fiscal and the current account in the economic literature.[4]

In conclusion, the evidence suggests that a number of factors underlie the considerable deterioration in the US current account, including a long-term decline in private saving, a sizable fiscal expansion in recent years and the substantial rise in oil prices.

---

3 The oil bill of the United States increased from 1.1 per cent of GDP in 2000 to 1.8 per cent of GDP in 2005.

4 See Bussière, Fratzscher and Müller (2005) for a review of these estimates.

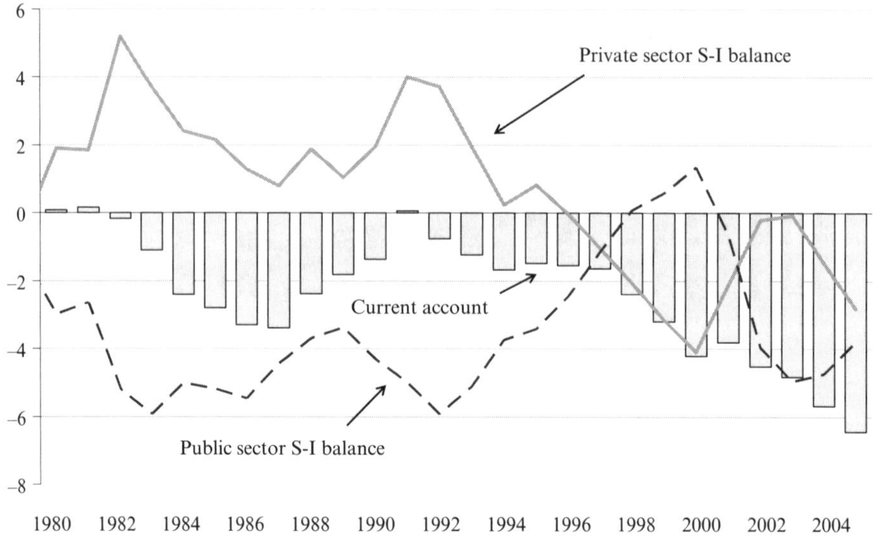

Figure 12.3 US Current Account and Saving–Investment Balance of the Private and Public Sectors, 1980–2005 (Per Cent of GDP)

Sources: US Bureau of Economic Analysis and ECB staff calculations.

Savings Glut: Asia and the Role of Oil Exporters

Since the global economy is closed, a large current account deficit in one country must find a counterpart in large surpluses somewhere else. So, it is intuitive to think that part of the reason for the US current account deficit may lie in developments and policies outside the United States. The most relevant explanations include: (1) the high saving rates in some Asian countries in relation to the decline in investment following the financial crises in 1997–1998; (2) very high saving, which is outpacing rising investment, in China and (3) the impact of the high oil prices, which have generated large surpluses in oil-producing countries and exacerbated the US deficit.

In East Asia, excluding China, IMF data indeed confirm that saving rates continue to be high, much higher than those observed in European and North American countries. The gross national saving rate of Japan and emerging Asian countries – excluding China – declined over the 1990s and has evened out at 28 per cent of GDP since 2000. Investment was also on a declining path over the 1990s in these countries and collapsed after the financial crises in 1997–1998, posting a modest recovery thereafter, but remaining well below saving and thus resulting in sizeable current account surpluses (see Figure 12.4a). The question of whether investment is "too low" or national savings are "excessive" is of course controversial. Recent analysis by the IMF suggests that some emerging Asian countries, such as the Philippines, Thailand and Indonesia, might be investing less than what would be needed to reach a steady-state capital–output ratio. In addition, the IMF's econometric analysis could not provide an explanation of the recent low investment growth in emerging countries (including oil exporters) and also, although to a lesser extent, in industrial countries (see IMF 2005b). Whatever the possible explanations may be, the key point remains that the growing gap between saving and investment in Asia has led to a significant current account surplus in the region in recent years.

4a) Japan and emerging Asia excl. China, 1991–2005

4b) China 1994–2005

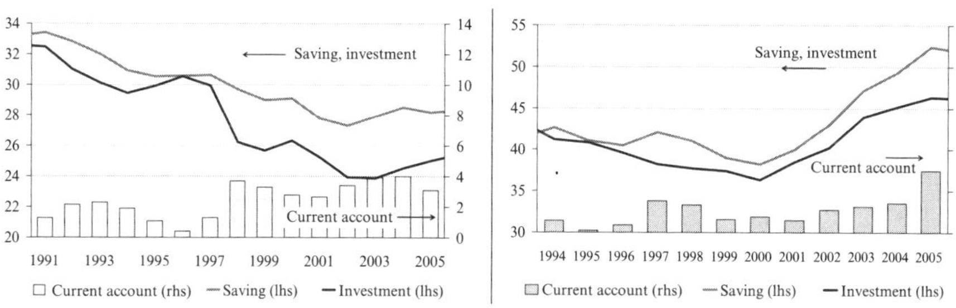

Figure 12.4 Saving, Investment and the Current Account (Per Cent of GDP)

Sources: IMF World Economic Outlook (September 2005) and ECB staff calculations.

The excess of saving over investment is also evident in China, where the current account surplus surged to around 7 per cent of GDP in 2005. Here, though, there could be a problem of overinvestment – and not underinvestment – coupled with an excess of saving of the population and state-owned firms. Household saving is very high due to adverse demographic developments and the lack of a social safety net. Moreover, the limited access to financial markets gives an incentive for both state-owned firms and households to increase their level of precautionary savings. As a result, China's gross domestic saving rate has reached the remarkable level of around 50 per cent of GDP (see Figure 12.4b).

Finally, the sudden rise in oil prices shifted part of the current account surplus from the East Asian countries to oil-producing nations.[5] Actually, the oil exporters have been replacing the Asian region as the group of countries with the largest current account surplus. For 2005 the current account surplus of oil exporters is projected to peak at around US$ 400 billion or around 14 per cent of oil exporters' GDP, corresponding to about half of the US external deficit. Oil exporters have saved most of the extra income generated by the oil price shock and the saving rate surged from 20 per cent of GDP in 1998 to around 35 per cent of GDP in

5 According to the IMF's September 2005 World Economic Outlook, the major oil exporters (for which data are available) ranked according to the size of their projected 2005 oil balance surplus in US dollars are: Saudi Arabia, Russia, Norway, Iran, Algeria, United Arab Emirates, Venezuela, Nigeria, Kuwait, Mexico, Libya and Qatar.

2005 for the countries as a group. By contrast, so far, investment does not seem to have been affected by the oil price shock and has remained on average at about 21 per cent of GDP (see Figure12.5).

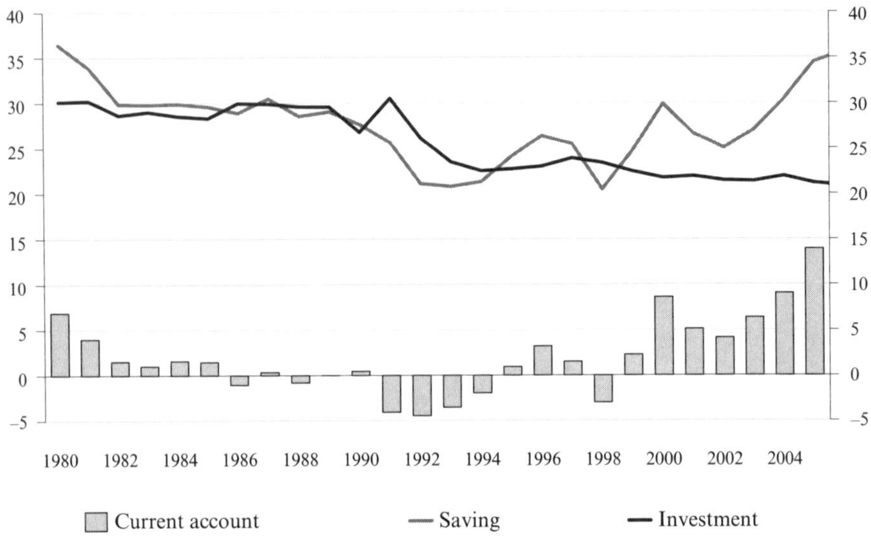

Figure 12.5 Oil Exporters' Saving, Investment and Current Accounts, 1980–2005 (Per Cent of GDP)

Sources: IMF World Economic Outlook (September 2005) and ECB staff calculations.

The rising oil bill has added to the problem of global imbalances, becoming an additional hurdle to the adjustment of the US current account deficit and partially explaining its worsening over the past few years. The oil bill (net imports) of the United States rose from 0.7 per cent of GDP per year from the mid-1980s until the end of the 1990s, to 1.8 per cent of GDP in 2005 or around one-fourth of the US trade deficit.

How Worried we Should be about Global Imbalances

The US current account has led to a steady deterioration of the net US international investment position. Back in 1980, the United States was a net creditor towards the rest of the world to the tune of US$360 billion, whereas at the end of 2004 it owed foreigners US$2.5 trillion or around 22 per cent of GDP. Between 2002 and 2004, this latter ratio remained stable in spite of large current account deficits mainly because of large valuation gains, which were prompted by the depreciation of the US dollar, which in turn boosted the dollar value of foreign currency-denominated assets. However, it is unlikely that a permanent net debt devaluation strategy is sustainable, since international investors could end up asking for higher interest rates on US debt.

In fact, these dynamics point to a need for a lower current account deficit in the United States. Let me illustrate this with the results from a simple arithmetic calculation. If the current account deficit of the United States continues to run at around 6 per cent of GDP and nominal GDP grows at 5.5 per cent a year – which is more or less the long-term consensus forecast for growth in the United States – the ratio of US net foreign debt to GDP would increase above 100 per cent in the very long run (if one excludes possible valuation effects).

In this context, the ability of the US economy to attract sufficiently large financial flows becomes crucial for the sustainability of the external deficit. Until 2000 the US current account deficit was financed by inflows into the domestic productive sector, taking the form of equity or direct investment. Recently, investors seem to have reassessed the longer-term profitability of US firms relative to earlier expectations and, as a result, net equity and foreign direct investment in the United States dried up and even went into reverse, being replaced by large net inflows into the US bond market. In the last two years, virtually all of the net foreign inflows into the United States have been debt-creating. The accumulation of foreign exchange reserves by Asian central banks and other reserve accumulators such as Russia, which mainly buy US government securities, played an important role in shaping this trend.

From a flow perspective, the growing stock of debt interacts with the current account dynamics. In fact, the United States is expected to face higher costs for servicing its rising debt. Over the past twenty years, the US income balance consistently recorded surpluses ranging between 0.1 per cent and 0.5 per cent of GDP, although in 2005 this surplus shrank to a tiny amount of US$1 billion (preliminary estimate), on the back of rising debt service obligations. Looking ahead, the income balance could turn negative as US interest rates have been rising.[6] A growing negative investment income would in turn imply a smaller sustainable trade deficit over the long run and complicate the current account adjustment.

Therefore, the relevant question is not whether, but when and how the adjustment will take place. In my view, the most likely scenario will be a gradual and orderly adjustment of these imbalances over the medium term, given the policy commitment restated recently by the main global players. However, should external imbalances persist for a fairly long period, there is a risk that this could lead to a purely market-led adjustment that might prove to be abrupt and would entail high costs. A disorderly adjustment could lead to a significant slowdown in economic growth, which is undesirable for all partners in the global economy.

In our view, the probability of an abrupt adjustment remains small. However, as the imbalances keep widening, the need for policy action becomes all the more

6 With rising yields in the United States, the differential between the rates of return paid to service US international liabilities and the return received on the stock of international assets is likely to diminish in the period ahead. This may potentially drive investment income into negative territory. See Higgins, Klitgaard and Tille (2005).

important. A sustainable resolution of external imbalances requires a rebalancing of resources and demand among different sectors of the economy that cannot be achieved effectively and durably through exchange rate flexibility alone. Therefore, it is in everybody's interest – as recognized in the G-7 communiqués over recent years – to work towards minimizing that risk.

The Need for Policy Adjustment

The orderly unwinding of global imbalances requires global policy efforts. By this I mean that the adjustment of global imbalances is a shared responsibility and requires the participation by all regions. This global process should aim at maximizing sustained growth, which requires strengthening policy and removing distortions to the rebalancing.

In the United States, savings should increase, both through further fiscal consolidation and through an increase in private savings. The direct impact of fiscal consolidation on the external balance of the United States can be significant. Fiscal tightening would also enhance the confidence of economic actors that policy makers are serious about tackling the issue of global imbalances. In addition, fiscal consolidation is also desirable from other perspectives, like the long-term sustainability of the US public finances. Household saving could be encouraged through reforms of the US tax system and the elimination of distortionary tax incentives, and the oil part of the US trade deficit could be reduced through a shift towards higher energy efficiency.

Emerging Asian countries are also expected to play a role in contributing to a smooth resolution of the global imbalances. The large current account surpluses and the unprecedented accumulation of foreign exchange reserves are as much a part of the global imbalances as is the US current account deficit. In this regard, exchange rate flexibility is an essential element to ensure that necessary adjustments take place. China's decision to shift to a new managed floating exchange rate regime was a welcome first step, though more flexibility is required to reduce the large current account surplus of China. This adjustment is also relevant from a domestic perspective, since there are growing signs that foreign exchange interventions are complicating domestic monetary policy and banking sector reform. In addition, reforms aimed at strengthening domestic demand and improving and deepening the financial sector would lead to a more efficient domestic allocation of assets and allow households to smooth consumption, reducing the incentives to hold large precautionary savings. This would facilitate the resolution of both internal and external imbalances.

Oil producers have become increasingly large current account surplus countries. Oil exporters may have an interest in saving part of the oil windfall, as they do through stabilization funds, even if oil prices are expected to remain durably high, to cushion against the future exhaustion of oil resources. Investment to enhance their oil extraction and refining capacity, to develop their infrastructure and to diversify their domestic production capacity away from oil is also important. Structural reforms in these economies – concerning product, labor as well as financial markets – will be instrumental in raising domestic demand, reducing imbalances and rebalancing global economic activity.

As for the euro area, our view is that our external position, with a roughly balanced current account, is broadly in line with the structure of our economy. Our external balance is also consistent with demographic developments in the euro area, which require net savings over the longer term.

We think that the euro area should play a contributing role in the resolution of global imbalances through the implementation of further structural reforms aimed at increasing our growth potential. The precise link between structural reforms and current account positions is admittedly complex. The impact of stronger growth on the current account will depend on two main factors: expectations and private consumption smoothing, and the sector targeted by the reforms. Structural reforms can induce higher import demand by raising expectations of higher income in the future, for example because of expected productivity gains through product and financial reforms. This underlines the importance of implementing structural reforms in a credible, consistent and well-communicated manner so that business and consumers can clearly identify the benefits of reform.

Structural reforms aiming at enhancing productivity in the euro area would contribute to the adjustment of the US current account deficit, especially if they primarily target the non-tradables sector. This is in line with the priorities for further reform in Europe, in particular in the services sector. Beyond the direct impact on external imbalances, lifting potential growth in the euro area, alleviating rigidities and facilitating efficient resource allocation are important to achieve a rebalancing of global growth and to increase the resilience of the euro area to potential external shocks.

A similar line of argumentation to that of the euro area applies to Japan. Further action is needed to ensure the recovery with fiscal soundness, promoting flexibility of the economy, especially in the non-tradables sector, and raising productivity growth.

In conclusion, this chapter has stressed three main messages. First, a number of factors throughout the world economy may have contributed to the global imbalances. Second, these global imbalances will sooner or later be corrected; the question is when and how. At present, the probability of an abrupt disorderly correction is low and the most likely scenario is a gradual correction over a number of years, and indeed the last year has already seen a slight improvement in the US current account deficit. Third, further progress in implementing the agreed international policy agenda – beyond what has already been done – is necessary to ensure that such an orderly adjustment takes place. The specific policies differ from country to country and also include some large emerging economies, but by and large one can say that the policies required to alleviate the global imbalances would also be beneficial for the resilience and long-term growth prospects of the economies in question. The present favorable global outlook provides the best opportunity for the implementation of such a policy strategy.

References

Bussière, M., Fratzscher, M. and Müller, G. (August 2005), "Productivity Shocks, Budget Deficits and the Current Account", ECB Working Paper No. 509.

Higgins, M., Klitgaard, T. and Tille, C. (December 2005), "The Income Implications of Rising US International Liabilities", *Current Issues in Economics and Finance*, Federal Reserve Bank of New York, vol. 11, no. 12.

IMF (2005a), "United States: 2005 Article IV Consultation–Staff Report", International Monetary Fund, Washington, DC, July. See http://www.imf.org/external/pubs/ft/scr/2005/cr05257.pdf.

IMF (2005b), "World Economic Outlook: Building Institutions", Chapter II. Global Imbalances: A Saving and Investment Perspective, International Monetary Fund, Washington, DC, September.

Kraay, A. and Ventura, J. (January 2005), "International Risk Sharing with Demand Shocks", mimeo, World Bank.

OECD (October 2005), "Economic Survey of the United States 2005" (Paris: OECD).

Chapter 13

The Euro and the Developing Countries

Francesc Granell

Introduction: The Euro and the Developing Countries

The United States dollar remains today the most important international currency for developing countries. Most of the prices of the commodities exported by developing countries are quoted in US dollars. Only a few developing countries have expressed interest in shifting to the euro for their international transactions. In some cases this is due to political reasons. In other cases it is to avoid the danger of a dollar weakened by the enormous external US deficit.

In this context this chapter discusses the opportunities that the importance of the European Union (EU) operations in the Third World, the eurozone's countries bilateral and multilateral transactions with poor countries, and the role played by the European countries in the governance and action of the international institutions, are offering for the internationalization of the euro.

The analysis considers that some African, Caribbean and Pacific countries and territories have their currency linked to the euro, that the EU is the most important ODA donor and that the European market is essential for exports from many developing countries.

At the same time, European investors are very active in many developing countries and millions of European tourists are visiting developing countries extensively.

A section of the chapter analyzes the contradictions that Latin American and Caribbean countries heavily connected with the US economy are facing regarding dollar/euro utilization. The paper also compares the importance of the euro and the IMF's SDR as an internationally accepted asset.

The US Dollar and the Bretton Woods System

The Bretton Woods Conference held in 1944 created a post-war International Monetary System which led to a privileged situation for the US dollar in the world economy.

The United States was, in fact, the only economic power emerging from the Second World War and the main creator of all world organizations created since. The contribution of the United States to the creation of the International Monetary Fund (IMF) was very important. Equally important was the role played by the United States in the recovery of the European economies through the Marshall Plan and the creation of the OEEC. After the decline of the pound sterling as an international currency, the US dollar remained, for years, the only international monetary asset together with gold.

Due to the prominence of the US dollar during the first twenty-five years of the Bretton Woods system, the American currency took a monopolistic position in the International Monetary System that created a "malaise" in the words of the French President General de Gaulle.

This pattern changed at the end of the 1960s and the beginning of the 1970s. As Robert Triffin pointed out, the system became unsustainable when the United States started having large external deficits while American gold reserves did not increase at the same pace as the enormous amount of "paper dollars" circulating around the world.

The expenditure of the Vietnam War, the weakness of the US trade balance and the continuous flow of American investment abroad obliged the IMF to find new sources of international unconditional liquidity in order to avoid the "Triffin Paradox". This was done by creating the Special Drawing Rights (SDR) as a reserve asset. This move was approved by the IMF in Rio de Janeiro in 1969 and started to operate in 1972 in an attempt to avoid the link between the creation of new international liquidity and new deficits in the US balance of payments.

The idea behind the creation of the SDR was to create a new international currency attractive enough to gradually change the central role played by the US dollar in the International Monetary System. The reality has been different.

SDR had been allocated to IMF members in proportion to their IMF quotas. A member may use SDRs to obtain foreign exchange reserves from other members and to make payments to the IMF. Such use does not constitute a loan because members are allocated SDRs unconditionally and may use them to meet balance of payments financing needs without undertaking economic policy measures or repayment obligations.

The SDR suffered several modifications in order to give it more recognition and acceptance as a substitute of the US dollar. In fact the SDR is the unit for the IMF operations but the SDR has never gone beyond being a bureaucratic currency, not having any practical interest for running international business and transactions out of the "official arena". All SDR transactions are conducted through the SDR Department of the IMF, but transactions are facilitated by fourteen voluntary arrangements under which parties stand ready to buy or sell SDRs for currencies that are readily usable in international transactions, provided that their own SDR holdings remain within certain limits.

The role of the SDR has never been very important even if this international asset is backed by the International Monetary Fund, the Bank for International Settlements, the central banks and some regional financial institutions.

Today the SDR represents less than 1 per cent of the international official holdings of reserve assets against 66 per cent in the US dollar and 24 per cent in the euro (see Table 13.1), even though the SDR has a very stable value because this unit is based on the weighted average of the values of a basket of currencies of the major international currencies.[1] That shows that the tradition and the inertia play in favor of the US dollar, regardless the good will of the IMF regarding the substitution of the US dollar by the SDR as the centre of the International Monetary System.

Table 13.1 Currency Breakdown of International Reserves (in Per Cent)

Currency	1999	2000	2001	2002	2003	2004	2005
US dollar	71.0	70.5	70.7	66.5	65.8	66.0	66.4
Euro	17.9	18.8	19.8	24.2	25.3	24.9	24.3
Yen	6.4	6.3	5.2	4.5	4.1	3.8	3.7
Pound	2.9	2.8	2.7	2.9	2.6	3.2	3.6
Other	1.8	1.7	1.5	1.8	2.1	2.1	2.0

Source: IMF and ECB.

After the recovery of the European economies and Japan in 1960s, other currencies like the deutschemark and the yen started gaining international acceptance for international transactions. But the predominance of the US dollar was practically total because no other big country accepted losing the control of its monetary policy, subordinating its currency to international events and accepting external unbalances.

Against this background, the Second Amendment of the IMF rules in 1978 confirmed the abandonment of gold as the official international monetary standard and reaffirmed the US dollar as the "unique" currency accepted as international liquidity.

Additional liquidity was demanded for financing the extraordinary expansion of the world transactions that followed the trade liberalization imposed by the GATT and the explosion of service and investment transactions under the open economic policies adopted by most of the countries in accordance with the Liberalization Codes of the OECD.

Dollars and petrodollars generated by the Oil Crisis of the 1970s financed the expansion of world transactions of that time. Due to the dominance of the sometimes weak US dollar a project to create a "substitution account" to absorb the enormous dollar liquidity was launched as early as 1979. This project was never pursued because the liberalization of international transactions and the

1 The SDR valuation is based in a basket comprised of the US dollar, the pound sterling, the euro and the Japanese yen, most widely used currencies in international transactions and those that are widely traded in the principal foreign exchange markets. The IMF establishes the weekly interest rate for the SDR on the basis of a weighted average of interest rates on short-term interests in the markets for the currencies included in the SDR valuation basket.

continuous erosion of IMF and governments control over the financial markets made such a project useless.

The US dollar continuously increased its share in the total of identified official holdings of foreign exchange in the hands of the central banks. From 1995 to 1998 (the last year before the launch of the euro) the deutschemark fell from 15.8 per cent of official holding reserves to 13.8 per cent while the US dollar climbed from 59.0 per cent to 69.4 per cent and the French franc fell from 2.4 per cent to 1.6 per cent. At the same time the predecessor of the euro, the ECU, fell from 8.5 per cent to 1.2 per cent.

The Creation of the Euro

In this context the launching of euro and the European Central Bank[2] created expectations of a better diversification of international assets. When the European Communities began with the European Coal and Steel Community in the 1950s, the world financial system was ruled by the Bretton Woods regulations with a discipline of fixed exchange rates imposed by the IMF. Therefore, there was no room to discuss the need to establish special monetary mechanisms to avoid excessive fluctuations of currencies inside the common market.

The situation changed dramatically by the end of the 1960s at a time in which the international monetary discipline relaxed. In 1969 (when the International Monetary System was threatening to collapse) the European heads of state decided at The Hague Summit that the Community should progressively transform itself into an economic and monetary union. The Werner Report (October 1970) proposed to achieve this monetary union in three stages.

The dollar's convertibility into gold ended on August 15, 1971 and, after a period of reflection, the IMF approved a Second Amendment of their Rules in 1978. In accordance with this amendment, the currencies were allowed to float. At the same time that the world monetary rules changed, the European governments pushed for a rapid process of deepening for European integration to complete the internal market. This was done mainly via the concept of creating a single market (Single European Act, 1986) and the establishment of a European Economic and Monetary Union with a new European single currency backed by a new European Central Bank (Maastricht Treaty on European Union, 1992). The European single common currency was created in January 1999 and the paper euro went into circulation on January 2002.

The eurozone was built with the participation of twelve out of the then-fifteen member countries. The national currencies of the twelve participating countries since that moment have been irrevocably locked into the euro. These twelve became

2 The European Central Bank and the US Federal Reserve are quite similar in functions and powers. The US Federal Reserve was created in 1914, 138 years after the creation of the United States. The European Central Bank, the first EU federal institution, was created fewer than fifty years after the start of the European integration.

thirteen in January 2007 when Slovenia joined the eurozone; and the Slovenian tolar disappeared.[3]

But a monetary union and a monetary policy cannot create a stable currency without fiscal rules aimed at safeguarding a stable macroeconomic framework. As the Maastricht Treaty provided only for the quantitative criteria for the adoption of the single currency with only a simple protocol on excessive deficit that was annexed (Granell April 2004), and it did not provide for any definition of a budgetary policy to be conducted after the changeover to the euro, it was considered necessary to adopt a Stability and Growth Pact in June 1997.

This pact (reformed at the March 2005 European Council) is supposed to ensure sound management of public finances in the euro area in order to prevent a situation from arising in which one member state's lax budgetary policy penalizes the other member states via interest rates, which would also undermine confidence in the common single currency.

Seven years after its creation and four years after euro banknotes and euro coins started circulating, the euro has provided much needed stability in the individual member state economies, even if its value against the dollar and other world currencies has fluctuated considerably.

The euro is presently the world's second most important currency and the internationalization has been apparent in global capital markets and euro-denominated securities.

The President of the ECB referred to the "gradual development of the international role of the euro" (Trichet May 14, 2004), but the reality is that the role of the euro is proportional with the importance of the EU in world affairs and the success of the policies linked to the Maastricht Treaty that created the EMU.

The literature has identified a number of key factors that were at the basis of the Maastricht success in creating the EMU and the euro and that can influence the future. These factors have been outlined by the Report Sapir as follows:

1 *Public visibility* The objective of meeting the Maastricht convergence criteria became the centerpiece of government strategy in many EU countries. The objective of reducing inflation was explicitly factored into wage negotiations. In the public finance area, public visibility was greatly facilitated by the simplicity of the 3% GDP deficit criterion which provided a clear signpost for economic policies regardless of political color of national governments.
2 *Clear structure of incentives* Politically, meeting the convergence criteria would allow countries characterized traditionally by unstable macroeconomic conditions to join their virtuous partners in the new policy regime, while

3 The eurozone is presently (2007), in fact, composed by sixteen countries because Monaco, San Marino and the Vatican are also participating in the euro through monetary arrangement with, respectively, the Bank of France and the Bank of Italy. Andorra is presently negotiating its participation in the eurozone. Some of the countries that became members of the EU in May 2004 will adopt the euro as soon as they fulfil the Maastricht criteria for membership to the EMU.

failing to comply carried the penalty of exclusion from the euro area. This was considered too harsh a political sanction.

3 *Political ownership* Strong macroeconomic stability came to be regarded as an essential precondition for countries to accept merging monetary sovereignty into a single currency.
4 *Constraining calendar* The Maastricht Treaty set very clear deadlines for moving to the final stage of the European Economic and Monetary Union. Countries willing to join with the first wave had no choice but to complete the convergence requirements.
5 *Effective monitoring* The simplicity and the unambiguous definition of the convergence requirements – especially those concerning the budget deficit and inflation – allowed an effective monitoring on the part of the European Commission which played the role of external agent commonly entrusted with the correct interpretation and implementation of the treaty criteria.
6 *Collegial culture* The process of convergence contributed to the progressive building of a collegial culture of stability through personal contact amongst policy makers and national and EU officials. This new climate contributed to peer pressure between national authorities and enhanced the role and authority of the European institutions (European Commission 2003).

The EMU and euro practices are still young and there is still considerable room for the "learning by doing process" as well as for advancing in the downgrading of the purely national competences in this field.

So far the euro is considered a reliable international currency. In addition, the acceptance of the present EMU and *euro acquis* by the new EU member countries during the enlargement negotiations conducive to the Athens Treaty of 2003 meant that the potential advantages of monetary integration and the existence of the euro were fully appreciated inside and outside the EU.

Among the sixteen pre-2004 EU members only UK, Sweden and Denmark do not use the euro. In fact the problems experienced by these three countries in accepting the common currency are more political than economic. The same is true for the new 2004 and 2007 EU members, which have shown their readiness to surrender their national monetary sovereignty in this area once they fulfill the conditions established by the Maastricht Treaty. All of them are expected to adopt the euro once they fulfill the conditions established by the Maastricht Treaty.

The Limits to the Progressive Internationalization of the Euro

When launched in 1999, the euro took the EU to a new plane both within its own territory and in its dealings with the rest of the world. The euro is playing a role commensurate to that of the dollar in world trade and financial markets, and has been gradually adopted by economic operators as a currency through which trade may be conducted and in which financial assets may be denominated.

In the eurozone internal front, the euro has entailed big changes helping to eliminate distortions and differences that used to be hidden by currency fluctuations, creating a level playing field in which everything – prices, costs, taxes and social security payments – becomes instantly comparable from one country to another. In fact the euro has opened up a much wider market for stronger competition within the eurozone.

On the external front, the progressive introduction of the euro would depend on the possibilities offered by the European single currency regarding the evolution, the perception and the reality of the three major determining elements for the use of an international currency: the function of "means of payment", the function of "store of value" and the function of "unit of account."

Means of Payment

With the "means of payment" function many European multinational firms have invited foreign suppliers to invoice them in euros. A handful of world companies have already begun to integrate the euro into their operations. Most business sectors, however, will only change to the euro once some of the major players decide to shift, taking their customers and suppliers with them. It is all a question of critical mass still to be reached.

In the commodity markets, currently priced in US dollars, the impact of the euro has been very limited. At some moment the oil and other commodity producers manifested their intention to shift to the euro to avoid the weakness of the US dollar but at the end of the day they have decided not to denominate their goods in euros.

Inertia and tradition play an important role in sustaining the status quo of the US dollar and the pound sterling at the main boards of trade and commodity exchanges.

The dollar remains the most important international currency even though currency diversification has taken place since 1973. Currency diversification is progressing at a slow pace because the Bretton Woods System, coupled with the Marshall Plan, boosted the USA's role as the major economy and turned the dollar into the "universal currency".

Today capital flows are forty times larger than trade flows. Thus the most important "means of payment" function that a currency can have is to be used as international currency in transactions between third currencies at a lowest possible cost. The key determinants are the size of the market, the exchange restrictions and the aforementioned inertia/tradition. Thereby an established "international currency", like the US dollar, benefits from positive externalities stemming from lower transaction costs, lower information costs and network effects. Conversely, an emerging currency with international ambitions, like the euro, is faced with indirect limitative effects in its internationalization process. This applies particularly to the potential use of the euro as a reference currency for quotation of raw materials.

Store of Value

The second determining element of the importance of a currency is the use of it a "store of value" (composition of international reserves, composition of the debt of developing countries, and so on). In this sense some diversification of the foreign exchange reserves in favor of the euro is taking place, showing that diversification out of the US dollar is more dynamic for the "store of value" function than the other functions (such as invoicing practice by multinational companies or quotation of raw materials). Table 13.1 (above) shows the currency breakdown of the international reserves in accordance with the statistics of the IMF and the ECB.

The future trends in this second international function of the euro as a "store of value" would depend on the "euro intrinsic" qualities demonstrated to the markets, and the political will of the national authorities of the third countries to diversify to the euro to avoid overdependence on the US dollar if the United States continues to run an enormous external imbalance.

Unit of Account

The third element to push the international function of a currency is its use as a unit of account in the post–Bretton Woods system in which crawling-pegs, managed floats and floating regimes have expanded. According to the IMF's 2005 Annual Report on Exchange Arrangements and Exchange Restrictions the exchange rate arrangements followed by the IMF members are distributed as follows:

- thirty-five countries have an independently floating policy;
- fifty-three have managed floating with no predetermined path for the exchange rate;
- thirty-seven have conventional fixed peg arrangements (out of those, twenty-four with the US dollar, three with the euro);
- forty-one have exchange arrangements with no separate legal tender – six Caribbean countries with US dollar, fourteen CFA franc zone with euro, thirteen of which are members of the eurozone (including San Marino), eight are using the dollar as national currency.

It is difficult to assess the hierarchy in the functions of the euro compared with the US dollar as international currency because of:

- inertia and market traditions;
- the larger US dollar market;
- the exchange risks; and
- the network effects.

Observing the evolution we can see that the euro has increased its use moderately compared with the role played before by the addition of the deutschemark and the French franc.

Until 1999 the deutschemark was the *de facto* anchor currency for Western Europe. The French franc was the anchor currency for the African Monetary Unions linked to France by means of the CFA franc.

The European Central Bank has bought the former Bundesbank "credibility" on low inflation, fiscal stability and wage grown in line with productivity.

In addition, the growing unification of Europe's capital markets and the enlargement of the EU – even if enlargement of the eurozone has not yet occurred – would probably boost the role of the euro as a currency of denomination for foreign financing even if the US dollar retains its advantage in terms of transaction costs.

We assume, of course, that the euro will continue to be a solid nominal anchor. At the same time the extent to which the euro will continue to emerge as an international currency will depend very much on the position taken by the ECB as regards its own targets and the loss of control of the money supply outside the eurozone.

Can the ECB have a similar behavior to the United States during the 1960s in terms of allowing external deficits?

More than 60 per cent of the US dollars in circulation are held by foreigners. General De Gaulle referred to this as a "huge privilege", allowing the United States to run-up external deficits and buy European industries. Immediately the United States encountered a problem in controlling the money supply.

Assuming that the eurozone is ready to follow the 1960s dollar model, Europe's balance of payments basic account would have to move from surplus to deficit in order to provide enough euro-liquidity for the international monetary system to enhance the use of euros in international transactions and to provide euro-liquidity to third parties. This idea is in conflict with the ECB objectives of maintaining low inflation and making the euro a strong and stable currency.

The enlargement of the eurozone with possible future membership of the United Kingdom and most of the EU's new members will help the development of the euro as a better international currency.

Up until the present day central banks have followed the rest of the investment community by moving parts of their foreign exchange reserves into riskier assets in the search for higher returns, but in actions that reflect the strength of the US dollar.

During 2005 only a small number of central banks diversified their holdings of foreign currency out of dollar-denominated assets and into euro assets, as explained by the *Financial Times* taking into consideration a survey conducted from 56 central banks around the world (*Financial Times*, February 14, 2006).

The Euro and Developing Countries

The statistics produced by the Bank for International Settlements (BIS) and the IMF are continuously showing that the developing countries have a greater preference for the euro in the context of their official holdings.

In 2004 the share of national currencies in total identified official holdings of foreign exchange was of 71.5 per cent (US dollar) to 20.9 per cent (euro) for industrial countries, and 59.9 per cent to 29.2 per cent for developing countries.

The development of the euro into a major international currency for developing countries is following a clear pattern: from 19.9 per cent of share in 1999 to 29.2 per cent in 2004.

According to the BIS that move has been helped by a tendency of the rich OPEC petroleum exporting countries to move smoothly towards the euro. In 2001 75 per cent of the reserves of the OPEP countries were denominated in US dollars and 12 per cent in euro. This percentage has change to 69.5 per cent and 16 per cent respectively in 2005.

This relative greater preference of the developing countries for the euro is a consequence of a series of factors: historical links, trade, aid flows and other elements that relate Europe and the developing countries as well as the loss of value of the US dollar and its weakness due to the enormous external deficit of the American economy.

Colonial Monetary Links

In the colonial era the countries of Central and West African sub-regions operated some form of monetary integration with the colonial powers. The French-speaking countries had their local CFA franc fixed to the French franc at par, while the English-speaking countries had their local pound fixed to the pound sterling at par. The arrangements in both zones were purely currency board systems. The French-speaking countries maintained the arrangement beyond independence and advanced it to a full economic union. The arrangement was abandoned in the English-speaking countries, with each one introducing its own national currency.

The CFA zones comprise today fourteen countries: Benin, Burkina Faso, Côte d'Ivoire, Guinea-Bissau, Mali, Niger, Senegal and Togo forming the WAEMU (West Africa Economic and Monetary Union) and Cameroon, Central Africa, Chad, Congo Republic, Equatorial Guinea and Gabon forming the CAEMC (Central Africa Economic and Monetary Community). These areas are linked to the eurozone through the French treasury. The participation of the English-speaking West African countries is also envisaged but the advancement of a West African Monetary Zone (as a Second Monetary Zone in the West) has been hindered by the creation of UEMOA by the countries of the Western African Economic and Monetary Union CFA zone in 1994.

The CFA zones have had one of the longest experiences with a fixed exchange rate for a convertible currency and with regional integration, including both common currency areas and preferential regional trade arrangements, of any group of developing countries. Since their establishment in the aftermath of the Second World War, the franc zones have survived decolonization, the collapse of the Bretton Woods exchange rate system, debt crises and the end of the Cold War.

Economic Links

In addition to this direct euro-link for some developing African countries and the use of the euro in the French and Dutch departments and territories in the Caribbean, Indian and Pacific Oceans, another element relevant to a further possible greater internationalization of the euro among the developing countries is the fact that the EU is the biggest donor of international aid and the biggest customer of the exports from developing countries.

It is also clear that, in terms of relations with the EU and the eurozone, the developing group of nations is not homogeneous. The United States is the most important economic and financial partner of most Caribbean and Latin American countries while Japan and Australia are major partners for much of the Pacific developing countries. The EU is the bigger partner for most of the Mediterranean and sub-Saharan countries.

Trade

Concerning trade, Europe absorbs 43 per cent of African exports while the United States absorbs 19 per cent and Asia 17 per cent.

On top of these statistics it is necessary to say that the EU aims to contribute to a more equitable integration of developing countries into the international trading system through coherent action on three levels:

- the multilateral participation in the WTO talks to advance the Doha Development Agenda;
- the bilateral agreements with plenty of developing countries and groupings of developing countries; and
- through autonomous measures like the Generalized Systems of Preferences.

This means that Europe is an open economy for exports from developing countries. Nevertheless, improving market access is not in itself sufficient to help the internationalization of the euro in developing countries because most of the transactions are quoted in US dollars. Eighty per cent of the African exports to Europe are oil and other commodities quoted in US dollars.

Inertia and tradition in the commodity markets are preventing further expansion of the euro in trade transactions between the EU and developing world.

Aid Flows

As far as the question of aid, 55 per cent of the world's development assistance was provided by the EU in 2005. EU assistance goes to more than 160 countries, territories and organizations and focuses on the global challenges of the twenty-first century: tackling poverty, promoting democracy and security, social equity, economic prosperity and environmental sustainability. Seventy-seven Commission delegation offices are now managing external assistance programs on the ground, in closer cooperation with countries concerned.

What is the influence that such a predominant situation may have for enhancing the role of the Euro as an international currency? The first answer is the limited relevance of the developing countries more largely assisted by the EU aid flows (basically sub-Saharan and Mediterranean countries) in terms of world population and GDP (see Table 13.2).

Table 13.2 The World Economy 2000

	Population (million habitants)	GDP (billion €)
UE–25	452	8.935
Other Europe	339	1.064
Mediterranean countries	154	388
Sub-Saharan countries	671	345
China and India	2.310	1.685
Latin America	520	2.315
Japan	127	5.163
USA	286	10.806
Other countries	1.261	3.313
World total	6.133	34.015

Source: Report Sapir.

This reality is not helping the development of the euro as an international currency even considering the relative preference for the euro that developing countries are showing for the European single currency (see Table 13.3).

Table 13.3 Share of National Currencies in Total Identified Official Holdings of Foreign Exchange (Per Cent)

	Developed countries		Developing countries	
	US dollar	Euro	US dollar	Euro
1999	73.5	16.1	68.2	19.9
2000	72.5	17.1	68.2	20.6
2001	72.7	18.0	68.6	21.8
2002	68.9	22.4	64.0	26.1
2003	70.5	22.1	60.7	28.9
2004	71.5	20.9	59.9	29.2

Source: IMF.

In addition, the critical mass of the amount involved in foreign aid is not sufficient to allow a bigger role for the euro except in cases in which political will to exclude the US dollar in foreign transactions has been expressed (the case of Cuba that is penalizing the use of dollars by tourists).

In accordance with the results of the 2002 UN Monterrey Conference of Financing for Development, the European countries would make additional efforts in the field of aid following the agreement reached during the Barcelona European Council of March 2002.

As stated by the Financial Perspectives 2007–2013 approved by the Brussels European Council of December 2005, "The Union is a global player. It needs to be ready to share in the responsibility for helping to reduce global poverty, including by contributing to the achievement of the Millennium Development Goals, and to improve global security, and to have adequate funding to enable it to do so."

On the basis of these commitments, the Union's external actions and policies would include amounts between 6.280 and 8.070 million euros every year between 2007–2013 and a financial envelope of 22.682 million euros for the period 2008–2013 under the existing inter-governmental European Development Fund Framework in favor of the Africa-Caribbean-Pacific (ACP) states.

Among the countries receiving some aid from the EU only a shift by China to the euro would change the possibilities of internationalization of the single European currency, but this country is set to remain the dollar's best friend because currency diversification requires a great currency flexibility that China does not have at this moment (*Financial Times*, January 9, 2006). Due to the weakness of the US dollar vis-à-vis the euro, China has announced its intention to "optimize the currency and asset structure" of the country's enormous foreign currency reserves and some observers consider that further move to the euro would be possible.

China is today the world's largest single holder of official reserves having more than a half of the international foreign reserves of the developing world (about 950 billion US dollars out of 2,000 billion); 75 per cent of it is believed to be in dollar denominated assets.

Migrant Remittances

Migration is a rising issue on the policy agenda in most European countries. Policy makers and the general public are confronted with a substantial degree of confusion related to issues of legal and illegal migration.

There are between 34 and 37 million foreign-born migrants in the EU–25. Overall the number of migrants leads to a share of around 8 per cent of the total EU–25 population (Krieger 2005).

Migrants in Europe are expending and investing most of their revenue in the EU itself. Therefore one should not expect any substantial shock in order to help internationalization of the euro due to migrant remittances in the developing countries because few people coming from these countries have good business or job opportunities that allow them to send money back home in substantial amounts.

Relative Level of International Reserves

One element that is helping the internationalization of the euro but that at the same time is disturbing the expansion of the euro as an international currency among developing countries in the future is that some of the most connected countries with the EU (the CFA countries) hold more international reserves than needed.

The reserve cover ratio (putting in relation gross official reserves and short-term liabilities) amounted for these countries to an estimated 120 per cent while the requirement for this ratio is only a minimum 20 per cent.

This obviously limits the expected benefits to them of reserves in terms of shock smoothing. It is conceivable that this ratio could be safely reduced without undue pressure being put on the exchange rate, thereby freeing resources for enhanced consumption smoothing and development in the zone. This can be contrary to the idea of a greater internationalization of the euro but can show a good image of sound financial governance for the countries not linked to CFA/eurozone.

Direct and Indirect Effects

Even if limited in amount, the consequences of the introduction of euro for countries that have trade, tourism and financial links with Europe have been both direct and indirect (Granell May–June 1999).

The direct effects relate to trade creation, trade diversion and the impact of establishing a single financial market in euros for the foreign debt of non–EU countries. The indirect effects relate to the global or systemic effects of the euro as a new international currency. It is worth saying that some ACP countries receive significant amounts of aid from the EU, and the denomination of this aid has been switched to euros. According to OECD statistics, the impact of this is limited and only applies to a very few sub-Saharan countries heavily dependent on EU assistance for the financing of their public sector.

Caribbean countries maintaining close US dollar links would not shift to the euro even if the euro were less volatile against other world currencies. This is because it is not clear for them what the real positive or negative impact on their economy of a move in the EU/dollar exchange rate relation or volatility would be.

The Weakness of the Dollar, Developing Countries, and the Internationalization of the Euro

Beyond volatility itself, developing countries actively trading with the eurozone have an interest in the movement of the euro/dollar and euro/yen exchange rates.

Of course there is no reason to expect that – in the long run – the euro will be either too strong or too weak against other currencies if the major partners also pursue sound monetary and fiscal policies. But the tendency to the depreciation of the dollar against the euro that has started at the beginning of 2001 is supposed to continue due to the magnitude of the US external deficit.

All central banks know that a big depreciation of the US dollar would be a danger for the stability of the world economy and the Group of Ten and the G–7 are trying to avoid an excessive depreciation of the US dollar vis-à-vis the euro and the rest of major currencies. The main economies are the most interested in not creating additional problems in this respect, even if the present euro/dollar relation is not the most satisfactory for the competitiveness of the European goods and services. This message is true for the developed countries managing the world economy, yet the same cannot be said for the developing countries.

Even if the new US Federal Reserve President were to continue the increase in US interest rates that began in June 2004 under Mr. Greenspan, some investors and central banks from developing countries may consider shifting from dollars to euros because of the foreseen decline in value of the US dollar due to the enormous US foreign debt (*Wall Street Journal*, March 23, 2006). By keeping the European interest rates lower than US interest rates, the ECB is contributing to avoiding a bigger shift from the US dollar to the euro, but it is necessary to remember that the ECB is not pursuing a policy of having a more internationalized euro, but following the mandate of taking care only of inflation and stability in Europe.

Of course, when the membership of EMU exceeds twelve countries (with the participation of Slovenia since January 1, 2007) there will be a modest increase in the international role of the euro that only would be radically changed if the UK finally decides to surrender the pound sterling to the euro. Nevertheless, the tendency towards firm policies against inflation may also be encouraged by the fact that some of the new smaller EU members have stronger inflationary pressures compared with the actual biggest three core EMU countries.

In conclusion, the expansion of the euro among developing countries would not be supported by the attractiveness of high European interest rates, but by a progressive engagement of the European countries in the Third World through trade, investment, aid and other economic relations. The pace will depend on the future performance of the European economy and will depend as well of the level of solidarity that European taxpayers would be able to show vis-à-vis the developing countries. In any case the change to an additional internationalization of the euro would never be dramatic enough to change the monetary traditions and inertia that would continue to play in favor of the US dollar.

References

European Commission (2003), "An Agenda for a Growing Europe: Making the EU Economic System Deliver", Report of an Independent High-Level Study Group Established on the Initiative of the President of the European Commission, Chairman: André Sapir (Brussels).

Financial Times (January 9, 2006), "China Is Set to Remain the Dollar's Best Friend".

Financial Times (February 14, 2006), "Central Banks Opt for Riskier Assets but Stick by the Dollar".

Granell, Francesc (May–June 1999), "The Euro and Its Significance for the ACP Countries", *The Courier ACP*, no. 175.

Granell, Francesc (April 2004), "The European Stability and Growth Pact Debate and the Future of Europe", Miami European Union Center Conference on the European Union Constitution and the Future of Europe.

Krieger, H. (2005), "Who Is Going Where? Migration Trends in the EU Context" (Dublin: European Foundation for The Improvement of Living and Working Conditions).

Trichet, Jean-Claude (May 14, 2004), "The International Role of the Euro", speech delivered at the Schierensee Gesprache on May 14, 2004.

Wall Street Journal (March 23, 2006), "US Debt Party: Investors Look Danger in The Eye".

Chapter 14

Currency Crises and Institutional Changes in Latin America: Lessons from Mexico

Angel Calderón-Madrid

Introduction

In 1982, 1985, 1987 and 1994 Mexico registered major exchange rate devaluations; in the first and in the last of these episodes it was the epicenter of an emerging markets' financial crisis that required international intervention. Our point of departure for an understanding of the determinants of Mexico's abrupt exchange rate movements is that the models to analyze them can be classified into three generations of models. This understanding is required to assess if the institutional reforms they instigated are effective to avoid their recurrence, to reduce vulnerability of the economy to external shocks and to induce market participants to internalize cost implied by exchange and interest rates uncertainty.

In first generation models a collapse of a fixed exchange rate is the foreseen result of unsustainable fiscal and monetary policies. In second generation models, exchange rate devaluations can occur as self-fulfilling events in which financial market participants, in an attempt to protect themselves, precipitate the very devaluation they fear. This occurs even though economic fundamentals are consistent with a no-crisis outcome. That is, as opposed to what happens with previous models, more than one equilibrium exchange rate is embedded for a same set of fundamentals. The multiple equilibrium possibility solution is shared by third generation models which, in turn, incorporate as key ingredients government bailout guarantees, moral hazard, contract enforceability problems and the effect of exchange rate movements on banks' balance sheets.[1] The depreciation of the French franc in 1993 is generally regarded as the event that forced economists to recognize the limits of the first generation currency crisis models, whose predictive power was most clearly shown in the now paradigmatic case of the 1982 Mexican peso devaluation. In turn, the 1998 Asian crisis made abundantly clear the need for a third generation of models. In this paper we show that relevant features for

1 A representative model of the first can be found in Flood and Garber (1984), of the second in Obstfeld (April 1998) and of the third in Schneider and Tornell (December 2000).

the development of second and third generation models were already provided by currency collapses that had previously occurred in Mexico.

We show that the collapse of the Mexican peso in 1987 was a self-fulfilling event that occurred in spite of a compatibility of fiscal fundamentals with the prevailing exchange rate regime. We consider the ingredients required to understand the 1994 crisis and argue that these are the core of third generation currency models, especially the government bailout guarantees offered by Mexican authorities before 1994 and the uncovered positions of banks' balance sheets. We add that another important ingredient to understanding this crisis was the prevailing lack of transparency of key indicators in the conduction of monetary policy and banking supervision – among them those related to commercial banks' solvency and to the extent that the Central Bank could back-up with international reserves domestic public debt that was denominated in US dollars (so-called *Tesobonos*). This lack of transparency misled private agents in their decisions concerning exchange rate and interest rate uncertainty.

We stress and discuss how the crises of 1985, 1987 and 1994 were powerful instigators of major institutional changes on the macroeconomic and financial regulatory fronts. After the 1985 exchange rate crisis, the economic administration introduced far-reaching fiscal reform, reduced government subsidies, privatized the majority of state owned enterprises and successfully renegotiated its foreign debt. The Central Bank's autonomous status resulted from a need to avoid the repetition of the circumstances that led to the 1987 exchange rate depreciation. In turn, after the 1994 crisis, measures were taken for the elimination of the blanket coverage on bank deposits and its replacement by a limited deposit guarantee scheme, for an adequate bank deposit insurance mechanism and for more transparency in indicators used by monetary authorities for the supervision of banks.

In addition to this introduction, the paper is structured into three sections. The first section presents an overview of the evolution of the Mexican economy. The following section examines three major exchange rate crises that occurred in Mexico in a period of only ten years. We posit that while first generation models adequately explain the 1985 crisis, the 1987 crisis belongs to the second generation and that the 1994–1995 episode provides the first case in the world that inspired the development of third generation crisis models. The section ends with a discussion of the 1998 episode – which could have resulted in another exchange rate depreciation, but did not – and asks what was different. The concluding remarks are left for the final section.

Background of the Mexican Economy

The so-called "populist" economic policy conducted in Mexico before 1982 led to an incontrovertible textbook case of "first-generation" exchange rate crisis (Bazdresch and Levy 1991). Although this episode was followed by a three-year lapse of temporary macroeconomic discipline, no effective fiscal reform was taken then. As a result, an abrupt 20 per cent loss in the value of the peso in 1985 made evident the need for measures that effectively address the incompatibility of fiscal fundamentals and the exchange rate regime. In spite of the fact that these were taken and solid macroeconomic fundamentals were achieved by 1987, another major currency crisis was registered at the end of that year. Since this occurred in an inflationary environment, the movement of the exchange rate made the indexation of the economy more likely. As a response to this situation, measures were taken to restore and maintain the credibility of monetary authorities – a process that culminated with the granting of autonomy to the Central Bank. With strict adherence, an announced management of the nominal exchange rate was implemented from 1988 onwards. This was the result of a monetary program, with continuing commitment to credit expansion taking place only as expectations and growth reactivation consolidated (Aspe 1993).

Privatization of publicly owned enterprises and banks,[2] financial de-regulation, sustained reductions in public debt, large surplus in the capital account of the balance of payments and the signing of a Free Trade Agreement with United States and Canada characterized the last two years of the 1980s and the first three of the 1990s. The funds obtained from the privatization of publicly owned enterprises were used to re-purchase government debt, which was also reduced with the sustained fiscal surplus of these years. As the share of public debt declined in banks' portfolios, the private one augmented.

During this period, Mexican firms had access to international capital markets on unprecedented favorable terms. This implied that, for the most dynamic and solvent of them, acquiring domestic loans was no longer an attractive option[3] and that Mexican banks had to turn to riskier clients as their lending capacity grew. Bankers making loans before the crisis erupted, as well as their custumers, were expecting higher real estate prices, lower interest rates and faster economic growth in subsequent years.

According to Krugman (1995: 30), "excessive market optimism on how the reforms adopted in Mexico after 1988 would generate a growth takeoff led to a temporarily self-fulfilling prophecy along with a more subtle political process through which the common beliefs of policy makers and investors proved mutually reinforcing".

The flip side of an apparently solid macroeconomic picture was a sustained private sector spending spree fueled by the increased lending capacity of banks. The five-year boom in household spending had an aggregate counterpart in terms of their holding of financial assets relative to their debts. By the first half of 1992 they were no longer net creditors with the banking sector, as their loans, taken as an aggregate, surpassed their deposits. Their holdings of public debt also declined as a counterpart of the wealth reduction implied by having expenditure flows above their earnings for a sustained number of periods. Due to this reduction in financial wealth and because foreigners increased their holding

2 The privatization of the commercial banks in 1991 took place following nine years under state ownership.

3 With the nominal exchange rate policy between 1991 and 1994 *ex-ante* cost of financing in dollars was very low vis-à-vis financing in pesos.

of peso-dominated Mexican debt, domestic residents ended up holding in 1994 a very low share of Mexican financial assets.[4]

Compared with previous crises, in 1994 the exchange rate regime was relatively more vulnerable. As the exchange rate crisis erupted in December 1994, the consequences of an inadequate supervision and regulation of domestic commercial banks became evident: This time a banking crisis and the fears of the cost it could imply for the government aggravated the collapse of the Mexican peso.

A sudden reversal of expectations concerning an optimistic growth scenario and the feasibility of avoiding an exchange-rate collapse was accentuated by three factors: the lack of transparency of indicators used by the monetary authorities in their decision making, the high exposure of banks to macroeconomic shocks and an associated government contingent liability in bailing out those who were distressed.

First, Second and Third Generation Currency Crisis Models in Mexico

We analyze next the determinants of the 1985, 1987 and 1994 currency crisis and stress that each of them illustrates a case study of first, second and third generation currency crisis models.

Unsustainable Macroeconomic Policies and the 1985 Peso Depreciation

A limited amount of international reserves and the perception that the authorities would not or could not change their expenditure and income patterns, prompted, as it had happened in 1982, major capital outflows that caused the collapse of the Mexican currency in 1985. As in the preceding depreciation of 1982, first generation models adequately explain the 1985 depreciation as the result of forward-looking agents reacting to the perception that fiscal imbalances were no longer sustainable.

Market participants' expectations concerning the incompatibility of economic fundamentals and the ability of the Mexican government to sustain its exchange-rate regime were reinforced by four major factors:

1 Before 1985, the authorities reduced public expenditures across the board to reduce fiscal deficits, instead of eliminating or consolidating state functions. This led many observers to believe that – as happened to be the case – the 1982–1984 reduction in public expenditures was transitory in nature, and that the omnipresent role of the state in the economy had not really changed.

---

4 *Cfr.* Calderón-Madrid (1999). Since foreigners have, relative to domestic residents, more investment opportunities in other countries to which they can quickly move into this might have been an additional source of vulnerability of the exchange rate regime.

2 The uncertainty prevailing in oil markets made oil export revenues an unstable source of revenue, a problem aggravated by the fact that it represented 26 per cent of public sector income in 1985.
3 The semester prior to the exchange rate depreciation was characterized by a relaxation of fiscal spending.
4 It was not clear yet that ongoing negotiations with international bankers to reduce Mexico's debt overhang – initiated in the wake of the 1982 debt crisis – would come to a favorable conclusion; discussions concerning reductions in interest payment on foreign debt and changes in its amortization dates were still taking place.

Changes in the composition of fiscal accounts and a debt renegotiation program that altered perceptions of fiscal solvency and thus of the feasibility of announced exchange rate programs occurred only after the crisis episode. Although these changes were sustainable, the exchange rate regime would collapse two years later.

Self-Fulfilling Confidence Crisis and the Collapse of the Peso in 1987

In spite of solid macroeconomic fundamentals in 1987, a major currency crisis was registered at the end of that year. During 1987 the balance of payments was quite strong and the possibility of multiple equilibria in second-generation models is consistent with puzzles such as the one expressed in relation to that episode:

> It is paradoxical that financial crisis should have occurred when international reserves were at a historical peak [at the end of 1987] and the balance of payments was recording a substantial surplus. But there is also little doubt that the inflationary environment amplified the nervousness of financial markets. Once more it became apparent that, in times of high inflation, expectations are extremely volatile and can easily destabilize what appeared to be an otherwise sound financial situation. (Ortiz 1991: 289)

In early 1987 inflation rates increased to unprecedented levels and were already exhibiting an upward trend. The government reacted by allowing the nominal exchange rate to depreciate at a controlled rate, and by varying the rhythm of this daily crawling-peg in an attempt to balance two conflicting aims: to reduce domestic inflation and to counteract the effect of cumulative domestic inflation on export competitiveness. From July to October, the daily rate of depreciation was reduced relative to the previous six months. Then, in a clear change of policy, during the six weeks before the devaluation took place, the monetary authorities reacted by accelerating the rate of nominal exchange rate depreciation. It was increased from a monthly rate of 6.6 per cent in the third week of October to over 10 per cent in less than forty days, thereby partly compensating lost export competitiveness, but signaling that the exchange rate would no longer be used as nominal anchor to achieve disinflation.

In theory, as in a model developed by Obstfeld (1988), monetary authorities can provoke a speculative attack on the balance of payments if they lead agents to believe that they are prepared to use the exchange rate as an instrument to make up for reductions in export competitiveness. He showed that the following is possible: When forward-looking speculators think that the monetary authorities are prepared to use the exchange rate if inflation hits a certain threshold, the result can be a forced devaluation followed by inflation whereby this threshold or an even higher rate is registered. Thus, instead of inflation reaching the threshold and causing the bank to act, a speculative attack of agents anticipating the behavior of the bank forces an abrupt depreciation before inflation actually approaches the limit, leading to further inflation.

The monthly rate of inflation increased to almost 15 per cent in December – almost twice as high as the average monthly rate of inflation of the previous eleven months, as a result of a speculative attack that caused a 21 per cent devaluation of the peso. It is our contention that an inflation threshold that would have led monetary authorities to adjust the nominal exchange rate was largely superseded in December 1987 in Mexico, not because of the actions of the authorities, but as a result of a forced devaluation precipitated by the actions of forward-looking financial market participants. To explain this abrupt exchange-rate depreciation, the insight of the Obstfeld model referred to above is useful; hence we consider next the relationship between changes in domestic interest rates and in the exchange rate to show how the monetary authorities were the ones that provoked the speculative attack that forced the collapse of the exchange rate.

Consider the monthly nominal interest rates on short-term (twenty-eight day) peso-denominated government bonds – the so-called *Cetes* – that are shown in Table 14.1. These rates increased steadily from October 21 onwards. This upward trend is consistent with the hypothesis that an upward revision of expectations about the monthly rate of exchange rate depreciation had taken place. It is also compatible with effects associated with a reduction in the credibility of the announcements of monetary authorities (an extra return was demanded to compensate for the risk that rates of return would again become lower than expected in terms of an alternative asset denominated in US dollars).

During the period in which exchange rate depreciation was not accelerated by the Central Bank (July, August, September and the first half of October) the annualized *ex-post* rate of return was twenty-four points above returns to comparable bonds in international markets.[5] In contrast, the return on bonds issued on October 21, which matured four weeks later (November 18) was only one-fourth the average rate obtained for bonds maturing during the four previous weeks (second column in Table 14.1).[6]

A return to US dollars, lower than what market participants were expecting, was the result of a rate of exchange-rate depreciation that was – at least 1.83 points – faster than what they thought would be the case, when they bought the

5 *Viz.*, subtracting the twenty-eight days' observed nominal exchange-rate depreciation from the nominal interest rate on *Cetes*. Not shown in Table 14.1, corresponding returns for July and August were on average 2.46 per cent and 2.20 per cent.

6 We concentrated on the dates of primary offers, which took place once a week.

Table 14.1 Rates of Return of *Cetes* During September–December 1987

Auction date	Nominal rate of return in pesos at the day of the auction	*Ex-post* rate a month later, when converted to return in US$	Auction date	Nominal rate of return in pesos at the day of the auction	*Ex-post* rate a month later, when converted to return in US$
September 2	6.98	2.06	October 28	7.26	0.87
September 9	6.95	2.18	November 4	7.37	0.51
September 16	7.00	2.36	November 11	7.76	0.61
September 23	7.05	2.57	November 18	8.31	–15.5
September 30	6.97	2.61	November 25	8.89	–14.19
October 7	6.9	2.26	December 2	8.88	–12.68
October 14	6.9	1.79	December 9	9.36	–10.72
October 21	7.00	0.57			

Source: Bank of Mexico.

bond (no factors determining the risk of holding pesos changed). This story was repeated during the following three weekly auctions.[7]

Due to the fact that the Central Bank depreciated the exchange rate at a faster rate than that expected by financial market participants holding Mexican government debt, during these weeks *Cetes* returns ended up below expectations.

That is, as a result of successive surprises of this kind, and given expectations that a further acceleration of exchange rate depreciation could be on its way, a major speculative attack on the peso gained momentum and the abrupt exchange rate adjustment ensued. This caused capital losses and currency depreciation well above what financial market participants had feared.

Uncovered Banks' Balance-Sheet Risk-Exposure and the 1994 Crisis

In December 1994 an exchange rate crisis erupted after a seven-year period in which a commitment to keep inflation low using the exchange rate as a nominal anchor was observed.[8] There was an initial attempt to have a 10 per cent fall of the peso within the limits of an exchange rate band controlled by the Central Bank. Over the next two days, following this initial realignment, no major increase in interest rate occurred and more reserves were lost than in the previous month.[9]

7 International interest rates did not fall in these weeks and factors determining country risk in Mexico – such as presidential elections in 1988 – contributed, if at all, towards an upward revision of the *ex ante* dollar return.

8 For a discussion of "reputation building" process that characterized the 1998–1993 exchange and interest rate management, *cfr.* Calderón-Madrid (1997): 138–140.

9 At the time of the crisis, the Central Bank did not use to disclose information on the level of international reserves.

This speculative attack forced the Central Bank to withdraw from the foreign exchange-rate market, allowing the currency to float freely.

According to information that is now publicly available, the previous large decline in international reserves occurred a month before the exchange rate collapse, as a result of a relatively minor political scandal (the resignation of the attorney general in mid-November).[10] This was the first time that the authorities of the Central Bank opted to loosen international reserves, rather than tighten interest rates as a policy to stop capital outflows. During the two days that the authorities attempted to keep the exchange rate within a larger band, they also opted to loosen international reserves, rather than letting interest rates skyrocket as an attempt to stop the speculative attack.

Market participants might have perceived this policy stance to signal the authorities' fears in avoiding potential costs implied to them by raising interest rates and deteriorating the solvency of banks. If this were the case, the capital outflows and the exchange rate depreciation could be seen partly as a result of a self-fulfilling currency crisis of the type suggested by Bensaid and Jeanne (1997). In these crises, raising the nominal interest rate helps maintain the parity, but is costly for the government. The speculators are aware that this cost gives incentives for the government to stop defending the parity, which in turn reinforces the speculation against the currency.

A two-month downward trend of the exchange rate, accompanied by increasing domestic interest rates followed the exhaustion of international reserves.[11] This time, a climate of uncertainty due to the overexposure of banks and potential bailing-out of those in distress created conditions for further exchange-rate movements to be determined less by market fundamentals than by the expectations of financial market participants.[12]

A major component aggravating the crisis was the prevailing government guarantee that bank depositors and other senior bank creditors would be protected in full in the event of bank insolvency. This created incentives to undertake risky lending practices, with high profits in the event of an optimistic scenario and limited losses otherwise.

As a result, banks had an uncovered position of their balance sheets in 1994 against macroeconomic risk – a risky position aptly described as being "in effect long [in] real wages, short [in] nominal interest rates and long [in] real property".[13]

---

10 This behavior contrasts with the one adopted by the Central Bank in April of that year; their reaction then to an attack on the peso was to raise interest rates significantly.

11 This result contrasts with previous episodes, for example, 1985 and 1987, in which the nominal exchange rate initially "overshot" its level and no further real exchange rate depreciation occurred.

12 A stabilization package put together by the US Treasury and the IMF in 1995 helped to stabilize expectations.

13 Lacoursiere (1999). Domestic banks had a "potential" currency mismatch that did not occur. This was because their dollar liabilities were "backed" with Tesobonos and there were doubts as to the government fully honoring their value in dollars. A point raised by Garber (1988) is that domestic banking sector's off–balance sheet operations played an important role in increasing the vulnerability of the economy to an exchange rate attack.

The developments on the exchange rate front exposed and intensified the potential insolvency of most banks, which in turn aggravated fiscal and balance of payments problems. Financial market participants' *perceptions* about the fragility of the banks' balances and of the lack of an adequate institutional mechanism to reduce the potential fiscal cost of a major banking crisis further precipitated the loss in value of the Mexican peso.[14] Moreover, by acting initially on the exchange-rate front, the authorities led market participants to fear that, since the monetary program had been discredited, domestic interest rates would have to increase and that economic slowdown would follow.

Once the crisis began in December of that year, it became apparent that banks had portfolios with badly assessed or non-existing credit collateral and with very inefficient administrative records. This situation – attributable to a great extent to lax banking supervision and lack of transparency – was severely aggravated by the prevailing system of imperfect enforceability of contracts which encouraged a culture of non-payment of debts.

This relatively lax regulatory and supervisory context implied that, with the prevailing institutional framework, neither bank owners nor their managers had incentives to improve risk-assessment strategies and accounting practices. It also meant that incentives for the circumvention of regulations for related lending were implicitly offered.

According to calculations by Guerra (1997), in 1994 a non-negligible share of the mortgage loan portfolio either had, or was close to having, a negative capital value (because of interest-rate increases and a decrease in real estate prices during the two preceding years). Thus, the ratio of the amount of the loan relative to the house value was close to one for many borrowers.

These figures led Guerra to suggest that "[t]he mortgage loan problem is frequently pointed out as caused by the crisis, [n]evertheless ... the problem of non-performing mortgage portfolio had already been generated [by 1994], it was the crisis which created the conditions under which it will be developed" (Guerra 1997: 44).

Since most mortgage loans had interest payments of 5 or 6 percentage points above the equilibrium inter-bank interest rate, debtors saw their debt increase sharply when this rate increased to values above 50 per cent in 1995, as a result of the exchange rate collapse in December 1994. This increase in the real value of mortgages, together with a fall in housing values and the highly leveraged position of debtors (in view of their small initial down payments), caused the ratio of the

---

He argued that commercial banks "inflated" capital inflows before the crisis by means of derivatives and other off–balance sheets instruments and automatically reversed them after the crisis, thereby accentuating the sharp turnaround in foreign currency flows that was to occur, as soon as perceptions changed.

14 In third generation crisis models it is possible to explain a situation in which an attack can provoke a crisis that would not have occurred with such strength otherwise. For example, in the model deployed by Burnside, Eichenbaum and Rebelo (2000), self-fulfilling devaluations are possible because devaluations transform the government's contingent liabilities into actual liabilities and deplete government reserves.

value of the credit relative to the value of the property to approach or pass one. Between 1995 and 1999, these ratios continued to worsen. The extent to which the evolution of the non-performing mortgage portfolio was linked to the lack of recovery of property prices in Mexico is reflected in Table 14.2: Contrary to expectations when mortgages were granted, the real value of houses did not increase more quickly than consumer prices. In addition, homeowners could not service their debt any longer, since their income was stagnant or declining as a result of the economic recession that followed the 1994 crisis.

Table 14.2 Variations in the Prices of Houses Relative to the Consumer Price Index (Relative to the So-Called *Udis*)

Type of house	1995	1996	1997	1998	1999
Social	1.03	0.98	1.00	0.93	0.85
Economic	1.06	0.87	0.89	0.79	0.77
Average	0.97	0.87	0.92	0.89	0.8
Residential	0.92	0.87	0.95	0.85	0.76
Residential plus	0.99	0.94	0.95	0.89	1.21

Source: FOVI, Bank of Mexico.

Some authors, most notably Sachs *et al.* (1996), have suggested that the financially vulnerable position of the government was a major detonator of the exchange rate depreciation. According to them, "[i]liquidity exposed Mexico to a self-fulfilling panic. Investors realized that if other investors stopped lending money to the Mexican Government, the Government would be unable to repay its debt – particularly the dollar-denominated Tesobonos – as they fell due. Therefore, each individual investor could do no better than to withdraw its funds when other investors started to withdraw their funds".

Together with the government's un-hedged position we argue next that private firms with debt in foreign currency as well as domestic banks with liabilities in dollars were also major contributors to the severity of the crisis. Mexico's minister of finance five years later recalled the situation he had to face as follows:

> We started doing some rough back-of-the-envelope calculations of what was the amount of amortizations due in '95 and it came out to pretty much staggering amounts. We were running a current account deficit of about 7 per cent of GDP – that was about 40 billion dollars. Plus we had another 35 billion worth of Tesobonos, and about 7–8 billion of sovereign debt due. *And amortizations of private debt for another 40–45 billion dollars.* So, the number was pretty big, as we sat there. (Ortiz 2002, italics added)

This reveals the relevance of private market participants. Moreover, as a result of a market optimism that resulted without basis, private firms and banks participating in international financial markets were unwilling to issue long-term debt or hedge their positions, even days before the crisis erupted. This reluctance was due to prevailing expectations that Mexican liabilities were about to receive a lower-risk qualification by international grading companies – hence for funding costs to fall down. Due to these expectations, not only were most of them very liquid in their exposure, but they were also un-hedged against macroeconomic crisis.

On the one hand, as they attempted to move against an unfavorable scenario and pay debts in foreign currency, they increased the pressure on the Mexican peso. On the other hand, due to the liquid positions of the holders of these assets, once the crisis started, it was difficult to renew them, even at much higher rates; they were either rationed or offered unacceptable terms.

As a result of 1994 crisis, the regulatory and supervision frameworks for commercial banks were substantially reformed: The elimination of the blanket coverage on bank deposits and its replacement by a limited deposit guarantee scheme; the implementation of an efficient bank deposit insurance mechanism embedded with early warning and prompter intervention mechanisms[15] and easing remaining barriers to foreign ownership in the financial sector, to the effect that foreign investors gained the right to acquire equity holdings in the three largest commercial banks.

These features and the institutional changes that have occurred as a result of the other two crises discussed in this paper have helped to avoid an exchange rate collapse in the last decade. (Since 1985 fiscal sustainability has been part of the macroeconomic agenda and – with the exception of the bailing-out of banks in the 1995–1998 period – has no longer been a source of incompatibility with exchange rate stability. In light of the 1987 exchange rate crisis experience, the Central Bank has been concerned with keeping domestic inflation within a targeted figure – becoming an autonomous institution has enhanced its credibility in achieving them).

This appears to have been shown in 1998 and 1999, when seven of Mexico's important competitors in the US market – Indonesia, Thailand, Malaysia, Philippines, Korea, Taiwan and Singapore – had major exchange rate depreciations.[16] In clear contrast to what happened in 1987, there was no doubt that the Central Bank's position was that the expansion and sheltering of export markets should not be achieved at the expense of monetary policy credibility, but by means of sustained productivity gains in the production of goods and services. The monetary program for inflation control and financial stability was not modified and after relatively minor exchange and interest rates movements, they recovered their 1997 levels.[17]

15 *Cfr*. Calomiris (1999).

16 During the first months of the Asian crisis (Jun 1997–January 1998), their currencies had depreciated by 198 per cent, 104 per cent, 77 per cent, 67 per cent, 85 per cent, 20 per cent and 23 per cent respectively. In the same period, the Mexican peso depreciated 1.4 per cent.

17 As a result, in spite of their more favorable exchange rates, Southeastern Asian countries could not increase their exports to the United States at the expense of Mexican products by more than the amount in which Mexican products displaced products from these countries during the same period.

Conclusion

A working hypothesis in this chapter is that the Mexican economy has become less prone to exchange rate crisis as a result of institutional changes on the macroeconomic and financial regulatory fronts, instigated by previous collapses of the peso. We suggested and have demonstrated that this was the case. Moreover, a floating exchange rate regime has been followed in Mexico since 1995 – unlike what happened with a regulated exchange rate regime that subsidized one-sided bets against the peso, market participants have since been induced to hedge against macroeconomic risks.

A process towards transparency adopted by the Bank of Mexico – required to achieve its inflation targets within a flexible exchange rate regime – has also played a key role in allowing private agents to plan their financial decisions.[18] As it has been pointed out by Martínez Trigueros (2005), this regime has a feature not so evidently present in previous years: It forces market participants to internalize risks taken in their investment and indebtedness decisions.

References

Aspe, P. (1993), *Economic Transformation the Mexican Way* (Cambridge: MIT Press).

Bazdresch, C. and Levy, S. (1991), "Populism and Economic Policy in Mexico, 1970–1982", in Dornbusch, R. and Edwards, S., eds, *The Macroeconomics of Populism in Latin America* (Chicago: University of Chicago Press).

Bensaid, B. and Jeanne, O. (1997), "The Instability of Fixed Exchange Rate Regimes When Raising the Nominal Rate Is Costly", *European Economic Review*.

Burnside, C., Eichenbaum, M. and Rebelo, S. (2000), *On the Fundamentals of Self-Fulfilling Speculative Attacks*, NBER Working Paper No. 7554.

Calderón-Madrid, A. (1997), "Incomplete Adjustment: Fiscal Policy, Private Savings and Current Account Deficits in Mexico Since 1982", in Jansen, K. and Vos, R., eds, *External Finance and Adjustment, Failure and Success in the Developing World* (London: Macmillan).

Calderón-Madrid, A. (1999), "Why Did Private Saving in Mexico Fall in Advance of the 1994 Crisis?", in Reinhart, C. (comp.), *Accounting for Savings: Financial Liberalization, Capital Flows and Growth in Latin America and Europe* (Washington, DC: Interamerican Development Bank).

Calomiris, C. (1999), *The Postmodern Bank Safety Net: Lessons from Developed and Developing Economies* (Washington, DC: The AEI Press).

Flood, R.P. and Garber, P.M. (1984), "Collapsing Exchange Rates Regimes: Some Linear Examples", *Journal of International Economics*, 17, 1–13.

Garber, P. (1988), "Derivatives in International Capital Flows", NBER Working Papers, No. 6623.

Guerra de Luna, A. (1997), "La Relevancia Macroeconómica de los Bienes Raíces en México", Banco de México, *Documento de Investigación*, No. 9707.

---

18 Also helping to cope with interest and exchange rate uncertainty is that, since 1995, a market for futures and derivatives on the Mexican peso has been operating in Chicago.

Krugman, P. (July/August 1995), "Dutch Tulips and Emerging Markets", in *Foreign Affairs*.

Lacoursiere, R. (April 1999), "Mexico: Banking Sector", *Bear Stearns Emerging Markets Equity Research Report*.

Mackey, W. (1999), *Report on the Comprehensive Evaluation of the Operations and Functions of the FOBAPROA and Quality of Supervision of the FOBAPROA Program 1995–1998*. Mimeo.

Martínez Trigueros, L. (March/April 2005), "La Política Cambiaria y Monetaria en México: Lecciones de una Década de Flotación Cambiaria", *Información Comercial Española 821*, Marzo-Abril.

Obstfeld, M. (1988), "Competitiveness, Realignment, and Speculation: The Role of Financial Markets", in Giavazzi, F., Miccossi, S. and Miller, M. (eds), *The European Monetary System* (Cambridge: Cambridge University Press).

Obstfeld, M. (April 1998), "Models of Currency Crises with Self-fulfilling Features", in *European Economic Review* 40, 1037–1047.

Ortiz, G. (1991), "Mexico Beyond the Debt Crisis: Toward Sustainable Growth with Price Stability" in *Lessons of Economic Stabilization and Its Aftermath* (Cambridge: MIT Press).

Ortiz, G. (2002), Comments to Cline, W. "Credit Relations", in Feldstein, M., ed., *Economic and Financial Crisis in Emerging Market Economies*, Institute of International Finance (Chicago: University of Chicago Press).

Sachs, J., Tornell, A. and Velasco, A. (1996), "The Collapse of the Mexican Peso: What Have We Learned?", in *Economic Policy*, 13–63.

Schneider, M. and Tornell, A. (December 2000), "Balance Sheet Effects, Bailout Guarantees and Financial Crisis", NBER Working Paper No. 8060.

Conclusions

Is There a Future for the Euro in the Global Economy?

Pedro Gomis-Porqueras and Joaquín Roy

Given the long process required to create the euro, it is not too surprising that the dollar has been the dominant currency of the world economy for almost a century. The dollar had no competition for a long time since no other economy block came close to the size or importance of the United States. As a result, the dollar had been the *de facto* world reserve currency. In the past, the US currency accounted for approximately two-thirds of all official exchange reserves. More than four-fifths of all foreign exchange transactions and half of all world exports are denominated in dollars.

Euro banknotes and coins have been in circulation since the first of January 2002 and are now a part of daily life for over 300 million Europeans living in the euro area. Since 2002 the euro has gained widespread international acceptance resulting in important institutional, economic and financial changes both for the euro zone, the United States and the world economies, affecting foreign exchange and financial markets as well as economic activities around the world.

The main purpose of the euro is to be the currency of the citizens of the European Union, and as such to serve them well in their financial transactions. Whether it develops a role as an international currency is not a direct policy objective. It is just a consequence of the ability of the European Central Bank to maintain price stability and financial stability in the euro area. In order words, the international role for the euro is left to market forces. This means that all elements and developments are determined by the market and these developments provide us with valuable information on how effective and competitive a currency the euro is perceived to be by international market participants.

The selection of an international currency is conventional in nature. This means that it is chosen by the accord of participants in the market. As a result, the choice of an international currency is not determined by the issuer of the currency, but by the final users. The choice of an international currency or currencies is the result of competition between the various national or domestic currencies on the basis of how well a particular currency serves the purpose of a medium of exchange, a unit of account and a store of value for the international market.

Nowadays, the euro is used as a currency of investment and funding by both private and public sector entities. It is also used as an anchor currency for several currencies and as a foreign reserve and intervention currency by authorities in several countries. Moreover, the euro is also used as a parallel currency by private individuals in a few countries neighboring the European Union. Finally, it is important to note that in order to buy some goods and services from the countries that have adopted the European currency, the euro is needed. Moreover, the degree of openness of an economy and its share in international trade naturally influence the use of the euro internationally. As a result, the euro is used for invoicing in international trade transactions, and as a vehicle currency in some segments of the global foreign exchange markets.

A different role of the euro is to be a symbol of common identity, shared values and the success of European integration in bringing the peoples and nations of Europe together. The euro acts as a stimulus to further integration by showing that common action by member states can bring widespread benefits to all those who take part. A clear example of this shared vision is that as of January 1, 2007, the euro has also been the currency of Slovenia.

The potential future attractiveness and effectiveness of the euro can be increased through the improvement, and especially the simplification, of the decision-making process in the European Union. It is also important to have in place a simple and enforceable institutional framework for economic policy co-ordination between the euro area member states. In years to come we need to consider and study to what extent medium-term economic prospects in the euro area are being threatened by the timidity of the reforms of pension systems in different euro area countries. The current context of an ageing population is obviously putting the current social security arrangements at risk and is threatening the income developments and income expectations of the current wage earners. Finally, there is the important issue of the labor market. With more flexible labor markets, fewer restrictions and lower taxes on labor, many people would decide to work more than at present. Structural reforms in labor and product markets in order to make the economy more flexible and productive also yield a stronger currency. By increasing the speed with which labor and product markets respond to shocks and policies and by raising the long term rate of sustainable growth, structural reforms to boost productivity and flexibility in the euro area economy enhance the effectiveness of monetary policy to preserve price stability under monetary and financial conditions fostering faster growth.

In the future, the international role of the euro will eventually hinge on the validity of the fundamental idea underlying its creation, namely the idea that important components of sovereignty can be pooled and shared among nations in the pursuit of common economic and political objectives. The perception of the euro as a store of value also depends, of course, on the ability of policy makers to implement consistent and sustainable economic policies that can promote economic growth.

Index